11/00

Good Marriages Don't Just Happen

**Keeping Our
Relationship Alive
While Raising
Our Ten Sons**

Prayer of a Husband and Wife

Keep us, O Lord, from pettiness.
Let us be thoughtful in word and deed.

Help us to put away pretense, and face each other
in deep trust without fear and self-pity.

Help us to guard against fault-finding, and be quick to discover
the best in each other and in every situation.

Guard us from ill temper and hasty judgment; encourage us
to take time for all things, to grow calm, serene, and gentle.

Help us to be generous with kind words and compliments.

Teach us never to ignore, never to hurt, never to take each other
for granted.

Engrave charity and compassion on our hearts.

—1979, Columban Fathers, St. Columbans, NE

Good Marriages

Don't Just Happen

**Keeping Our
Relationship Alive
While Raising
Our Ten Sons**

*Catherine Musco Garcia-Prats
& Joseph A. Garcia-Prats, M.D.*

ThomasMore®
Allen, Texas

Acknowledgments

To Maria Illich with our heartfelt appreciation for your help in fine-tuning our words. Your green pen flowed with wisdom, love, and laughter.

To Jeanne Weaver with genuine gratitude for your kind gestures of support and encouragement as well as your willingness to take on a few extra children during our book-writing crunch time.

To Debra Hampton, our editor, with sincere thankfulness for your support, advice, spirit, and patience from beginning to end.

To our sons—Tony, David, Christopher, Joe Pat, Matthew, Mark, Tommy, Danny, Jamie, and Timmy—for being understanding and supportive of our efforts. We love you!

Send all inquiries to:

THOMAS MORE PUBLISHING
200 East Bethany Drive
Allen, Texas 75002-3804

Telephone: 877-275-4725 / 972-390-6300

Fax: 800-688-8356 / 972-390-6560

Customer Service e-mail:
cservice@rcl-enterprises.com

Web site: **www.ThomasMore.com**

Printed in the United States of America

Library of Congress Catalog Number 00133317

ISBN 0-88347-461-1

1 2 3 4 5   04 03 02 01 00

To our parents,
Jane and Anthony Musco
and
Luisa and Jose Garcia,
who gave us the gifts of life and love

"Joe and Cathy Garcia-Prats offer a simple recipe for marriage: love, respect, commitment, and faith . . . and share their personal covenant, a rich sign and symbol of God's faithful and permanent love."

—Winnie Honeywell
Director of Family Life Ministry
Diocese of Galveston-Houston

"I guess it was never easy to keep a marriage alive. It has always required a lot of work. In this day and age, long marriages may indeed be little miracles. It has never been truer that *'Good Marriages Don't Just Happen.'* The Garcia-Prats tell us of things we know but need to be reminded of, mention things we don't really like to talk about, and nudge us to be better partners."

—Ron Stone
TV broadcaster and President
Stonefilms of Texas

"This is a wonderful story about the adventures of a wonderful couple during a long and happy marriage. The Garcia-Prats' marriage is a portrait of a couple and a family who approached marriage as a covenant rather than as a contract. Contracts define business relationships, whereas covenants describe eternal commitment. This book should be read by all individuals who are contemplating marriage and as a constructive guide to happiness for all currently married couples."

—Judith Z. Feigin, Ed.D., and Ralph D. Feigin, M.D.
Texas Children's Hospital

Table of Contents

Life is either a daring adventure or nothing.
            —Helen Keller

He who desires to see the living God face to face
should not seek Him in the empty firmament of his mind,
but in human love.
            —Dostoevsky

Your reason and your passion are the rudder and the sails
of your seafaring soul.
            —Kahlil Gibran

Prologue

Marriage: The Ultimate Adventure

*A*s we circuit the country speaking to parents about parenting and family life, many of the questions and comments that follow our presentations center on the couple—the spousal relationship. Parents and couples frequently want to know how we, having built a solid foundation, sustain our relationship while balancing the constant demands of children, careers, individual and spousal needs. How do we find time for each other in the midst of ten sons, hectic schedules, and numerous responsibilities?

When we began our marriage, we were idealistic and excited about the adventure we were embarking upon. We were young, in love, and ready to make our impact on the world as individuals and as a couple. Joe was the young, eager, pediatric intern, and Cathy was the new college grad anxiously awaiting her first class of students. That was twenty-six years ago. Today, Joe is a loving, dedicated husband and father as well as a mature, competent neonatologist; Cathy is a committed, passionate, devoted wife and mother as well as a homemaker, writer, speaker, and volunteer. Needless to say, much has happened in twenty-six years. Older and (hopefully) wiser, we are still in love, and ready to make an impact on the world, not only as individuals and as a couple, but also as a family with ten sons. We continue to be idealistic, although our idealism is tempered with a healthy dose of realism. How quickly we learned that "good marriages don't just happen."

Once you have exchanged your vows, the "adventure" truly begins, an adventure that encompasses almost every emotion and feeling we as human beings can share. Adventure can be defined in several ways: an unusual and exciting experience, a risky under-taking, or a business venture. The manner in which we define and approach the marriage adventure makes a difference.

In society today, too often the marital relationship is approached as a business venture. Contracts are signed, stipulations made, expectations defined—all in the "unlikely" event of one or both parties not holding up to his or her part of the bargain—thus divorce. We believe that, with this mentality, the marriage is destined to failure. By mutual agreement divorce is seen as an acceptable end to the relationship. We do not believe a relationship, such as marriage, can grow and strengthen when entered under those restricted expectations.

Rather than a contract, our marriage was approached as a covenant made with each other—a permanent and unconditional commitment. We *chose* to commit our lives to each other "for better and for worse, for richer and for poorer, in sickness and in health, till death do us part." We *chose* to be with each other in a never-ending relationship. We *chose* to love the other in a relationship that would strive to make each of us better individuals. We also *chose* to integrate God into all aspects of our lives, not understanding at the time of our wedding how integral God's love and spirit would be in the growth of our relationship. We've experienced the richer and the poorer, the good times and the bad, health and illness, sadness and joy, fulfillment and disappointments. The commitment we both made to our relationship enabled us to weather the hard times and grow stronger in our love. Building a loving, lasting, joy-filled relationship entails effort and a constant commitment by *both* spouses. Good marriages don't just happen.

Is marriage a risky undertaking? Sure it is. Most couples, like ourselves, begin this adventure with confidence and high expectations, anticipating a strong, loving, long-lasting, mutually beneficial and satisfying relationship. Yet, as a couple lives and shares day-to-day experiences, many aspects of our individuality will surface that were not obvious before we married. The impact of expectations past experiences and the influence of our families of origin become more evident.

We often hear people say that they did not know what they were getting into when they got married. That is probably true of most couples. We need trust and love to guide us through these new-found characteristics and acknowledgments, as well as the conflicts that will surely surface. We also cannot know what the future holds regarding our health, finances, children, and/or careers. That's why an unconditional commitment, although difficult to maintain at times, is so important to the growth and strengthening of the marriage.

And we do believe marriage is an unusual and exciting experience—the ultimate adventure. Unusual in that no other relationship is as unique as the one shared by a married couple: physically, emotionally, intellectually, and spiritually. Exciting in that every day offers new challenges and areas of growth for the individuals and the couple. The manner in which we approach the challenges and experiences we encounter determines our level of peace and happiness in our marriage.

We are glad we are not the same couple we were twenty-six years ago. We have come so far. First and foremost, we are not just a couple anymore. We are now the proud parents of ten sons who presently range in age from six to twenty-four years. We still share the same goals, values and ideals we did then, but we better understand how to make those ideals a reality and to incorporate them into our ever-changing family. Over the years, we have laughed, cried, worked hard, worried, struggled, loved, and grown as a couple and as a family. We have learned to enjoy our time together, in spite of the challenges and demands we face. The love and commitment we vowed to each other during our marriage ceremony continues to provide the foundation for our relationship and for our family. Many people tell us we are lucky, but we don't believe it is luck that has strengthened our relationship over the years. We are blessed with the fact that both of us are committed to our marriage. We consciously decided what we wanted our relationship to be and then strove to bring it to fruition. It is a never-ending process—we can't stop working on it, even after twenty-six years! It is an active process that needs daily nurturing to deal with the constant changes that emerge.

In writing this book, we share with you our experiences, challenges, joys, and insights into married life. Each marriage relationship is unique because of the individuals who make up the relationship. Therefore, we know and accept that we are not perfect and do not have all the answers. Everything that works for us may not be conducive to others. At the same time, we do understand and believe from our own experience, the experiences of friends and families, and the many engaged couples we have worked with over seventeen years, that there are characteristics that are essential to having a loving, joy-filled, lasting relationship: love, respect, commitment, and faith.

The philosophy we share with you in this book is a philosophy that has worked for us. A philosophy, though, only works if we live it. So the choices we make each and every day are essential to building and sustaining a strong marriage relationship. These choices affect each other, our children, and society.

Marriage is the ultimate adventure—full of laughter, sorrow, smooth sailing, and rough waters. Enjoy, enrich, and nourish your relationship. Make time for each other in the midst of every day demands. As Brian Zinnamon, S.J., stated: "Your success will ultimately depend on your faith in God, the value and dignity you place on each other, and the consistency in how you love." The joys and rewards for your efforts last a lifetime and beyond.

Catherine Musco Garcia-Prats
Joseph A. Garcia-Prats
Houston, Texas

A faithful friend is a sturdy shelter;
he who finds one finds a treasure.
                              —Sirach 6:14

And in the sweetness of friendship let there be
laughter, and sharing of pleasures.
For in the dew of little things the heart
finds its morning and is refreshed.
                              —Kahlil Gibran

Chapter One

Building a Relationship—Being Friends!

*W*e may not have experienced love at first sight, but we were friends after our first date. Twenty-six years later, we continue to be friends and nourish our friendship because this is an essential part of a strong, lasting marriage. You may meet someone and quickly become friends, but it takes time to build and sustain a meaningful relationship. Sharing time together as well as experiences, dreams, goals, joys, sorrows, and frustrations all contribute to the growth of a friendship and, ultimately, a marriage. You begin to know and understand the other person more intimately, just as the other person begins to know and understand you. You accept and appreciate your similarities and differences. You believe you will help each other develop intellectually, emotionally, physically, and spiritually. You commit to help the other person reach his or her full potential, and he or she does the same for you. The marital relationship requires this level of respect, commitment, and unconditional love by both persons to reap long-lasting joy and peace.

In the Beginning— Friends

True friendships and relationships develop and strengthen over time. You can't rush them. The two and a half years that we dated before we were married provided us many opportunities to know each other in a way we didn't—and couldn't—on our first date. During the first months of our marriage, we discovered that there were still many aspects of our lives we didn't fully know and understand. How we wish we knew then what we know now. Such knowledge and understanding would have saved us many conflicts and heartaches in the early years of our marriage.

Too often couples rush the process of building a relationship. They meet, enjoy being with each other, and impetuously decide to marry. They may not have taken the time to discuss with each other those areas of their own lives that are the most important and intimate. In many instances, couples may not realize which areas of their lives they *should* be talking about. They frequently confuse intimacy with sexuality, especially since society places so much emphasis on the physical dimension of the relationship. They eclipse the developmental process by skipping ahead to a sexual relationship before they have established the necessary bonds that foster a lasting relationship. In short, couples often become lovers before they become friends.

(Joe): While I was in medical school at Tulane, opportunities to meet young ladies who had the kind of qualities that I would consider "admirable" were quite limited. Unfortunately, the medical school was located in downtown New Orleans, rather than on the university's campus. Most young women who worked in the area, then, were either nurses (who didn't pay attention to medical students) or young women who worked at the medical school itself and were already married to medical or surgical residents in training or to other medical students. Thus, quests for eligible young ladies to go out with were very limited. Medical student friends frequently became the primary source for meeting young ladies— usually as blind dates. Most blind dates, though, were a big gamble for both parties involved.

When Lynne, who was dating a good medical student friend, insisted on a blind date with Cathy, I hesitated. Lynne described Cathy as cute (she was a cheerleader at Loyola University) and nice, and assured me we would have a good time together. Not a much different description from the many previous blind dates that had ended in disaster. But it was Lynne, and I knew the kind of person she was. Likewise, she knew me pretty well, so I decided to risk a date with Cathy. To my great surprise, this blind date was wonderful! We really did have a good time on that first date. We still reminisce about the Mexican restaurant in New Orleans where we ate dinner and the rather large, boisterous waitress assigned to our table who literally yelled our order into the kitchen. Referring to the appetizer of tostitos placed on our table as "chips," she continuously returned to the table to demand: "Youse guys ready for some more chips?" We laughed at the time and still wonder, how with all the good restaurants available in New Orleans, we ended up there.

Little did I know that my date with Cathy was the beginning of a very special relationship. She was cute, neatly dressed, fun loving, intelligent, and a very good dancer—all wonderful traits in my book. However, as we spent more time together after that first date, certain differences made this togetherness very special. Why was Cathy so different from the other young ladies I had dated? They also were cute, neatly dressed, fun loving, intelligent and good dancers. I believe the difference stemmed from the similarities in our values, similarities that made us both long to learn more about each other. Education and family were so important to both of us, as well as our faith, personal honesty and the importance of being kind and respectful to others. It was the discovery of those common, deep-seated values that made me realize why Cathy was different. There was a comfort in talking and being with her.

In retrospect, I also changed because of her. Did I change to gain her approval or garner her acceptance? Maybe to a certain extent I did. I do believe, however, that she stimulated me to revisit and rededicate myself to those deep-seated values that were so important to me. Also, this was a very different relationship from other friendships. While growing up, I did not have female friends. The closest I ever came to that kind of relationship was with my cousins, Patsy and Tessy. We shared many stories and feelings over our teenage years. I approached most other young ladies romantically, always as possible dates. This romantic aspect of the relationship, always present, prohibited the relationship from moving to a level of comfortable acceptance. Fortunately, I eventually experienced this kind of familial relationship with Judy and Charlene, the wives of some of my close medical school friends. These women were friends in the truest sense. They were accepting of me, and I of them, without any "romantic overtones" to the relationship. These friends gave me the first insight into what a male-female friendship could be and how much comfort, peace and happiness this could bring. When I met Cathy, then, I think I finally understood what a true friendship could be. This understanding was another factor in why this was different from before. Maybe it was just my maturity and the fact that I was ready to share who I was with a special friend. I firmly believe that Divine Providence had a hand in it as well.

(Cathy): Joe and I met on a blind date while Joe was attending medical school at Tulane University School of Medicine and I was pursing my undergraduate degree at Loyola University New Orleans. A mutual friend, Lynne, invited me to go to dinner with a good friend of hers. I had had my share of blind dates and was not interested in another uncomfortable and pleasureless evening. Lynne was persistent, though, and convinced me that I would have a good time with Joe, although none of us envisioned that the good time would continue for as long as it has.

Joe picked me up at the dorm. We went with another couple to a Mexican restaurant, an unusual cuisine for New Orleans especially in the early 1970s. To my surprise, I found myself relaxing and enjoying the evening. In fact, laughter was the rule of the night, from the unusual mannerisms of the restaurant personnel to the sharing of stories from our own experiences. Lynne was right—the evening with Joe was a joy! And only the beginning of many more to come.

I emphasize the word "beginning" because after that first date,

I knew I was comfortable and enjoyed being with Joe although, in reality, we were still strangers. I knew little more about his background, values, dreams or moods than I did before we met. His last name even confused me—was it Garcia or Prats? (For clarification, Joe's last name is Garcia-Prats: Garcia is his father's surname; Prats is his mother's maiden name.) I did know that I was pleased he had not "attacked" me on the way home or even expected a good night kiss. What a welcome change!

I rarely went out a second time with someone I met on a blind date. When Joe called and asked me out again, I eagerly accepted. I felt comfortable talking and being with him. After several dates, we realized that we had many similar interests and values that brought us closer together. Sharing common bonds was important to me because I knew from a previous relationship that certain characteristics when absent create an uncomfortable void. I wanted to be with someone I could easily talk with about more than sports and weather. And being with someone who shared a similar religious background and commitment was also an advantage. Joe understood the importance of faith in my daily life because faith was an integral part of his life.

Joe and I did not date exclusively for the first year of our relationship, more my choice than his. I was seven years younger than Joe; I was not interested in a commitment at that point in my life. Marriage was definitely not on my immediate agenda. I intended to take advantage of the many opportunities that were available to me: graduate school, fellowships, teaching positions, and new locales. I wanted to meet and be with lots of different people.

As we dated longer and longer, my time with Joe became more relaxed and enjoyable. We didn't have to go anywhere fancy or do anything in particular—just being together was a delight. Since neither of us had much money at that point in our lives, we had to keep our choices simple. For example, when we first started dating, I volunteered on Saturday mornings in the pediatric ward at Charity Hospital in New Orleans. As a medical student, Joe often made rounds on Saturday mornings. Many Saturdays he came by the pediatric ward after he finished rounds and I completed my shift. We picked up "po' boy" sandwiches and picnicked in Audubon Park. We talked and laughed the afternoon away. I have fond memories of those Saturdays because it is during those lazy afternoons that Joe and I became closer and closer friends. As we learned more about each other, we liked what we learned. I increasingly looked forward to the times he called as well as to the times we were together.

Not all the times we were together, though, were perfect, dream-filled encounters. I remember certain outings when I felt out of place with his friends and what they were doing. They were older than I was and thus had experienced many of the things I was still enjoying. Joe and his friends did not want to reverse course and reexperience their college years, and I wasn't ready to skip over mine. I remember one evening in particular when I asked Joe to take me straight home after leaving a party. He sensed something was wrong because it was still early in the evening. I felt extremely uncomfortable during the evening and realized I had some thinking to do about our relationship. I questioned whether Joe and I were just too far apart in age and experience. While he understandably wanted to participate in the medical school activities and be with his friends, I wanted to be involved at Loyola. My commitments at Loyola fostered development in many aspects of my life, and I wanted this growth to continue in that atmosphere. Since I was not interested in a long-term relationship, I built up the courage to tell Joe that maybe it was better for both of us if we didn't see each other as often.

What surprised me, after telling Joe this, was how much I missed him almost immediately: our talks, our walks, the laughter, and the sharing. Without my conscious recognition, Joe had become an integral part of my life. What a void enveloped my days! Although I had many friends and was busier than busy, I missed him tremendously. I came to the realization that he meant more to me than "just a friend."

Fortunately, Joe recognized and understood my feelings of

insecurity. Most of us have experienced feeling out of place at one time or another. Joe allowed me some "space," but not too much. He wanted us to talk about our individual feelings and needs. It was our ability to talk about our feelings that enabled us to grow through the experience and understand each other in a new way. We became closer because of our sharing. I grew to appreciate Joe's many talents and gifts, but his gifts of understanding and sensitivity impacted and strengthened our relationship the most—and still do. I needed those characteristics to be at the forefront of a meaningful relationship.

During the years we dated, we continued to share our goals, dreams, values, concerns, fears, and day-to-day ups and downs. Through this sharing we learned what was important to us as individuals and as a couple. We also learned how we handled and reacted to our daily experiences. We asked questions (although we later learned not enough questions) and talked about specific items that were important in our lives: faith, children, family, education, and service to others. Gradually, the dreams became *our* dreams versus his or hers. We were ready for our relationship to proceed to the next level.

More than Friends— Engaged!

Joe graduated from Tulane Medical School and moved to Houston for his pediatric training. Cathy remained at Loyola to complete her student teaching and other undergraduate requirements. We discussed getting married soon after Joe's graduation, but Cathy wanted to receive her degree from Loyola University. We became officially engaged the following fall with the wedding scheduled in May. We wanted this engagement period to be a time of growth in our relationship. In retrospect, our separation during this time hampered the process. We were not together sharing day-to-day experiences. Joe's life and responsibilities in Houston differed from those in medical school; Cathy's student teaching presented new experiences as well. Unfortunately, many of the present means of communication were not available in the mid 70s. We were dependent on the U.S. Mail, Ma Bell, and quick trips to Houston—no e-mail or "instant messenger." We were determined, though, to build on the strengths already present in our relationship.

Once we were engaged, other issues surfaced that were not directly related to our personal relationship. **How quickly we came to understand that while we were still the same couple, our decisions and choices, as simple as they seemed to be, now affected other people—starting with our immediate families and our wedding plans.** We wanted our wedding to be in New Orleans and as soon after Cathy's graduation from Loyola as possible. Graduation was on a Monday. Since we didn't want to wait until Saturday to be married, we decided on a Tuesday rehearsal and a Wednesday evening wedding. The plans seemed simple and reasonable to us; our parents disagreed. A Wednesday evening wedding? In New Orleans? All of a sudden, we were confronted with their wishes and desires as well as our own. We needed to blend the different needs, backgrounds and cultures of both families. (Joe is of Mexican and Spanish descent; Cathy is of Irish and Italian descent.) Until now, our families had not directly played a major role in our relationship. After all, Joe's parents lived in Texas and Cathy's parents lived in Virginia. We tried to appreciate their desires and concerns and be flexible while simultaneously addressing our needs, especially the timing of the wedding. Cathy's dad still teases us about our definition of "flexible."

We were married on a Wednesday evening in New Orleans at Our Lady of Guadalupe Church, a beautiful May evening shared with family and friends—a true celebration! While we spent a substantial amount of time organizing and planning for our wedding, we also invested significant time in preparing for our marriage. Marriage preparation in the Catholic church differs today from what the Church offered engaged couples in the mid '70s.

Fortunately, we attended a couple's retreat (a precursor to the engaged weekends presently offered) where married couples shared their experiences on the various aspects of married life, such as communication, sexuality, spirituality, and family life. We had the opportunity to ask questions, voice areas of concern, and spend time talking together as a couple. The weekend was an enriching and enlightening experience.

If you are a couple preparing for marriage, we strongly recommend that you participate in a marriage preparation program, ideally a program offered by your church. Avail yourselves of the opportunity to learn more about each other and the characteristics needed to build and sustain a marriage. **We spend way too much time *and* money worrying about the wedding but not enough time on preparing for marriage itself. The wedding is one day; the marriage commitment is for a lifetime.** Father Martin Carter, SA, pastor of Our Lady of Victory Church in Brooklyn, New York, offers sound words of advice to the couples he prepares for marriage: "Be honest *before* you get married. Know as much as you can about your future spouse; it's not fun to be blind sided. It's easier to work on the front end to resolve differences than to work extra hard on the back end."

If you're a married couple, remember the early stages of your relationship. What attracted you to each other? How did you spend your time? What brought joy and laughter to your relationship? What did you enjoy talking about? What did you enjoy about each other? What were the strengths of your relationship? What conflicts, if any, surfaced? Were the conflicts resolved? Were you friends? Were you lovers? Now ask the same questions in the present tense.

If you missed the opportunity to participate in a marriage preparation program before you married, find a program now that is specifically formulated for married couples: marriage encounters, seminars, or weekend retreats. We assure you that these programs can enrich and strengthen even the best of marriages.

(Cathy): During the months that followed our engagement in October, I resolved some personal issues that had kept me from making a commitment earlier. I realized I did not have to forego my dreams by being married to Joe; rather they would now be shared dreams—just in Houston or wherever we decided to establish roots. I felt confident that Joe would encourage and foster my goals, as well as his own.

I also learned an important life and love lesson: There are times when, out of love, you postpone your own immediate needs for the growth of the other person(s) you love. As a wife and mother of ten children, this lesson has guided me in loving Joe and our sons. Postponing one's needs is often described as "sacrificial" love, but I do not feel as if I'm sacrificing when the choices I freely make foster the growth of the individuals I love.

New doubts and some previous concerns surfaced during our engagement. When I visited Joe in Houston, I was again thrown into situations where I felt uncomfortable and out of place. While I again questioned the age factor, I was more concerned with the expectations of my role as a doctor's wife. I did not feel I could fulfill that role for Joe as I perceived it at the time. I am thankful we attended the couples' weekend and had the opportunity to settle my doubts as well as discuss other aspects of our relationship that we hadn't previously addressed. We were also able to tap the experience of married couples who understood the importance of expectations in a relationship. And, I was fortunate that Joe was willing to listen to my concerns. I would not have gone through with the wedding if he hadn't been understanding and accepting of my feelings. I owed that much to Joe and myself.

As I look back on that weekend, it was a gift for our relationship. I was so much more at peace the weeks following the retreat. The retreat experience benefited me during those first months after the wedding, too. I was better able to deal with many situations as they arose because of the words of wisdom shared by experienced couples. Yet there were those unexpected difficulties that arose that I did not feel equipped to handle. Our marriage *preparation, although better than most couples at the time, was still beset with myriad gaps.*

We realized we didn't know as much about each other as we thought we did. We also realized that we still had much to learn about each other in the days and years ahead. We *did* learn a lot that first year, mostly by trial and error—and hurt feelings and misunderstandings. How we wish we had had the skills and understanding we have now and *knew* then what we know now.

Today we share our marriage experience with engaged couples preparing for marriage in the church, much like the married couples did for us during our engaged retreat. We first became involved in marriage preparation seventeen years ago. We felt the need to get involved as we witnessed family and friends struggling with their relationships and too often divorcing. What amazes both of us is how much we learn about our relationship and how to continually strengthen it while administering the preparation program to other couples.

The marriage preparation program we use, *For Better and For Ever*, covers essential aspects of a marriage relationship and allows the couple time to talk and share their feelings on various issues: family backgrounds, religion, money, sexuality, expectations, communication, children, careers, and the difference between a "covenant" versus a "contract" marriage. The program provides us the avenue to address individual needs specific to the couple we are working with at the time. For example, some couples struggle with financial differences, other couples are anxious about the differences in their religious beliefs or commitment, while some worry about the impact their families of origin will have on their relationship or how their careers will impact their marriage. Not all issues are resolved or identified during the weeks we meet with the couples. We are confident, though, that the program provides a means for couples to learn more about themselves and each other, to interact and discuss important elements that build and sustain a relationship. Our goal is to provide the tools and knowledge the couple will need to establish a strong foundation on which to build their marriage and family.

Like Father Carter, we emphasize the importance of honesty in their sharing, not only during the sessions but throughout their lifetime. Maybe if couples are more honest with themselves and/or with each other before and after their wedding, many divorces and unhappy marriages could be avoided.

It is important to understand and ask: Why am I getting married? Am I ready, willing, and mature enough to accept the commitment and responsibilities inherent in a marriage relationship? Marriage is not just a continuation of the dating phase. Marriage entails a totally different commitment and level of responsibility. You are not just responsible for yourself anymore—you are now committed to the physical, emotional, intellectual, and spiritual development of another. Am I free to marry? Is my fiancé(e) aware of previous obligations: financial, spousal, parental? Do we share common values and goals and understand how we will attain those goals and live those values? Are there behavioral or attitudinal characteristics of my fiancé(e) that worry me: alcohol, drugs, free-spending, philandering, aggression, prejudices, immature behavior? How do we deal with conflicts and disagreements? How will in-laws affect the marriage? Will we make each other better people through our marriage?

Many questions to ask and answer or reconsider. Couples don't end up with all the answers by attending a marriage preparation class or solve all their problems by attending a marriage seminar or weekend retreat. Usually, though, couples become keenly aware of the role and the importance that shared goals and values, healthy communication skills, forgiveness, acceptance of each others' uniqueness, laughter, change, compromise, and family backgrounds play in the growth and strength of their relationship. Even mature, committed couples face unexpected, hard to deal with situations during their marriages. But two mature, committed, honest, prepared, faith-filled individuals will have a better chance at working out their difficulties and differences while reaping the joy and peace that marriage offers.

Our relationship has evolved over the years and still we remain friends. Friends appreciate and enjoy each other, share in good times and in bad, and are loving, accepting, and supportive of each other. Marriage does not end a couple's friendship but rather enhances it— we are best friends today. Each year of our marriage has added to the depth of the friendship we established twenty-six years ago.

God is love,
and those who abide in love
abide in God, and God abides in them.
                              —1 John 4:16

Let all that you do
be done in love.

                    —1 Corinthians 16:14

Chapter Two

The Foundation of a Relationship: Love, Respect, Commitment, and Faith

*W*e always seem to be looking for magic formulas and easy ways to make things work and solve problems. We want quick fixes and instant relief with as little time, energy, and commitment requirements as possible. When it comes to marriage, there are no magic formulas, good luck potions, or catchy aphorisms that enable us to have a good marriage. Couples frequently ask what are the two or three most important elements of a marriage. Although we can provide a quick answer, what couples need is a complex design similar to the specifications for a home that an architect would provide a builder. Much attention to details and to the building materials goes into the construction of a home. Marriages are likewise built. The strength of the marriage will depend on the foundation you establish, the design you follow, and the attention to details.

Our marriage's strength is grounded in the four principles of love, respect, commitment, and faith. All four are intertwined and inseparable. One does not exist without the others. From these four principles all other areas of our relationship flow: healthy communication skills, forgiveness, acceptance, appreciation, sexuality, and parenting. They guide our choices, they direct our values, and they shape our goals.

Our Vision

Businesses, schools, and organizations usually formulate vision and mission statements that encompass their objectives, plans, and long-term goals. Thus, they and others will understand who they are and what they strive to attain. Equally, a couple should consciously think about and verbalize what each of you wants in your marriage and how you intend to reach your goal, whatever stage of marriage you are currently in. Being on the same page, as they say, is essential.

We knew what we wanted in our marriage and, eventually, our family. (Yes, we did want a large family!) We may not have written our vision and goals down or memorized them by heart or completely understood that we had a mission, yet these goals guided the choices we made right from the beginning. Our vision as a couple evolved into our vision for our children and family. What we want and strive for in ourselves as individuals and a couple is what we endeavor to achieve with our children. We did not have the knowledge and experience during those early years of our marriage that we have now, but with our vision and a strong commitment in our hearts we were able to overcome and work through the conflicts and differences that emerged, and we continue to do so.

Our vision then and now is the same. We want to be loving, caring, compassionate, forgiving, respectful, responsible, well-educated, and faith-filled individuals. **We want our self-worth and success to be measured in nonmonetary terms: by who we are, what we do with the gifts God has given us, and how we live our lives.**

Our vision is contrary to how society appraises an individual's success and self-worth. With the tremendous and excessive focus in today's society on materialism, people measure success and self-worth by the cars they drive, the homes they live in, the possessions they own, the people with whom they associate, the clothes they wear, and the places they go. Robert Bellah, author of *Habits of the Heart,* tells us we are "chasing the more, the bigger and the better."

Goals are set outside ourselves (materialism) when we should be focusing on our inner qualities and a common good.

(Cathy): When I chose to be a teacher, I knew the teaching profession was not a lucrative field. I had always desired, though, to work with children. Teaching provided me the opportunity to combine my ability to motivate and guide children with my love for them. Following graduation from Loyola University, New Orleans, I taught first grade at Corpus Christi Catholic School in Houston, a small parish school in a middle income neighborhood. My salary was not much more than the tuition I paid at Loyola. If I measured my success and self-worth by my salary, I would not have considered myself successful or adopted a positive self-image. I knew, though, that I touched the intellectual, physical, emotional, and spiritual dimensions of the lives of the children I taught, and the students and their families did the same for me. **The years I taught school were rewarding and fulfilling. I met many wonderful parents who exemplified the family values Joe and I wanted to attain. I also learned many life lessons from the students' family experiences that reinforced the importance of faith, hope, and love in my daily choices.** *I may not have become rich teaching, but my life was definitely enriched.*

(Joe): I must admit that I was always considered a determined individual even as a young child. I tried very hard to accomplish my goals whether they were being a good athlete or a good student. This determination served me well in my efforts to get into medical school, get through medical school, and eventually to become a competent and caring physician. I do believe that I "followed my bliss" in choosing to become a physician and, ultimately, a neonatologist. I knew that there would be financial rewards associated with becoming a physician; but that was not the driving force that got me through the tough nights and weekends of studying and the thirteen years of preparing to become a neonatologist. What enabled me to get through the grueling schedule was the knowledge

*that I would ultimately help people. Likewise, it was this altruism that I saw in Cathy. Although for her it went much deeper than just altruism, there was always a true, heartfelt kindness at the core of why she extended so many kind acts to so many people. I think it was this common sentiment and core belief that may have attracted us. It certainly has guided us over our many years of marriage. To strive to have a bigger house, nicer cars, or extensive wardrobes has not been a driving force for us. **The priorities that our parents taught us remained at the top of our own list: God, family, education**. Although my dad and mom worked very hard to provide our family with food, clothing, and a loving home, they still stressed the value of education, the importance of family, and the central place of God in our home. These important priorities remain paramount in our home and lives as well and guide our choices.*

If you don't know what you want out of life or don't know where you're going, it is hard to know how to get there. ***Taking the time to consciously and concretely determine what your values, goals, and mission are will enable you to focus on making them happen.*** The choices you make, guided by your faith, love, respect, and commitment, become easier to make when you establish goals. The "sacrifices" don't seem like sacrifices because the choices are made for the good of another, in this case your spouse and children. "The feet find the road easy when the heart walks with them."

We continue to face the demands and challenges of our everyday life, even as these demands and challenges change from day to day and from week to week. ***The principles of love, respect, commitment, and faith strengthen and motivate us to do the best we can.*** As a couple, we share the path we want to follow. And when we fail or don't meet our own expectations, we know each new day provides us a fresh start and the opportunity to try again.

We assure you that we did not understand the impact of these principles when we first married. We learned through our experiences, fairly early on, how important love, respect, faith, and commitment are to the long-term peace and joy of the relationship. With them in our hearts we have grown as individuals, as a couple, and now as a family. As we share our experiences with you, visualize how you can practice these principles in your own life and the choices you make.

To Love— When Jesus was asked what is the greatest
A Decision commandment, He answered, "You shall love
and a Promise the Lord your God with all your heart, and with all your soul, and with all your mind." The second is like it: "You shall love your neighbor as yourself" (Matthew 22:37–39).

There are many facets to love and ways to love. The word "love" is used freely and in many contexts. But what is love? What does it mean to love another? To quote Erich Fromm: "To love somebody is not just a strong feeling—it is a decision, it is a judgment, it is a promise." If we believe that statement, then loving our spouse and our children is a decision and a promise. It is not just a feeling—feelings come and go. Along the same lines, St. Thomas Aquinas tells us: "To love is to will the good of another." *We must decide to make our spouse and children a priority in our lives and to make choices that enable and encourage them to become the best that they can be.* In the process, we become better individuals as well.

Love, thus, becomes a reflection of the choices we make and whether these choices are in the best interest of our family as a whole. Mother Teresa told us: "It is simple but not easy." How right she was. The choices we made over the years and continue to make in our marriage and for our children have not always been easy. At times, our self-interest and pride cloud and muddle our vision, creating conflicts and disappointments. We and the boys can feel when we're "out of sync." Getting back on track means refocusing on the principles we know work and striving again to live and love with humility and for the good of our marriage and family.

*(Joe): I have always desired to become an individual that would "make a difference" in this world. I thought it was important that my life would leave a positive mark on mankind. This is a lofty goal, you might say. Yet my parents and teachers never discouraged my efforts or gave me the impression it was an unattainable goal. Growing up I considered myself a good student, a good athlete, and a good son to my parents. I was fortunate to receive some recognition in high school and college for the hard work I had invested. My acceptance to medical school further encouraged me that there would be something that I could do to leave my mark on this world. Certainly by becoming a physician I might have an inside track on accomplishing something unique, such as discovering a cure for a disease or doing research that furthered medical science. There certainly were numerous avenues for my search to "leave my mark." Yet after twenty-eight years of being a physician and twenty-six years of marriage, **I am realizing that living a life that would influence the world has to begin within the individual. I must strive very hard each day to become a person who deals with the people in this world in a loving, respectful, and compassionate manner every step of my life.***

In her book A Simple Path, *Mother Teresa tells us that "if you want to change the world, go home and love your family." She comments further on the importance of love in the world in her book* No Greater Love: *"The poverty of the West is a different kind of poverty. . . . It is not just a poverty of loneliness . . . there is a hunger for love." My desire to leave a positive influence on this world begins with me and how I deal with the people I love in my own home: Cathy and the boys. This loving relationship that I develop at home will have a natural extension to those outside my home.*

My relationship with my God must be my starting point each day. *After the acknowledgment of the central role He plays in my life, as well as a request for His help and guidance, I am prepared to tackle the demands and joys of the day. The love I see in Cathy as she awakes and deals with the many responsibilities* of the day only inspires me to be a better individual. I find developing our relationship through our respectful sharing and loving strengthens us as individuals and as a couple. Likewise, giving of ourselves to the boys in so many ways throughout the day as parents further develops the family as I think God would want us to unfold. Making choices that mirror our love is part of my role as spouse and parent.

Dealing with these daily activities doesn't seem "earth shattering or as noble" as winning a Pulitzer Prize in medicine or literature or brokering a peace treaty or rescuing people from a flooded landscape. However, I do believe that it is the love we give to our spouse and to our children that has the greatest impact on our world. Choosing to be positive to each of the boys and recognizing and appreciating their individuality is a way of loving each one. Recognizing when Cathy has an important meeting in the morning or evening and doing all that I can to help with the boys and the house, so that she can go to her obligation feeling that she has not "abandoned" her children to her husband, is a way of showing her my love. Listening intently and not being distracted while one of the boys relates a story of what happened at school is a loving thing to do. **Making sure that I am a loving and respectful person in all that I do is one act that will eventually cause change in the world.**

(Cathy): *Each and every morning I am faced with the decision to love or not to love Joe and the boys. When I wake up, I can throw up my hands and lament about all the responsibilities I have to fulfill that day: eight loads of laundry to wash, fold, and put away, bills to be paid, children to transport to school, doctor and orthodontist appointments, soccer practices, school functions, meals, dishes, homework, and on and on. Or I can wake up each morning and thank God for the gift of Joe and our ten sons and ask for His guidance in taking care of them and the strength and patience to meet the demands and challenges of the day—both the planned activities and the unexpected surprises.*

My accepting and cheerful attitude and approach to the day right from the beginning is an expression of my love for Joe and the children. It shows Joe I am glad to be his wife and the boys I am glad to be their mother in spite of the demands, challenges, and constancy. How wonderful for your family to feel that they are an important, meaningful part of your life—and not a burden and another obligation to fulfill. Through my faith, I garnered an understanding of the importance of a positive, loving attitude in all I do. The words of St. Paul to the Corinthians reflect the significance of love being the essential ingredient in our everyday actions. "If I speak with human tongues and angelic as well, but do not have love, I am a noisy gong, a clanging cymbal. If I have the gift of prophecy and, with full knowledge comprehend all mysteries, if I have faith great enough to move mountains, but have not love, I am nothing. If I give everything I have to feed the poor and hand over my body to be burned, but have not love, I gain nothing" (1 Corinthians 13:1–3).

As a wife and mother I can easily relate to St. Paul's words. If I talk about the importance of my faith but do not have love, I am a noisy gong and a clanging cymbal. If I understand the importance of fulfilling responsibilities and sharing the gift of my time, talent, and treasures with my family and others but do not have love, I am nothing. *If I meet Joe's physical and emotional needs but do not have love in my heart, I gain nothing. If I prepare wonderful meals for my family every day, if I wash twenty-five loads of laundry a week and keep a spotless, picture-perfect home and volunteer countless hours but do not have love, I gain nothing in the eyes of the Lord.* **Love must be the driving force behind my words and actions.** *Otherwise, they are wasted and mean nothing. I might appear impressive to those around me, but if the things I do and the words I say are without love, I am probably an unhappy, unfulfilled individual. I believe the people closest to us feel and know when love is a part of the equation. When love is absent, those same people feel as if they are an inconvenience and a burden.* **The love behind the action is what brings joy and peace**

to the lover and the loved. *Mother Teresa reminds us, "It's not how much we do, it's how much love we put into the doing."*

Although I am a loving, compassionate person, I, too, struggle at times with choosing to give and do out of love. There are those occasions when the fulfillment of an obligation is done out of a sense of duty rather than love. For example, there are those evenings when I am exhausted and all I want is some quiet time and a break from being Mommy. I remember those long nights when the boys were younger and Joe was on call at the hospital. By eight o'clock, all I wanted was the boys bathed, stories read, prayers recited, and all of them quickly tucked into bed. When the odds are not in your favor—one adult to six, eight, or ten children—fatigue, feelings of frustration, and self-pity can easily suppress feelings of love. It was a matter of survival at that point in my day. What I learned, though, was that if I didn't stay calm and handle the boys with tenderness, quiet may have enveloped the house once they were in bed, but peace was not present in my heart.

The same feelings happened in my relationship to Joe. If I let my frustrations with his schedule and time demands take precedence over my love, I was not at peace—actually we were not at peace. I had many adjustments to make that first year of our marriage: my new life with Joe, my first teaching assignment, the move to Houston, and the building of new friendships. I tried desperately to adapt to his hours and not let negative feelings and thoughts surface. But it was hard. I remember the frustrations, for example, with preparing a simple dinner, another new experience for me. The challenge, especially since I was an inexperienced cook, was timing the dinner for Joe's arrival home. He would expect to be home by a certain time only to end up being delayed by hours. Many a piece of meat or chicken looked shriveled up and unappealing by the time he finally arrived home. I also wanted to eat dinner together, but I was famished waiting until eight, nine, or ten o'clock in the evening to eat. In addition, the late and unpredictable hours played havoc with my schedule. I had preparations to make for school and other things I wanted to do; the freedom to do them was often dictated by his hours. We only owned one car, so I needed to be available to pick Joe up when he finished at the hospital. I was often lonely, frustrated at the unpredictable hours, and disappointed by the reality of married life and my expectations.

I was grateful for my teaching and the children I taught. They brought much love and laughter to my days, as well as the need for many hours of preparation. I kept busy with school-related activities, but not having Joe around to share the experiences with created a void in my life. During the couples' retreat we attended before we were married, the priest giving the retreat told me, when I voiced my concerns about being married to a doctor, that it was going to take a lot of love and determination to be married to a doctor because of the unique demands and pulls of the profession. How right he was, and how scared I was by the reality of the situation. This was not going to be easy. When your husband is constantly late for dinner because he stopped off to have a beer with the guys or to play another round of golf or a game of tennis, that's one issue. But when he's constantly arriving home late because he needed to wait for lab results, meet with the parents of a sick child, or attend to the needs of a child, it is harder to justify the frustration and anger. I felt guilty and selfish being annoyed with him.

Another area of frustration involved Joe and the television. **Joe loved to come home and vegetate in front of the TV after the stresses of his day. I wanted to spend that time talking and finding out about his day and sharing what had happened in mine. I felt like a side-order in his life instead of the entree. I asked myself many questions: "Where did I fit into his life?" "Why had he married me?" "What was I offering him that he didn't have before we were married, with the exception of the obvious answer of sex?" "How was this relationship making me a better person?" I was not at peace with myself or our marriage. I knew, though, that I had made a commitment to work at our relationship and the ideals we had set before ourselves. So work we did!**

Joe sensed my frustrations and anger; it was hard to disguise my emotions day after day. He hadn't realized how empty my life had become. He assumed that because I was busy with school I was fulfilled. His perspective and his needs were different from mine. In order to move forward, though, we had to deal with our individual feelings and needs. Knowing what we wanted for our relationship and understanding the importance of love, respect, commitment, and faith provided us the means to move forward and grow from the situation.

Sharing our feelings and our needs allowed us to understand each other in a new way, and in the process we strengthened our relationship. We learned that what may have worked for us as individuals before we were married may not be conducive to our growth as a couple. We both chose to make changes that were in our best interest—a little less individuality and a lot more commonality. **For a marriage to grow and strengthen, choices must be made that benefit the couple and family as a whole. If one person's wants are the central focus to the detriment of the rest of the family, the marriage and family will struggle. It is essential to find a balance between individual and marital needs.**

*(Cathy): It is this balancing act and the choices we make that continue to work for us. Joe's choice early on to watch less television and spend more time with me was an act of love. And later his choice to read to the boys versus watching Monday Night Football was also a choice made with love. My acceptance and understanding of Joe's late arrival home because of the needs of a patient or the patient's parents is a choice made with love in my heart. I try to understand the pressures and demands he is facing while appreciating the fact that when he is home he gives his all and all. Knowing Joe will be an integral part of my life when he is home makes the long hours alone as a wife and mother easier to accept and tolerate. My decision to love Joe becomes a true concern for his fulfillment along with my own. **Our love is not self-driven, but***

driven instead by a strong sense of what is best for us as a couple and a family.

My decision to stay home, for example, with our children instead of continuing to teach was a choice I made for our family. We both felt it was what would work best for us. The decision was as controversial and difficult in the mid-1970s as it is today. I enjoyed teaching and knew I would miss the children, the adult interaction, and the sense of accomplishment. Yet, during the years I taught, I observed how stressful and difficult it was for families when both parents worked outside the home. Even though we knew we would struggle financially with only Joe's fellowship salary, I decided to stay home.

The decision to stay home entailed making additional choices. Since we would only have one salary, we needed to agree on our lifestyle. It meant waiting longer to buy a house, another car (we only had one car until our second son, David, was born), furnishings for our apartment, eating out, entertainment, and the purchasing of nonessentials. Those early years of budgeting and living within our means enabled us to make similar choices as our family grew. The children, we often feel, helped us keep our priorities in the right place.

(Joe): So often we naively believe that our choices only affect ourselves. This is an unrealistic belief. I learned that my actions intertwine and affect the lives of my spouse and my family. My choice to unexpectedly spend an extra hour at the office working on a project instead of going home makes me sound as if I am a hard-working, dedicated professional. While in one sense that may be true, in another sense my arriving home late is disruptive to Cathy, the boys, and the evening schedule. Cathy may have dinner to prepare as well as other responsibilities to complete at home. The boys may have "a ton" of homework, as well as their athletic practices and other commitments. My "simple" choice (self-centered focus) has consequences for Cathy and the boys. For this reason, I have chosen to minimize my late meetings and, whenever

possible, plan those "stay later times" with advanced notice. That way Cathy and the boys can adapt the evening routine to accommodate my absence. My choice to control my hours when possible makes the unexpected delays more handleable. So when I am confronted with a very sick infant and cannot leave the hospital until the baby's condition is stable, Cathy and the boys are more accepting and sympathetic, even though it is still disruptive to the evening routine. They know that my attention must be with my patient and they are supportive.

This "self-centered focus" had a very sobering effect on me when I understood and realized how my choices impacted Cathy and the rest of the family. During college and medical school, I watched TV as a form of relaxation. Spending a Saturday and Sunday afternoon watching sports was really enjoyable, especially if a few friends came over and joined in the "vegging out." After we were married, such blocks of time spent in front of the TV created conflicts for Cathy and me. I felt that I needed a break from the rigors of a resident's stressful day, whereas Cathy needed to share her experiences with me. Initially, I didn't understand why watching TV was such an issue. As I look back, I realize I was a slow learner. The constant watching of TV instead of spending time with Cathy really affected our relationship. Once the boys started arriving in quick succession, there was not much available time to spend in front of the TV. Fortunately, but more importantly, I realized how much I was missing. I was missing the opportunity to know Cathy even better than before, and I was missing the opportunity to know and share my time with my growing boys. Little by little, I found that the time I shared with Cathy and the boys was more enjoyable and fulfilling than time spent watching TV. My decision to be actively involved with Cathy and my children allowed our relationships to grow. Understanding how my self-centeredness affected Cathy and the boys, and moving from the "me" to the "we" with its positive effects on my marriage and family was a maturing process for me. Choosing the boys and Cathy over the TV was a loving choice that I do not regret making.

The Principle of Respect Respect in a relationship is paramount to its success. Respect flows from the previous principle of love being a choice. If we love another, we choose to respect that individual in their uniqueness. We choose to appreciate the dignity that is inherent in each of us.

We respect each other for the individuals we are. When we chose each other to love and honor from our wedding date on, we did so because the qualities each of us possessed were qualities we appreciated and wanted to strive for in our own lives or qualities we too possessed and wanted to strengthen or develop. Although we did not know and understand every aspect of each other's personality and life, we did not enter into our marriage blindly. Much thought and prayer went into the decision to marry. The principle of respect was determinant in our decision.

Acting and Speaking with Respect

One way we demonstrate respect to our spouse is in the way we verbally and nonverbally communicate with him/her on a day-to-day basis. The words we say and the tone of voice we use exemplify respect. "Please" should always precede a request and "thank you" should follow a thoughtful statement or act. Even after twenty-six years of marriage, we still say "please" and "thank you." It may sound simplistic, but we believe it demonstrates appreciation and affirmation of each other. Many couples drop these signs of respect because they assume the spouse knows how they feel. We believe couples should not only foster "please" and "thank you" in their vocabularies but many more words of appreciation, affirmation, and kindness. Affirming and appreciating each other becomes second nature when done repeatedly. In addition, if respectful communication is practiced in the marriage, children will naturally learn and understand the importance of respect in the way they speak to their parents, siblings, and friends. The strengths of the marriage will trickle down to the children.

(Cathy): Each of us wants to be spoken to and treated with respect, especially in our homes. We just need to remember "to do unto others as we want them to do unto us"—beginning with our spouse and children. I can feel Joe's words of affirmation and appreciation are sincere and come from the heart: "Thank you for the nice dinner you prepared." "I appreciate you handling the car repair today." "How thoughtful of you to go to the bank this morning for me." My words to Joe are similar: "I appreciate you mailing those letters for me." "Your phone call this afternoon picked me up. Thanks for taking the time to call." "Thank you for stopping on the way home and picking up some more milk." (Since the boys drink five gallons of milk a day when they are all home, Joe is often stopping to pick up more milk!)

They are simple statements, nothing elaborate or eloquent, yet they convey respect and love. They are words that build up and strengthen the other.

Beyond the "please's" and the "thank you's," we need to be conscious of the day-to-day conversations with our spouse. Are our comments and conversations positive, uplifting, and loving? Or are they curt, demoralizing, and sarcastic? What tone of voice are we using? The words may be positive, but the words become insignificant if the tone of voice does not match. ***Remember, love and respect are conveyed through your words and tone of voice.***

Our actions also convey the level of respect we have for our spouse.

(Cathy): From Joe's hugs when he arrives home in the evening to the dinners he prepared when I was too nauseated from a pregnancy to do so, Joe's actions demonstrate respect for me as a person. He could just as easily come home after the stresses of his day, walk in the door, grab a beer, plop down on the sofa, and demand dinner. I assure you that has never happened. He may ask what's for dinner, but only after he's given me a hug and a kiss and asked about my day. These days Joe usually knows what's for

dinner before he arrives home because we sit down together on Sundays and plan our meals for the week.

I remember the story I read in Dr. Ed Young's book, Romancing the Home, about St. Peter coming home after a long, hard day preaching and bearing the responsibility of building the early church. He walked in the door and yelled, "I'm home. What's for dinner?" When his wife answered, "Fish," Peter retorted, "Again?" That was not what Peter's wife needed; she had had a long day, too. She would have appreciated Peter acknowledging her, asking how her day went, and then being grateful that dinner was being prepared. Now, instead of a calm, relaxing evening, Peter was trying to undo the hurt he had caused by not being attuned to his wife's needs.

Joe and I know how often comments, statements, reactions, or lack of action can affect the other. We may not intentionally set out to make the other feel hurt or inferior, but in some way we have. We must be sensitive, learning and reminding ourselves to consciously respect our spouse in all we do and say. For example, if we know our spouse is weight conscious, we will not make teasing or disparaging remarks about weight. If we realize our spouse needs some extra TLC one day, we will be ready to provide it. If our spouse has had an extra stressful day at work, we will work hard to provide as calm a home environment as possible. **Being conscious of your spouse's feelings, moods, and needs goes a long way to consciously respecting and loving your spouse. And just like practicing respectful communication, the more often we treat our spouse with respect, the more opportunities we have to build and strengthen the relationship. Our children, again, observe the way we treat each other and will model our behavior.**

Respecting Our Individuality

Respect also involves appreciating and affirming our spouse's individuality. We may share similar values and goals, but we are unique individuals blessed by God with our own strengths, weaknesses, personalities, interests, and abilities.

(Cathy): *Joe exhibits many admirable qualities. He is sensitive and compassionate. He makes strong commitments to what he holds important: his faith, family, friends, work, and education. He enjoys life and being with people. He is calm and easy-going.*

While I have similar qualities, with the exception of being as calm and easy-going as Joe, we approach and handle situations differently. In addition, we have different strengths. For example, I like to complete tasks right away and have them behind me; Joe is content with things being done in the time frame provided. If taxes are not due until April 15, Joe will wait until April to prepare them. I, on the other hand, want them prepared as soon as the necessary paperwork is available. If the boys bring a paper home on Monday to be signed and returned by Friday, Joe will make sure it is signed by the end of the week; I will sign it when the boys hand it to me and be done with it. The tasks get done and we fulfill our responsibilities, but we approach the process differently.

We both share a love and respect for children. Joe's love and expertise is in the area of pediatrics and neonatology, while my love and expertise is in the field of elementary education. Although we believe God wanted us both to work with children, He gifted us with different abilities and interests.

Around the house, Joe is excellent at building, repairing, and creating; I have a better understanding of financial matters. Our sons seek Joe out to help them with science and creative projects; I assist them in math, reading, and social studies. Joe can usually answer their computer-related questions; I can only listen to the questions.

We are distinct individuals. **We both want to be loved, respected, appreciated, and accepted for who we are. It is essential in a marriage relationship that spouses respect, appreciate, and accept the unique gifts bestowed on them as individuals.** We always tease that, if we were exactly alike, we would have many gaps to fill in our daily lives. And talk about boring!

The Principle of Commitment Marriage is about commitment. We commit and entrust our lives to each other "for better and for worse, for richer and for poorer, in sickness and in health, till death do us part." These words must be spoken sincerely and with conviction not only on our wedding day but also in our hearts every day after that. All the preparation during our engagement should help prepare us for making this solemn vow. The commitment is permanent and unconditional—a covenant versus a contract. It means we will be faithful to each other, work with each other, solve our problems together, and make changes when necessary to strengthen our marriage and to make each other better individuals.

Living the commitment entails making choices. We keep coming back to "choices." But the choices we make as we face the joys and struggles of everyday life determine the level of commitment we have to each other and our marriage. Stop and ask yourself some important questions: "What are the priorities in my life?" "What commitments do I have?" "How will I prioritize these commitments so I will continue to grow as an individual as we likewise continue to grow as a couple and a family?" We have asked ourselves these questions many times over the course of our marriage. They are not questions to be asked once and put aside. Why? Because change is an inevitable part of life. There are many ways change enters our lives, and we need to focus on our commitments and priorities with each new experience: a new job, the loss of a job, a new career, each new child, financial difficulties or financial security, the illness or death of a family member or friend.

We have many commitments: God, marriage, children, family, friends, career, church, community, and schools. ***Where we fit these commitments into our daily life demonstrates to the ones we love the importance and significance we bestow on them.*** We can talk about how much we love our spouse and/or our children, but if we are not living the talk, then the words mean nothing.

The importance of balance in our lives is essential. While careers and work, for example, are important because we need to support ourselves, they become a negative when they dominate our every waking thought, action, and minute. Our loved ones may enjoy the material things a job provides, but we know from experience, in our own home and from people we have met, that our loved ones want our time and attention even more than material goods. We may try to convince ourselves that we are good providers because we have bought our spouse and children many "things." But have we provided for their emotional and physical needs in the process? *"Things" cannot replace our love, time, and attention.* M. Scott Peck reinforces that concept with this statement: "When we love something it is of value to us, and when something is of value to us we spend time with it, time enjoying it, and time taking care of it."

The valuable commodity of time seems to be in short supply in today's world. We do not believe, though, that lack of time is the real problem but, rather, the distribution of our time. Too many of us are rushing around chasing the wrong dreams. Work, social functions, and the accumulation of wealth and "things" are more important than time spent with our spouse and our children.

We are often asked: "How with ten children and with all your other commitments do you find time for each other?" We answer simply and honestly: "We make time for each other." It is a choice we make each and every day. In our previous book, *Good Families Don't Just Happen,* we define "quality time" as any time we're with our children. The same concept applies to our marriage: "quality time" is any time we're with our spouse. We take every opportunity to share and talk during the day, whether talking on the telephone, preparing dinner, or folding clothes at ten o'clock at night. We learned early in our marriage how detrimental the television and other forms of technology can be to couple time. We rarely have the television on in the evenings, except to watch the news. We need to honestly evaluate how we spend our discretionary time because it reflects our priorities.

We also learned how important it is to set aside time for each other with as few outside distractions as possible. The need to reserve time for each other became even more important and difficult to accomplish as we had children. But, as the old saying goes, "where there's a will, there's a way."

Our first two sons are eleven months apart. When we went out, we needed a baby-sitter who was comfortable taking care of both boys. The nursing students from the Texas Medical Center emerged as the answer to our prayers. (We quickly discovered, too, the advantage of finding students who had boyfriends out of town.) We did not have to go anywhere fancy or spend a lot of money to enjoy time together replenishing our spirits and our love. As our family grew, we continued to set aside one evening a week for ourselves. Again, we usually kept it simple: coffee and dessert, an evening playing board games with friends, a movie or a dinner out when we could afford it.

We still try to keep one evening a week for ourselves. We have more flexibility in the schedule now with the older boys available to watch their brothers. At the same time, we are working around the older boys' schedules and activities in determining our plans. One other noticeable difference from our early years as parents as compared to now is that, when the boys were all younger, they went to bed earlier. The house was quieter sooner and we had that time together. As the boys grew older and stayed up later, we found that our quiet, alone time dwindled. Since we relish our time together, however, we continue to be creative in finding moments alone. It may be a little later in the evening or a little earlier in the morning, but we are both committed to finding the time we need to nourish our relationship. The status of our relationship is a priority in our lives.

We shared with you our definition of success and self-worth as part of our vision. Our definition was not tied up in monetary terms but, rather, defined by who we are, what we do with the gifts God has given us, and how we live our lives. When we remain focused on that concept, we are better able to make the commitments in our daily lives that draw us closer to our spouse and family. In the process, we become more loving individuals as well.

(Cathy): *When I decided to marry Joe, I had thought and prayed long and hard about the permanent commitment I was making. I saw marriages dissolve or marriages that existed in name only. The joy and fulfillment that I wanted in a marital relationship were not evident in many marriages. I also witnessed marriages where that joy and fulfillment were present, in spite of the challenges they obviously faced. As a person who observes situations and tries to learn from those observations, I noticed how couples interacted, conversed, and treated each other in routine activities and experiences.* **The love and respect that Joe and I know are essential in a relationship were an integral part of the healthy marriages.** *There was an unspoken bond between those spouses that indicated to me that they were committed to their relationship. The choices they made were for their growth as individuals and as a couple.*

Over the years, Joe and I have made many choices that have involved commitment to our relationship: the daily choices to love and respect each other, and the more involved choices that require greater change and acceptance. *One such instance was during our second year of marriage. I decided to return to school to work on my master's degree in education. I was still teaching a class of thirty active first graders with all the preparation time that involved. At home, I was shouldering most of the responsibilities of maintaining the household. It did not take long for the "too much to do and too little time" syndrome to set in. When I approached Joe with the situation, he initially thought I should either teach or go to school; it didn't seem as if I could handle both. That was not the answer I expected or the solution I had in mind or found acceptable. If Joe would shoulder more of the at-home responsibilities, I could successfully do both. He had juggled doing laundry, grocery shopping, banking, and bill paying before we were married. I did not see any reason why he could not assume some of these tasks now. The situation necessitated Joe and me to sit down and work out a shared commitment. Adjustments were made that recognized the needs and responsibilities of both of us. Joe willingly acknowledged that there were times he would need to buy groceries or pay* the bills. He accepted this fact out of love and commitment to me and our relationship.

Likewise, I had to make a commitment to Joe regarding his choice to pursue neonatology. When Joe came home several months prior to the completion of his pediatric residency and told me he was interested in continuing his medical training with a fellowship in neonatology, I cried. The thought of two more years of long days and nights and living from paycheck to paycheck was not exciting. (We had already started our family and I was no longer working.) But Joe was excited about the opportunity to specialize in neonatology, as well as to study and train under Dr. Arnold J. Rudolph, one of the premier neonatologists in the world. Joe had worked hard for many years and deserved the opportunity to pursue his dreams. Joe had supported my decision to work on my master's degree; now that the roles were reversed, I needed to be understanding and supportive as well. The two years of his fellowship were exhausting and stressful, but our commitment to each other made the difficult times workable and growth-filled.

(Joe): We keep stressing over and over again how choices reflect and support our priorities. When I was in the last year of my fellowship, I needed to make a decision as to what I would do after the completion of my training. The opportunities were many, but they boiled down to either going into a lucrative private practice or staying in an academic setting with a medical school. I had observed my friends and other neonatologists in private practice and noted how much of their time was spent at the hospital. It indeed was, in my opinion, a tremendous commitment to the practice of neonatology. It was attractive because of the professional independence that came with it, as well as the significant financial rewards for the time spent at the patient's bedside. On the down side, there was a lot more night and weekend call. In the practices that I was considering, it meant night-call every second or third night and the same for weekends. The job offer from the medical school meant joining a large group of neonatologists with much less *night-call but also less independence and less financial reward. It meant that I would have more teaching responsibilities for medical students, residents, and fellows (which I loved) but, more importantly, there would be more control of the time I could spend with Cathy and the boys. It was a decision that was not really a decision. The choice to stay with the academic practice has never been a disappointment to me because of the supportive bosses and the wonderful colleagues I have had in addition to the time it has allowed me with Cathy and the boys. To be a part of the boys' activities has been important to them and a validation of my decision. To have time with Cathy on our Friday nights has been a reward for us that cannot be assigned a true monetary value.*

Other significant commitments arose that likewise impacted our family and my relationship with Cathy. As our family grew, each unfolding life meant new challenges for all of us. Although Cathy notes how different each pregnancy was, there was one common element with each of them: her morning sickness, which wasn't always only in the morning and differed in duration with each pregnancy. In addition, certain smells aggravated her nausea. To this day, certain smells (syrup, especially) are not pleasant. It was not uncommon for me to arrive home to find Cathy not only tired from being pregnant and caring for our sons but also terribly nauseated. Cathy had developed into a good cook over the years, whereas I did little in the kitchen outside of helping to clean up. Now, however, I was frequently relegated to the cooking duties. Observing Cathy's expression of "I don't think I can look at food, not to mention prepare it" meant I needed to cook dinner or anticipate a lot of hungry faces. (When we only had a couple children, I could stop and pick something up for dinner. As our family grew, though, stopping and picking up dinner cost a small fortune.) At first it was just a duty performed out of necessity, but soon preparing dinner became an additional way for me to help Cathy through the pregnancy. She was already handling the more demanding responsibilities of taking care of herself and the new baby, not to mention the sons we already had, so it was the least

I could do to make her day a little more comfortable. It was my choice to cook on those nights that Cathy couldn't, a choice initially made out of necessity. Eventually, my heart caught up with my head and the choice was made out of love. That was my commitment to Cathy, to the new baby, and to the boys.

Making these commitments in the early years of our marriage ultimately prepared and strengthened us for the many other choices we would make in the years to come. Like most people, we are pulled in many directions by the needs and demands of our children, career, church, and schools, our social and volunteer obligations, as well as our individual needs and our needs as a couple. This is where having a vision and goals for our marriage and family makes a tremendous difference. **By keeping our marriage at the forefront of our commitments, we are able to prioritize these many other needs and demands.**

As much as all of us want to think we can do it all, something, or more often someone, usually suffers. Before we accept or make a commitment, whether a one-time activity such as a dinner engagement or a long-term involvement as a board member, we discuss the amount of time and energy the commitment will require, not only of the person directly involved in the activity, but also of the one who must fulfill the responsibilities at home while the other is away.

We had seven of the boys playing soccer at one time a few years ago. To say we had children coming and going is putting it mildly. We had to carefully organize the drop-offs and pick-ups for practices so that dinner would still be prepared, the meal eaten as a family (at least all those who were home), and our other responsibilities fulfilled, such as monitoring homework and reading to the younger boys. It entailed older brothers sometimes driving younger ones to practice for us, or one son arriving a little early for his practice and another staying a little later at his. We were fortunate at this time because the older boys were able to help us out. They understood that it would take all of us working together to enable each of them to be involved in the activities they enjoyed. When one of us was out of pocket because of another commitment, the juggling increased, and the need for the older boys to pitch in was paramount. We also relied on other parents to help us out when needed. Many families very willingly dropped off or picked up a son for us; when we could reciprocate the help, we eagerly did. Even today, although we have "only" five sons playing soccer, we coordinate our schedules in ways that are beneficial to our family as a whole.

(Cathy): Two experiences come to mind as I think about coordinating schedules and working around commitments; both of them occurred during the time we had seven of the boys playing soccer. One evening, Joe was on call in-house at the hospital, which meant he would not be home that night. I was running two of the boys to practice when I received a phone call from Joe Pat, who had arrived home from high school after I had already left. He wanted to know how he could start dinner so that, when I returned home, we could eat. I explained to him how to prepare the chicken and the vegetables over the phone; when I walked in the door, the meal was being served. Joe Pat's initiative significantly impacted the rest of the evening for all of us.

The second occasion revolved around an unexpected change in plans. Joe called late in the afternoon to inform me that the doctor on call for the night had a family emergency; Joe would need to cover for him. In turn, the plans for the evening would need to be revised. Chris was in the kitchen when Joe called. He could tell from my "okay, what do I do now" expression that something was up. When I explained that his dad needed to take call for one of the other physicians and would not be home, he immediately asked, "What do we have tonight and how can I help?"

People often ask me: "Cathy, how do you do it all?" I can honestly answer: "It is not just a 'me' that gets it all done; it is a 'we'—Dad, Mom, and the boys!" *How I appreciate Joe Pat's initiative and help as well as Chris's emotional support and active participation in the evening's commitments.*

(Joe): *When Cathy says it's a "we" in handling the many commitments of our family, she speaks from the many experiences that we confront as a family. When Timmy was three years old, he developed some stomach cramps on a Friday evening in June that kept Cathy up most of the night (I was on call at the hospital). The next morning when I arrived home, I surmised that he had eaten too much pizza the night before and awaited other symptoms to surface. The other symptoms did not materialize and, by late Saturday night, he was in excruciating pain. Cathy and I put him in the car and rushed to the emergency room. As we left the house for the emergency room, the older boys could read the worry on our faces. They told us to take care of Timmy; they would look after everything else. When we arrived at the hospital, the doctors determined that Timmy had an appendicitis, pretty unusual for his age. Not only was it an appendicitis, explained Dr. Mary Brandt, our "family" pediatric surgeon (she operated on David's appendicitis the following summer), but the appendix had ruptured as well. We called the boys and told them that, while Timmy was okay, he would need to remain in the hospital for ten days of antibiotic treatment due to the appendix having ruptured. The older boys got the boys to church the next morning and took over the running of the house. Soccer games, swimming pool time, lunch, etc., were all handled with the total cooperation of the boys. (And friends jumped in with dinners and many, many other acts of kindness.) Cathy and I were able to comfortably concentrate on Timmy's needs. Significantly, this all happened on Father's Day.* **When people ask what is the best Father's Day present I have ever received, I tell them this story: how the boys took care of each other so we could be with Timmy. It is not only the "me" commitment that gets things done but, more importantly, the "we" commitment that makes it all possible.**

Accepting Outside Commitments

The ability to accept outside commitments changed as our family responsibilities grew. We learned to be highly selective about any activities outside the home. Our family needs and responsibilities are a priority. We try to schedule meetings and appointments around hospital call schedules and the boys' activities. We have some flexibility now because our older sons pitch in to help at home and drive a carpool or two, but we still prefer one of us home to review schoolwork and read stories to the younger boys. We strive for one of us to be at the boys' school programs, athletic and academic competitions, and other functions in which they may be involved. Our commitment of time and energy, more powerfully than any words can possibly convey, demonstrates to our sons that they are loved and important to us.

Financial Commitments

Financial commitments and demands often strain many marriages. **We realize that when we focus on our financial goals as part of our value system and live within our means, the financial struggles are minimized.** Although our income is higher than that of the average family, the financial responsibilities inherent in a large family are also significant in comparison to the average family. For example, our sons drink four to five gallons of milk a day when they are all home. We not only have one or two sons who have required orthodontia, but five. We will have four sons in higher education next year: one in medical school and three in college. It is imperative that we remain focused on our needs and our goals.

One of our goals is to educate the boys in the Catholic school system since it offers a strong academic program in a faith-filled environment. We commit a large percentage of our financial resources to that end. This choice, like the choice made earlier in our marriage for me to stay home with the children, entails making additional choices. In order to pay the tuition, we need to maintain a simpler lifestyle. We focus on necessities versus wants. We drive cars for several years to avoid car payments. We fix rather than replace appliances—our Maytag washing machine is twenty-five years old. Finally, we do not feel compelled to buy every new gadget or technological invention that becomes available—our GE hand mixer is the one we received at one of our wedding showers, and it still makes great birthday cakes and mashed potatoes. Remarkably, our nineteen-inch television set is ten years old (and, as we remind the boys, at least it's color).

How easy it is to get caught up in "the more, the bigger and the better." It used to be described as "keeping up with the Joneses." Today it is keeping up with the mass media and the prevailing attitude that we "need" everything that we see advertised. Families are living beyond their means and incurring substantial debt—and incurring the stress that accompanies it. We strive to focus on our goals, live within our means, and save for large-ticket items in order to meet the financial responsibilities of our family.

All the commitments we make to each other, to our children, and to the other areas of our lives, strengthen our marriage and help us fulfill our vow to love each other "for better and for worse, for richer and for poorer, in sickness and in health, till death do us part."

The Principle of Faith

Our marriage is a unique relationship when understood in the context of our faith. **Our faith unfolds and gives meaning to the principles of love, respect, and commitment that we embrace.** We did not comprehend on our wedding day the impact and influence our faith would have on the growth and development of our relationship. While our faith was important to us as individuals and a bond between us as an engaged couple, our faith today is the core and foundation of our relationship and our family. We realize that living out our marriage vows and our responsibilities as parents is living out our faith. They become one and the same. While we practice the Catholic faith, we believe that all faiths and religions inspire a similar interrelationship.

Our faith is woven through each chapter of our marriage—at different degrees depending on the level of our development as individuals and a couple, but nevertheless present. Although one chapter of this book concentrates on how we integrate faith in our marriage, family, and community, faith is also woven through the other chapters of the book because it cannot be separated from who we are and how we live our lives. In today's society, the effort is made to separate our personal and private actions and words from our public persona. We contend, again, that our words and actions—day and night, public and private—are an expression of who we are—an expression of our faith.

We said previously that our commitment is permanent and unconditional—a covenant versus a contract. What exactly does that mean in the framework of our faith? The dictionary defines a covenant as a contract. In a Christian context, specifically in reference to the marital relationship and our relationship to God, the word "covenant" expresses a deeper meaning. Fr. Paul Palmer, S.J., distinguishes covenant from contract by comparing the two. He states (as quoted from an article by Carl Arico in the Fall 1979 *Chicago Studies*): ". . . contracts deal with things or the services of people. But covenants engage persons. Contracts are made for a stipulated period of time; covenants are forever. Contracts can be broken with material loss to the contracting parties. Covenants can be violated, but not broken, and when violated, they result in broken hearts. Contracts are secular affairs and belong to the market place; covenants are sacred affairs and belong to the hearth, the temple, the church. Contracts are witnessed and guaranteed by the state; covenants are witnessed and guaranteed by God. Contracts can be made by children who know the value of a penny; covenants can be made only by adults who are physically, emotionally, and spiritually mature."

Our covenant was made with the understanding that God was a part of the relationship. The "we" of husband and wife is not a duo, but a trio: husband, wife, and God. God is an integral part of our relationship. As Fr. Robert Ruhnke, C.SS.R., phrases it: "Christian marriage is a formal and conscious decision to include God as a 'third party' to the marriage." It is only with God as the third party in our relationship that we have been able to sustain both the planned and the unexpected events that have inevitably touched our lives.

The covenant we made as husband and wife and our commitment to love each other is beautifully compared to the covenant between God and His people and Christ and His church. Michael Lawler in his book *Family* relates how this comparison is a model for us in our marriages. "In a truly Christian marriage, which is not just a marriage between two people who say they are Christian but between two Christian believers, the symbolic meaning takes precedence over the physical meaning, in the sense that the steadfast love of God and of Christ is explicitly present as the model for the mutual love of the spouses. In and through the love of the spouses, God and God's Christ are present in a Christian marriage, providing for them models of steadfast love."

The steadfast love described in the above passage is a faithful and unconditional love. We are presented with this model to emulate in our own marriages. We may have entered the marriage on our wedding day with a true commitment to love and cherish our spouse from that day forward, but what we may not have completely understood is that it would require an ongoing commitment on the part of both spouses for the marriage to be sustained. There is a risk involved in making a commitment to another for life; we may understand what that commitment entails on our wedding day, but there is no way for us to totally comprehend what that commitment will demand of us in the months and years to follow. **We know that without God woven through the daily joys and struggles we encountered over the last twenty-six years, our marriage would not be the relationship it is today.**

Many of the biblical verses we read and heard since childhood took on a new relevance and understanding when placed in the context of our marriage. More importantly, though, and of greater challenge, was applying our new understanding and knowledge to our relationship and family. "What good is it to profess faith without practicing it?" (James 1:14) It has been a gradual and continuous process for us of learning, understanding, and applying the teachings of Christ and His command to "love one another as I have loved you."

The Building of a Good Marriage from a Strong Foundation

The principles of love, respect, commitment, and faith, interwoven and inseparable, are the foundation of our marriage and our family. Our marriage does not stop at the foundation, though. Rather it is built and strengthened from there. We hope as we share our experiences that we are able to demonstrate how we have integrated these foundational principles into the emotional, physical, intellectual, and spiritual dimensions of our relationship. We also want to show how the marriage relationship is an active process that demands constant time and attention for it to grow and mature into the loving, fulfilling relationship God intends it to be.

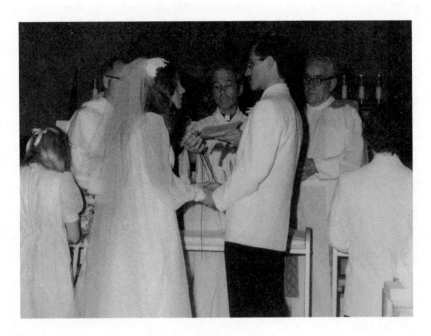

*That is why a man leaves his father and mother
and clings to his wife, and the two of them
become one body.*
> —Genesis 2:24

*You give but little when you give of your possessions.
It is when you give of yourself that you truly give.*
> —Kahlil Gibran

*We are fully ourselves only in relation to each other. . . .
I must begin with myself, true;
But I must not end with myself:
The truth begins with two.*
> —Walter Tubb

Chapter Three

Two Become One

*L*ike most couples, we entered our marriage with great confidence and high expectations. When we professed our vows, we believed that they were forever and that we would continue to grow in our love for each other. There was no way we could predict what the next day would bring, but we were confident our love for each other would see us through whatever life had to offer us.

What confidence! What trust! What hope! What love! Confidence, trust, hope, and love were a part of our relationship, but it took a lot of maturing and growing to appreciate what is truly meant by "two become one." While two becoming one is easily understood in respect to the physical, sexual dimension of our relationship, it is harder to comprehend the more profound and significant meaning of the mutual giving of our whole selves to each other: emotionally, intellectually, and spiritually as well as physically. Yet, giving of our whole selves to each other is what must happen in order to have a good marriage that is mutually satisfying and mutually beneficial for both spouses.

Our relationship has evolved over the twenty-eight years we have known each other. We know our love for each other has also evolved and matured over this same period of time. With each new experience we share together, a more realistic understanding unfolds of what marital love entails. Our love is fuller, richer, and more mutually satisfying and mutually beneficial than we ever dreamed possible, especially after the struggles and adjustments of our first years of marriage.

It is how we approach and handle each situation that enables us to grow as individuals and as a couple. We had to learn (and we emphasize "learn"), though, to merge our "I's" into a "we"—a "we" that was mutually loving, giving, forgiving, and supportive. It took the "we" to reach each new plateau in our relationship. The two becoming one didn't just happen on our wedding night but evolved over the years. Some couples achieve the "oneness" sooner than other couples, but we believe that it is possible for all couples to reach that level in their relationship when both spouses are committed and willing to follow through with the changes that are necessary to make in order for the "oneness" to happen.

*(Joe): Two becoming one didn't just happen for us overnight or even in the first few years of our marriage. In retrospect, we probably can say we were happy, but not to the extent of the happiness we have now. **It has taken time to mature and to learn to truly listen, to forgive and to ask for forgiveness, and to communicate. I could be entered in the Guinness Book of World Records for the many times I have asked Cathy for forgiveness.** But again, this is a process—it takes time. As Mother Teresa tells us, the most important step to achieving your goal is, "You must will it." Once that step has been taken, all is possible.*

After a family talk Cathy and I gave in Dallas to a large church group of young married couples, we joined a few of the couples for lunch. The lunch conversation, generated by experiences we had shared at the presentation, focused primarily on the marital relationship. As we were getting ready to leave, one of the young mothers came and sat down beside me. She asked me how long it had taken me to really be involved with Cathy and the boys. She was almost in tears as she shared that this closeness was not happening in her relationship with her husband. He spent many hours at work, to the dismay of his wife. They had been married four years and were very much in love, yet she was frustrated with her husband's lack of wanting to spend more time with her and their young child. He didn't feel the same sense of need for closeness (intimacy) as she did. Her statement made me wonder how often Cathy had the same thoughts about me. I responded that in actuality I was a fairly slow learner. It was Cathy's loving persistence and my love and respect for her and the boys that finally brought about my decision "to will it." I told her to persist in the good she does for her husband, her child, and herself, and that in time the "oneness" will happen.

We want to return to the early stages of our relationship to explain the process of developing our love. When we first met and decided to continue to date, we were attracted to each other because of the many qualities we each possessed—the outward physical features as well as the inner character and heart. Finding each other attractive in physical and nonphysical ways is a necessary, good, and positive development, a part of God's plan for us and the growth of our relationship. This attraction and desire to be with each other allowed us the possibility of moving to a higher level in the development of our relationship—we became friends.

As friends we cared deeply about each other. The desire to be with each other and the attractions we felt didn't wane or end but increased and became stronger as we learned more about the other. We gradually moved from just the "me" of the friendship to the "we." We wanted to spend time together sharing our experiences, our moods, our dreams, and even our disappointments. We moved from primarily needing to fulfill our own needs to wanting to enrich the life of the other. As we learned more about each other, we realized we wanted to develop our relationship even further. We wanted not only to spend more time together but to commit ourselves to each other in marriage.

The decision to marry was a choice and a commitment to love each other unconditionally and permanently. But even more than that, it was a choice we made to give ourselves to each other in a totally and mutually fulfilling way. Our love initially was naïve and untested. Although our intentions and goals were to love unconditionally and sacrificially, actually living this sacrificial love took many more shared experiences to understand, develop, and unfold. We are still in the process of our love unfolding, still working to attain a love that St. Francis of Assisi tells us is a love where "we may not so much seek to be consoled as to console, to be understood as to understand, to be loved as to love." Equally important is our realization and belief that "it is in giving that we receive; it is in pardoning that we are pardoned." If we are to model Christ's love in our marriage, then, it requires a love that focuses on serving rather than on being served.

In contrast, the society in which we live and grew up in is a society that highly values and stresses individualism. It is a society that focuses on and preoccupies itself with the gratification of the "me." In a marriage relationship, this emphasis on individualism is contrary to the concept of self-giving and sacrificial love. Any talk about squelching one's desires, one's wants, and one's needs in favor of someone else, even someone we love, is not readily received. **Yet for a good marriage to happen, the "I" must become a little "i." That is not to say that in becoming "one" either or both of us must lose our identity. Rather, it means we use our uniqueness to build up the other, and, in the process of building up our spouse, we build up ourselves.**

It may appear to be just semantics on the surface, but it makes sense when you understand the importance of knowing, accepting, and loving yourself as a means to love your spouse completely. "Fill yourselves first and then only will you be able to give to others," advises St. Augustine. A strong self-knowledge and self-love actually strengthen the marriage; self-centered, selfish love weakens the relationship.

(Cathy): *I know it sounds like we're contradicting ourselves when one minute we say become a little "i" and the next we are encouraging self-love. I hope as you read on, the difference in self-love and self-centeredness becomes clear.*

*Joe and I were strong individuals when we got married. We both had worked hard in our respective disciplines and were both respected for our accomplishments in our own right. When, as an independent woman of the 70s, I would read St. Paul's words to the Ephesians: "Wives should be submissive to their husbands as if to the Lord, because the husband is head of his wife just as Christ is head of his body the church, as well as its savior," I had a hard time comprehending how being submissive was important to our marriage or beneficial to me as a person. I looked only at the words "submissive" and "head" and failed to acknowledge the words that came before and after them. I erroneously interpreted the passage to mean that once I was married to Joe, contrary to before taking our vows, I would become inferior and unequal in status to him. How wrong I was! I no longer believe that St. Paul's words mean that women are to be swallowed up by the identity of their husbands or that women, once they are married, instantaneously become inferior individuals. Rather, when you read on in St. Paul's letter to the Ephesians, he tells husbands: "Love your wives, as Christ loved the church. He gave himself up for her to make her holy." St. Paul continues, "Husbands should love their wives as they do their own bodies. He who loves his wife loves himself." None of St. Paul's words imply that husbands have unbridled control over their wives or that husbands have the right to treat their wives with indignities of any kind. Instead, wives are to be respected and loved, not treated as doormats, as less intelligent, less productive, or less worthwhile individuals. **The love between a husband and wife is to be mutually giving, mutually respectful, and mutually satisfying. It is not a matter of being served but of serving the other. If we are to imitate Christ's love, we must remember that He came to serve, not to be served.***

I struggled with this concept of serving versus being served as well as loving myself versus loving others, especially once I became a mother. Balancing the needs of Joe, the boys, and myself became harder—and pretty soon my needs were left behind. I found I was giving to everyone but myself, and gradually that takes its toll. I resented in some ways that Joe could leave every morning and still pursue his interests. Although I knew in my heart I wanted to stay home with the boys, I also knew I needed "something" for me. My prayers were answered when our Sunday church bulletin announced the need for an assistant to one of the preschool religion teachers. The program ran on Sunday mornings for an hour or so. I called the director of religious education for more information. When Joe came home that evening, I told him that I wanted to volunteer on Sunday mornings in the Sunday school program. He was surprised; I hadn't mentioned my interest in teaching or doing anything outside the home to him. In fact, I don't think I had even shared with him my inner conflicts, because some of the conflict dealt with my relationship with him and fulfilling my needs. I accepted the teaching assistant position, and it made a wonderful difference in my life and our family's life. Any doubts Joe may have had about my being pulled away from my responsibilities at home vanished when he saw the difference the few hours of teaching provided for me and, ultimately, for the family.

I came to realize that in order to love Joe and our sons, I have to be a strong "me"—not in a selfish way, but in a loving way. I believe that if God created me, He created me with the same dignity that He created Joe and all persons. And, if I am to follow Christ's command to "love your neighbor as yourself," I must love myself in order to love my neighbor—my neighbor in this case being Joe. They go hand in hand.

I do not believe that once a woman marries she should stop or stall her own development. She must continue to strive to grow in all areas of her life: emotionally, physically, spiritually, and intellectually. **Self-respect and self-love enable me to respect and love the people in my life and to help them reach their full**

potential. *As a wife and mother of ten children, I have to find a balance between taking care of my needs and the needs of my family—a challenging endeavor each and every day. When I deprive myself of my needs (and it is imperative that I distinguish the difference in my needs and my wants), I struggle as a wife and a mother. So it is important for me to take care of me. By taking the time to walk on a regular basis, I feel better, I have more energy, and I enjoy a more positive mental and spiritual outlook. By building friendships and staying in touch with family, I gain another avenue of support in handling the day-to-day commitments in my life. By reading and attending lectures, I continue to learn and stimulate my mind. By praying or spending time in the chapel, I continue to develop and strengthen my relationship with God. I want to reemphasize that I'm not talking about being selfish, uncaring, or putting my needs first. Joe and the boys appreciate my taking care of my needs—loving myself—because they are rewarded with a happier wife and mother who is better able to in turn meet their needs.*

Theologian Richard Hauser, S.J., in his book Moving in the Spirit, *summarizes these thoughts beautifully: "True self-love is different from selfishness. Selfishness ends in the self; true self-love is integrated with a desire to love and serve God and others. And Jesus commands us to love our neighbor as our self. Jesus understood that if we loved ourselves because of our dignity as God's children, this love would naturally affect our attitudes toward all other people who are also God's children. True self-love is based on a desire to better serve God and others."*

As a child of God, I must love and accept who I am. And, I must remember that God made me who I am—Catherine Musco Garcia-Prats—with all my characteristics. He did not make me my sister Linda or my sister Patrice. He did not make me Katharine Hepburn or Catherine Deneuve. I believe He made me the way He did since He wants me to use the qualities He gave me to bring His love to others. In his book Happiness Is an Inside Job, *John Powell, S.J., shares his interpretation of our uniqueness: "God sends each of us into this world with a special message to deliver, with a special act of love to bestow. Your message and your act of love are entrusted only to you, mine to me. Whether this message is to reach only a few or all the folks in a small town or all the people in the whole world depends totally on God's choice."* Some of us He gifts as teachers, some of us as doctors, some of us as carpenters, some of us as bankers. **Each of us has a purpose under heaven. I am called by God to develop the special gifts He has given me and then to share them with others. Jesus makes it clear in the parable of the silver pieces: He does not want us to bury our talents. Jesus also does not make an exception to His expectations because I am a wife and/or a mother.**

In loving myself, I reemphasize that I must accept who I am: my physical characteristics, my intellectual abilities, my personality, my feelings, and my spirituality. I must understand and be able to differentiate between aspects of my being that I can change and those I cannot change. For example, physically God made me a petite five feet one inch tall woman. No matter what I do, I will never be five feet, ten inches tall. To harp on the fact or be dissatisfied with my height is wasted energy. As a matter of fact, the only times I wish I were taller is when I need to reach an item beyond my grasp. (But then, God has blessed me with sons that are taller than I am and can reach for me.) I have had many problems with my eyes over the years. During childhood it was a matter of wearing "coke-bottle" glasses to correct myopia. A few months after our second son, David, was born, it was determined that I had a detached retina in my right eye and tears in the left retina. With two small children at home, I spent two weeks in the hospital to reattach the retina and seal the tears in both eyes. Then a year ago, the ophthalmologist diagnosed a fast-growing cataract in one eye, unusual for someone my age. This entailed more surgery, although less involved than that with the retina. While it would be nice to have 20-20 vision, I accept the fact that my eyes require more care than usual; at the same time, I thank God every day for the gift of sight.

Intellectually, God has blessed me with a good mind. That does not mean that I am an expert or competent in all academic fields; when I was in school I was strong in reading, social studies, and math, but struggled with science. I still recognize my strengths and interests in certain areas. I may love music, but I am not gifted musically. I also recognize that I have to challenge myself in the areas where I have limited knowledge or ability, such as dealing with the computer and other technological advances. Learning is a lifelong process, so it is important for me to continue to challenge my mind, learn new skills, accept my abilities, and use the intellectual gifts God has given me.

A person's self-esteem and self-respect play an important role in an individual's emotional stability. I have been blessed over the years with parents, sisters, relatives, friends, teachers, Joe, and my sons who have all encouraged me, loved me, and accepted me for who I am—with the good and the bad, my weaknesses and my strengths. These individuals influenced my life at different periods of my development and in different ways. My parents' and sisters' influence were most profound in the first two decades of my life; they still encourage and support who I am and the choices I've made. I remember the impact teachers had on me: Mrs. Moerings, for example, in eighth grade asked me to be the narrator of our United States Constitution program. I was probably the shyest student in the class; the thought of standing and speaking in front of a few hundred students and parents intimidated me. Yet her confidence in my ability to tackle this challenge provided the motivation I needed to succeed. Joe's constant reassurance and faith during our marriage has enabled me to stretch and grow in many areas of my life. He has encouraged me when I doubted my ability to accomplish a task or reach a goal. For instance, when I first received requests to speak to groups about family and parenting several years ago, I questioned my ability to be effective. I did not view public speaking as one of my strengths. Standing up in front of large groups of people was just as scary and intimidating at that point in my life as it was for me in eighth grade. Joe bolstered my confidence and encouraged me to give it a try. How thankful I am to Joe because speaking to groups on parenting and family has proven to be an extremely rewarding experience for me. Over the years, he and our sons have often been my loudest cheerleaders—what a wonderful feeling!

In the Winter 1999 Birthright newsletter, Dr. Alan R. Zimmerman identified three prerequisites to raising self-esteem: First, believe in the other person; second, believe in the other person's drive; and third, accept the other person. The people in my life fulfilled all three of the prerequisites for me, enabling me to believe in myself, to believe in my drive, and to accept myself. Now I try to do the same for the people in my life: Joe, the boys, my students, my friends and family.

Even with a strong self-esteem and self-respect, I found that there was still an element missing. I realized that in order to accept or change who I am, I must know who I am. So as well as loving and accepting myself, I must strive to know myself better. It is only one part of the equation, for example, to acknowledge that I am frustrated, angry, disappointed, or discouraged, but another to understand why I feel the way I do and then to identify healthy ways to deal with the emotions. I have to accept the fact that I may need to change or adjust my attitude or my approach in certain situations—and not the other person. **Changing is not always easy to accomplish because it may mean acknowledging our weaknesses and/or our mistakes.**

My marriage to Joe has generated the most extensive growth in my awareness and knowledge of who I am, primarily emotionally and spiritually. When I would get upset with Joe early in our marriage, I needed to understand why I was upset with him. Sometimes it was obvious and other times it wasn't obvious at all. Why did certain things he said or did cause me to have a negative response? Although in my heart I knew he wouldn't intentionally hurt me, his words and/or actions sometimes did just that. Being able to step back a little from the situation, reflect, and question myself as to why I felt or reacted the way I did, provided countless opportunities to understand and *know myself better. They were also opportunities to change and grow from the experience; I learned that to only acknowledge the "why" was not enough.*

*I have become a much happier individual because of knowing myself. I may not like everything about myself, but I can acknowledge those characteristics that I don't like and continue to work to improve them. For example, I am a patient individual yet I often find myself intolerant of laziness, inefficiency, and incompetency; therefore, I consciously strive to be less critical and more tolerant. I get very frustrated with my technological deficiencies, so I am trying to improve my computer skills—thanks to the help of Joe and my sons. I am a person with high expectations; I have to continually make sure, though, that those expectations for myself and others are realistic. And, while I enjoy being with people, I am still shy and uncomfortable in certain situations. **Amazingly, the greatest reward in knowing and understanding myself is the ability to be more loving and understanding of Joe and the boys. This understanding and love facilitates the process of two becoming one.***

(Joe): Christ's New Testament command to "love thy neighbor as thyself" is very familiar to most of us. It was taught in my home while I was growing up and in the schools that I attended. I interpreted that commandment to mean that I would love and respect all the members of my family as well as those people that I would meet or deal with during my day. The equally important concept espoused by Jesus of loving oneself struck me as almost being contradictory. I understood the importance of loving one's neighbor, but it appeared that loving oneself was a selfish entreaty. I assumed that the emphasis of God's commandment was to serve those people in our family, our community, our world. This service entailed self-sacrifice for the sake of others. Thus, I should be prepared to make choices that are in the best interest of my spouse and children, sometimes at the expense of myself, because they were the individuals I loved so much. Erich Fromm says in The Art of Loving: *"When you truly*

love, you want what is best for that person, sometimes at the expense of what is best for yourself." This to me was living Christ's commandment.

To love oneself did not seem consistent with what I thought Christ was asking me to do. I really struggled with this and still do on occasion to this very day. I believe that I am slowly realizing what this commandment means to me in my daily life. I am reminded often of what Cathy has already stated about self-love: self-love must not be a "selfish" love or a "self-centered" love but, rather, a love of oneself as a creature of God. Part of that loving of oneself means understanding and accepting who I am with the gifts that are my strengths and acknowledging the weaknesses that I need to improve. That whole package, with its strengths and weaknesses, is me, Joe Garcia-Prats. It is a good package worthy of respect and love. Likewise, that package was created by God and placed here in this world for His purpose. Each day I am discovering what God wants me to do, so I am obligated to take care of myself physically, spiritually, and emotionally so that I can lovingly give to Cathy and the boys.

I would like to explain this in another way. **We read so much about the "ecosystem" and that each element in it plays a pivotal and important role in preserving the balance of that ecosystem. The plants that grow in a pond, the fish and insects that inhabit it, the rain that provides water to preserve the pond, the animals that come to drink the water, and the foliage around the pond— all play an important part in that ecosystem. Each must do its part to preserve the balance. The fish must act as a fish and not try to be a deer or plant. In that way the fish contribute to the life of the pond, as do the plants, etc. If those fish do not fulfill their roles as fish, then the pond's very survival falters. Such is the case with our "human ecosystem," our relationship with our spouse, our family, and our community.** I must be the best Joe Garcia-Prats that God has made and utilize all of my gifts that I have been given because of my role in God's wonderful plan. If I am not my best, then I am disappointing Him and those around *me. I can positively or negatively affect how those individuals relate and develop in this world. God created us with a free will which differentiates us from the other components of the "ecosystem." Thus, it becomes imperative that I choose to respect myself and accept who I am for the sake of all those whom I love and interact with—my spouse, children, parents, friends, acquaintances, etc. It is in loving and respecting myself that I ultimately contribute to the human community as family or in my own spousal relationship.*

As we grew to appreciate our individual similarities and differences, we also began to realize that, although we shared similar backgrounds, we experienced many differences in our upbringing and family life. The family dynamics we grew up with in our families of origin influenced our daily interactions as well as the assumptions and expectations we had of each other and, at times, the expectations and assumptions our families had of us. We found that we sometimes reacted differently to the same situations. Some of the differences we discovered were minor or trivial, while others were more involved. It took time for us to understand these differences and then to accept, adapt, or change according to the context of these differences.

Deciding on one brand of shampoo or buying the brands we both individually preferred were minor adaptations. Adjusting our time clocks, organizing our morning and evening routines, and determining how to spend our discretionary time took a little more effort. Defining, or redefining if necessary, our roles, our responsibilities, our assumptions, and our expectations, which are more reflective of our family background, was another hurdle. We were gradually learning to blend our "I's" into what would work best for us as a "we." At a recent diocesan meeting I attended, one of the committee members, Cody Clark, commented that when he works with engaged and married couples he reminds them: "Marriage is a skill you learn." Joe and I had to learn to blend and accept our individual differences and family differences as well as our similarities in order to grow as a couple, to become a "we" that is more important than the "me."

(Cathy): It is important to point out that just because we acknowledge and understand our differences does not mean that those differences, and the conflicts that may arise because of them, necessarily disappear. Our individual styles, personalities, abilities, interests, and needs still remain a part of who we are. I still prefer to get tasks done promptly, while Joe is still content to take the time available. Joe's calm, determined nature hasn't changed, while my spirited and determined personality persists. Joe is still more capable in dealing with the medical needs of our children, and I am more comfortable dealing with the educational needs of the boys. We are both involved with the medical and educational concerns of our children, yet we use our individual strengths to our advantage.

What has transpired over the years of our marriage is not the dissolution of conflict or differences but, rather, our ability and willingness to recognize our strengths and weaknesses and work together to achieve whatever our goal may be. It often requires one or both of us to adapt our style, our wants, and sometimes our needs for the benefit of the whole. A simple example is in the filing of our income taxes. Although I gather and prepare the necessary financial information for our accountant, Joe needs to compile the data in a few specific areas. Since I prefer to have them done earlier than later and Joe prefers to wait until April, it meant we were at odds on getting them done. Joe's waiting to prepare his information meant I was working, often frantically, at the last minute to get our records to the accountant on time. In the early years of our marriage it was a matter of convenience and preference when we completed taxes. As our sons began entering college, we needed to prepare federal financial aid forms based on our tax information in order for them to receive scholarships and financial assistance. Suddenly, the importance of finishing the taxes earlier rather than later became more imperative. Joe realized the benefit in furnishing his documentation sooner: we could not only provide our financial information to the colleges by the dates required, but also reduce my stress level, thereby making both our lives easier.

We make the same adjustments in all areas of our lives, whether it is in the outside commitments we make, how we will spend our free time, or how we will spend our money. We work together for the benefit of our marriage and family. We blend our strengths to make us stronger. And, very importantly, we do not let our differences tear us apart. Too often couples view their differences as a negative. We encourage you to analyze your similarities and differences, your strengths and your weaknesses, and to determine how you can use them for the enrichment of your family.

It is the love, knowledge, and acceptance of ourselves in addition to the love, knowledge, and acceptance of our spouse that has enabled us to become a "we." Two—Cathy and Joe—became one—the Garcia-Prats. We will continue to share how this concept unfolded for us as we share our experiences in communication, intimacy and sexuality, parenting, conflict resolution, and the joys of family life. Two becoming one involves all areas of our relationship.

In our faith, this unity is expressed in the Trinity: Father, Son, and Holy Spirit. In God there are three divine persons, equal and distinct. In our marriage, we are one couple yet two equal and distinct individuals. It is in this unique and dynamic interaction of "two becoming one" that our marriage is mutually satisfying and mutually beneficial. We more fully appreciate our commitment to love each other "for better and for worse, for richer and for poorer, in sickness and in health, till death do us part." It enables us to face the day-to-day joys and challenges with confidence, trust, hope, and love because we are together—one—in our efforts and our goals.

If you want a happy family,
if you want a holy family,
give your hearts to love.

—Mother Teresa

You are the bows from which your children
as living arrows are sent forth.

—Kahlil Gibran

Chapter Four

We Are the Fruit of Our Family Trees

*W*e are a husband and a wife. We are a father and a mother. We are a son and a daughter. We are a brother and a sister. We are a grandson and a granddaughter. We are a nephew and a niece. We are cousins. We are friends.

All the relationships that evolve from being one or the other in any of the above affiliations encompass who we are as individuals. We are influenced by our parents, siblings, grandparents, aunts and uncles, cousins, and friends. The relationships and experiences of our individual lives mold the individuals we become. When we get married, we marry not only our spouse but also, in many ways, our spouse's family because our spouse is a product of his or her family.

The Influence of Our Families of Origin and Our Past Experiences

We entered our marriage understanding that we were influenced by our families. This understanding became obvious once we were engaged. Because our families lived a distance from New Orleans, they had very little direct impact on our relationship while we were dating. Their involvement, however, changed once we announced our engagement. Our parents had opinions concerning the choices we were making about our wedding: the date and timing (a Wednesday or Thursday evening), the location (New Orleans), and the arrangements (the church, the attire, the guest list, the reception, the ceremony, etc). Their ideas were not always in sync with ours. They had preconceived ideas about what they wanted and expected from the wedding ceremony of their son or daughter. We worked hard to blend the different cultures, needs, expectations, and wants of our parents with our own needs and desires for our wedding. We sincerely tried to be adaptable and "flexible," yet we knew we would not be able to make everyone happy with every choice we made. That was just the beginning of our awareness of the direct and indirect impact and influence our families of origin and our past experiences have on us as individuals and, ultimately, as a married couple.

Although we grew up in families with similar values and goals, such as family, faith, education, self-discipline, self-respect, and a compassion for others, these values and goals were transmitted in different ways with a different emphasis placed on certain ones. In addition, the day-to-day issues, such as responsibilities, roles, traditions, and communication were handled uniquely. One family's way wasn't necessarily better than the other, but there were distinct differences in our family upbringing.

Our basic attitudes, approaches, and values are primarily formed by our parents and family relationships. Understanding our families and the traits—physical and emotional—we have inherited from them enables us to better understand ourselves and our behaviors. We encourage all couples, whether in the process of getting married or already married, to take time to critically examine the way their families of origin interacted because this is how we determine in our relationship what is normal behavior. Our family relationships affect our assumptions and expectations of ourselves, our spouse, and our children. **Couples must determine which familial behaviors, values, attitudes, and approaches are beneficial to their relationship and which ones they may need to adapt and/or change.** We can all change and adapt, if we make the choice to do so. **Moreover, we must emphasize that we can only change ourselves; we cannot be in the business of changing our spouse or his/her family. Our spouse must make the decision to change on his/her own.** What evolves, we discovered, is that as one individual changes, the other chooses, on his or her own, to make changes too. It is a type of dual metamorphosis that continues throughout the life of the relationship as a couple faces new challenges and directions in their individual lives, their marriage, and with their children.

How we deal with the challenges and the changes that occur in our marriage is directly influenced by how our families of origin dealt with challenges and changes while we were growing up. Likewise, the assumptions and expectations of what marriage and family life will be like are determined by the experiences in our own family background. Growing up we may not know whether the choices our parents made were healthy or unhealthy attitudes or behaviors. In fact, how we lived may be all we know when defining a "normal" family. That is why we encourage you now as an adult to remember what your family relationships and experiences were like, so you can sit back and begin to understand the healthy and unhealthy characteristics, attitudes, assumptions, expectations, and behaviors that were lived in your home as well as the effect they have on who you are as an individual.

We have participated in our church's marriage preparation program for eighteen years. We use the program developed by Robert A. Ruhnke, C.SS.R., *For Better and For Ever*. Two of the five preparation sessions revolve around our family of origin. The engaged couple answers questions about their background and upbringing. For example, engaged couples are asked: "Who has been the most important member of my family? Who has been the key 'parent' in my life? To whom in the family do I feel closest? From whom in the family do I feel most distant? How have I related to my brothers and sisters? How do each of them treat me?" The couples then describe the major strengths and weaknesses of their families, as well as what they liked the most and least about them.

Common patterns of behavior are likewise identified so the couple can reflect on the presence of these patterns on their own families and determine whether such behavioral patterns are healthy or unhealthy. Key patterns examined include the role of the mother and father, the pressure to make good grades, the pursuit of social status, the degree of physical affection and emotional support, the presence of neglectful or overly permissive parents, the emphasis on being "the best," and insistence on being on time. Also discussed are joyful family gatherings, physical or psychological illnesses, traditions, unemployment, alcoholism, frequent yelling, harsh punishment, control of the family money, vacations, and several other topics. The purpose of this exercise is for the couple to understand the dynamics of their own family of origin and the impact it will have on their developing relationship.

We stressed in the previous chapters the importance of self-love and self-respect and that, in order to love yourself, you must know yourself. An essential part of knowing oneself is knowing one's family. Fr. Ruhnke tells us, "We will never fully understand our own selves and our own behaviors until we understand the family from which we came." As we discovered once we were married, our family upbringing affected many of the day-to-day choices we made, as well as our expectations and assumptions of who would do what, when, how, and where. Most of our expectations and assumptions were based on the role our parents played in our families. Moreover, many of these expectations and assumptions were unrealistic for the kind of marriage we wanted and the goals we shared during our engagement. Even so, how easy it is to fall into a pattern of what you know and have experienced for so many years!

We faced the need to make adjustments and changes as differences in our expectations and assumptions surfaced, some due to our family background and some from the goals we established. Some of these adjustments and changes were straightforward while numerous others were more involved and required greater compromise and understanding.

One of the first realizations we made was that we are two unique individuals merging two unique family backgrounds to form a new one. Although we are products of our family and influenced by them, we are not an exact mirror image of any particular family member. We may exhibit certain qualities of our parents or siblings, but that is not to say we share all the characteristics of any one person. This is important to realize and acknowledge in order to avoid blindly imitating the roles and decision styles learned in our family of origin. By trying to be our father or mother, for example, we are not being ourselves. As a couple, we must decide what is in our best interest and how to use our unique God-given talents to build and strengthen our relationship. Our experiences were different from those of our parents due to opportunities and experiences we had that they may not have had. We had to fulfill our goals, our values, and our dreams. We came to realize that what may have worked for our parents may not work for us.

We also learned that it is important to separate psychologically from our parents and family. We have to understand that we are building a new relationship that is a relationship where our spouse is our number one priority. Separating from our family of origin does not mean that we break all ties with our family and pretend they never existed. Rather, it is a matter of finding our own identity as a couple and establishing our goals, values, priorities, traditions, and lifestyle. Thomas A. Power in his book *Family Matters* strongly encourages "family members to strive to become separate from their families of origin but to remain connected to them." The separation process is twofold: spouses separate from their parents and parents separate from their children. Again, to use the words of Thomas Power, we separate but stay connected. Both sides must understand and change with the new role in their relationship. Our parents will always be our parents, but they no longer need to parent us. We, as a couple, will now make the decisions in our lives that we determine are best for us. Our choices and decisions may not be what our parents would do or advise, but they must learn to step back and understand their new role. This change in roles does not happen overnight and for some individuals, the couple or the parents, it does not occur easily. Moreover, one spouse may be able to separate sooner than the other or separate in some areas of the relationship while retaining other connections longer. Also, as different situations arise in the marriage, we may revert back to some earlier dependencies or roles. The transition must happen, though, for a couple to move forward in their relationship with its new priorities, responsibilities, and roles.

(Cathy): I attended college away from home. Due to the distance and expense, I only returned home during the Christmas break and during the summer. My college years were the initial separation period from my family. Since I couldn't call or run home whenever I faced a dilemma, I learned to resolve my problems and make decisions on my own. My parents and sisters were always available if I needed them, but they could not do from a distance what may have needed to be done. It was a time in my life to determine what values were important to me, to establish goals, to meet new people, and to experience new adventures. I made choices about religion, career, and my relationships, as well as the role each would play in my life. I decided how and where to spend my time, and with whom. I made choices regarding drugs, smoking, alcohol, and sex. I made my decisions by incorporating (or discarding as necessary) the values and influences of my family with my new experiences, understandings, and priorities. My years at Loyola University, New Orleans, were definitely years of growth and maturity for me as an individual in all areas of my life.

When Joe and I got married, I had already experienced a degree of separation from my family; I believe they had experienced it too with my being away at college for four years. Plus, they understood that their role in my life was changing. Emotionally, as during the college years, we remained involved. I never felt as if I could not call home if I needed to. We stayed connected and close. I shared with them my experiences with Joe and my students—and my new life in Houston. We made a smooth transition from the parent-child role.

The more difficult separation for me occurred once our oldest son, Tony, was born. I now had a new role to fulfill and, as would be natural, my mother provided me with a role model—fortunately, a wonderful role model. Anyone who knows my mother knows what an exceptional example she has been for all five of her daughters and many, many other young women. Her patience, her unconditional love, her understanding, her listening skills, her gentleness, her self-giving, her virtue, her laughter, her inner and outer beauty, and her faith are all qualities to emulate. I have always been proud to call her my mother. And now as a new mother, I wanted to follow in her footsteps. But before I could do that, I had to make a separation. I had to come to the realization that I was Cathy and not my mom. I needed to blend her example of motherhood with who I had become as an individual. This blending of my mom's qualities with my personality, abilities, interests, and needs formed the mother I am today. It was a process that began with Tony, the oldest son, and continues with Timmy, the youngest. **My mom's influence on who I am as a mother today is significant. Can I fill her shoes? That's not possible! I did find, however, a new pair of shoes to wear that fit me—all possible because of my mom's love and respect for me as an individual and her daughter. She gave me wings to fly! Now, with some of our sons moving on to new phases in their lives, I am still emulating her by providing them wings to fly.**

(Joe): I was quite ready to leave home for my college experience after my graduation from high school, even though I had never been away from home prior to leaving for Loyola University, New Orleans. Other than being very homesick the first couple months, my experiences away from home were positive. The premedical program at Loyola University was rigorous and structured in its demands and served as a "safe haven" for spreading one's wings. I still went home for summer vacations and Christmas but found that, although I enjoyed being home with my family, I missed the independence I experienced while away at school.

I continued the "separation" process from my parents while in medical school at Tulane; I was a bit "older and wiser." My financial independence culminated when I was accepted at Baylor College of Medicine as a pediatric intern with my first real job and salary. I was finally on my own—I thought so at least.

My dad and mom were tremendously influential in my life in many wonderful ways. For instance, my respect and appreciation for the importance of education, God, hard work, and family came from my dad. My mother, on the other hand, showed me the "other way" to discipline: how to give lovingly and how essential it is to keep laughter and fun in your life. Their positive influences in my life remain.

Attending college and medical school in New Orleans meant that my parents were not involved in my social life, so seeking their approval of whom I dated and where I went was never an issue. They were always curious about whom I was seeing but could not "meddle." Nonetheless, they were probably more intertwined with my life than I realized—at least I didn't feel their presence or maybe refused to acknowledge it since I was in New Orleans and then Houston making my own decisions. However, as Cathy and I dated and our relationship became more serious, I wanted to include my parents in my happiness. They had the opportunity to meet Cathy at my medical school graduation.

When we announced our engagement later in the year, the feelings of independence that I had garnered were challenged when my parents began volunteering their ideas regarding various issues involving our wedding: the ceremony, reception, choice of location, etc. Cathy felt some of the same pressures from her parents as well. Cathy planned a beautiful and meaningful wedding for us; it was a special day filled with wonderful memories. We both hoped the ceremony and the day touched our families in the same way. Although we listened to our respective parents, we planned the day of our wedding to be special for the two of us. This was the first of many episodes where I had to address the good intentions of my dad and mom's need to parent.

Luckily, we were able to deal with some of this because of the distance between us—literally.

Expectations and Assumptions

The expectations and assumptions we bring into our marriage are based on the different roles and experiences we witnessed in our families of origin, as well as the roles society deems appropriate.

During our engagement, we talked about the importance of sharing roles and responsibilities as a couple, but what unfolded tended to be similar to the roles performed by our families of origin. One spouse was content with the arrangement, while the other spouse grew frustrated with the situation. Guess who was who? In the 1970s, society's thinking had moved forward slightly in regards to men taking on more household responsibilities and the balancing of career and family life, but not as far as we've come today. It remains an issue with many couples in the year 2000. Old habits and family traditions are hard to break.

(Cathy): In our situation, the division of responsibilities was not a big issue the first year of our marriage. Although I was busy with teaching, I had more flexibility in my schedule and discretionary time, so I was comfortable with most of the routine. The only frustrating part of the routine for me was the after-dinner segment. I fixed dinner (Joe did not cook at all at that point in our marriage) and soon found that I was doing the cleaning up as well. I knew Joe was tired after his long day, but so was I. I felt that if we both cleaned up together, we could then both relax or pursue other activities. I resented the assumption that as the woman in the household it was my responsibility to prepare dinner and clean up afterward. Once I brought my concern to Joe's attention, he understood and willingly helped after dinner. It wasn't, as they say, "a big deal."

Roles and responsibilities became more of an issue when I decided to return to school to work on my master's degree. Since I was still teaching, I no longer had the same discretionary time or flexibility in my schedule to handle the majority of the household responsibilities. I felt the easy solution to the problem was for Joe and me to revise the responsibility chart so that what needed to get done would get done. Joe had successfully juggled doing laundry, grocery shopping, and bill paying before we were married; there was no reason he couldn't do it once in a while now. Joe initially felt that if I couldn't teach while attending school and still fulfill the home responsibilities, then I should choose to either go to school or teach—but not do both. To say that was not the response I expected is to put it mildly. Our expectations and assumptions were not on the same page—not even in the same sentence or same language. Likewise, I "assume" my reaction to his reaction was not what Joe expected. **After some healthy discussion of available options, we decided that I could handle both teaching and going to school with Joe participating more with the home responsibilities. By enabling each of us to cultivate our intellectual pursuits, this shift in responsibilities was mutually beneficial for both of us.**

(Joe): I grew up in El Paso in what I consider a loving home. My parents each assumed a very traditional Hispanic role in our home: My father was the "bread-winner" and "head of household"; my mother cared for the home and lovingly raised my brother, my sister, and me. Both parents worked hard, successfully fulfilling their responsibilities. As I grew older, especially as I entered high school, I noticed a pattern of responsibilities that seemed unjust. My mother worked hard every day caring for us and the home, including preparing us a wonderful meal each evening. My father, who also worked hard, expected my mother to have dinner ready for him when he arrived home tired each evening. Following dinner, my father would retire to watch television and read the newspaper, while my mother remained in the kitchen to clean up. I remember many nights when my mom, although extremely tired from her long day, was still in the kitchen cleaning up or fulfilling another "responsibility." By contrast, my dad spent his evenings relaxing. This delineation of roles appeared to make sense to me when I was

younger. The older I became, however, the more I questioned the fairness of the delegation of responsibilities. My mom had worked just as hard as my father, albeit in a different way, and deserved the time to relax as much as he did. I felt he should have helped out a little, thereby allowing my mom to enjoy the evening with him. Unfortunately, my father never saw it that way.

After Cathy and I were married, I found myself modeling my dad's after-dinner behavior: I was leaving the table expecting Cathy to clean up for both of us. It didn't take long for Cathy to point out what I was doing, or for me to change my behavior. I didn't find it a struggle to change and work with Cathy to clean up because I remembered my feelings when my mother was expected to do it all. But not every change for me came without a struggle.

As our family grew, we both accepted additional responsibilities, many of which were not consistent with the roles of our parents. It was not uncommon, for example, for Cathy to mow the yard during the week so that we would have more time as a family on Saturday. I'm not sure about Cathy's mom, but I never saw my mom mowing the yard. Likewise, I was fulfilling nontraditional male responsibilities around the home. I knew I needed to be more emotionally involved with my family, and that along with the commitment I had made to Cathy and the boys came the practical day-to-day necessities that had to be done. Sometimes, I was challenged by what I thought should be my role in the household. Frankly, it was hard for me. I certainly did what needed to be done for Cathy and the boys, but my heart wasn't always behind my actions. I assume my feelings derived from the "role" I had witnessed with my dad.

I distinctly remember waking up one Saturday morning to the "quiet whispers" of our sons; Cathy was pregnant and needed some extra rest. The boys quickly moved from watching Saturday morning cartoons to wanting breakfast. I fed them and then proceeded to clean up the kitchen. While standing over the kitchen sink, I remember thinking that I must be the only male—a physician no less—in Houston, Texas, doing dishes on a Saturday morning. Why was I doing this? Was I some wimp under the control of a demanding or unrealistic woman? As I was standing there questioning my role, a cool breeze struck me from the open window (Cathy tells me it was the Holy Spirit), and I came to the realization that the reason I was doing what I was doing was because I loved Cathy and the boys. My heart finally caught up with my head! This may not have been the role of my father on a Saturday morning, but this was my role, and it was right for me and my family.

We have continued to adjust our roles and responsibilities over the course of our marriage and family life, addressing differences concerning our assumptions and expectations on a daily basis. We are amazed that, even today, there are times when our assumptions and/or expectations cause confusion and conflict. We recognize that there are still some areas in our lives we don't fully understand and that there are times when we each react differently to the same situation. When we say it is an ongoing process, we mean it from our hearts. We continue to unravel our story day by day.

The Day-to-Day Influence of Our Families of Origin

It is often the day-to-day interactions of family life that most significantly influence us. Whether our home was filled with love and laughter or discontent and yelling makes a difference. It may not be until we are older that we realize all families don't interact the same way. "Normal" family life to us, then, is the family life we are living.

Take the time to reminisce about your family and ask yourself the following questions. What was the daily life of my family of origin like? Were we a happy family? Was my home environment loving and secure? How did my parents get along? Did they treat each other with love and respect? Did my parents treat their children with love and respect? How did the siblings treat each other? Were family members supportive of each other? How did the family solve problems? What were my family's strengths? What were my family's weaknesses? What significant events in my life had the greatest effect on me? Was alcoholism, drug abuse, physical abuse, sexual abuse, or infidelity a part of my family history? What role did spirituality play in my family? What emphasis was placed on education? What emphasis was placed on social status? How were money and financial issues handled in my family and by whom? What were the priorities of my family? Did my family communicate in a healthy or unhealthy manner?

Hopefully, as you reflect on these questions you can begin to see how the answers help unravel the parts of the puzzle that make up who you are: your attitudes and approach toward life, your behavior, your perceptions, and your choices. If respect, for example, was practiced in your home, parent to parent, parent to child, child to parent, and sibling to sibling, then you grew up with a sense of respect for yourself and others. If respect was not practiced in the home, then lack of respect for one's self, individual differences, and uniqueness evolved. If children were a source of joy to your parents in spite of life's challenges and demands, then you will regard children as a gift in your life. By contrast, if your parents constantly complained about the responsibilities and frustrations of parenting, then you will perceive children as a burden in your life. If faith was joyfully integrated into your family's routine, faith will likewise be a positive influence in your life. If faith was preached but never lived, however, faith may seem like a noose around your neck or a contradiction rather than a way of life and a source offering peace and joy.

We may appreciate many of the traditions of our family of origin—what our parents did and taught us—while discarding those that are inappropriate for our needs. Also, some attitudes and behaviors might require discontinuation insofar as they are emotionally or physically unhealthy. As we reflect on these issues, we have to decide if we are going to follow in our parents' footsteps or trod a new path. Which traditions do we want to keep and which traditions (or baggage) do we want to discard and/or change?

As adults, we must take responsibility for our lives today in spite of the events of the past. We can't change the past, but we can change the role the past plays in the present. Whether we had a healthy or unhealthy family life or a combination of both, we must now make our own choices about our relationships and how we live our lives. Hopefully, we choose to build the foundation of our marriage with the positive facets of our family of origin and strive to change the negative behaviors and attitudes that weaken marriage and family relationships. Importantly, we have to remember that the process of blending our experiences takes time and effort; we have two families of origin to consider as we make these choices to build our marriage and our family.

(Cathy): I grew up in a family of five girls; I was the middle sister. My dad was in the Navy and my mom stayed at home until we all entered school. By the time I was in third grade, we had moved eight times and lived in quite diverse locales: Rhode Island, Alaska, Washington, California, Morocco, Spain, and Florida. I was exceptionally shy, so the experience of picking up and reestablishing myself and making new friendships was hard for me. I was fortunate to be close to my sisters; I considered them my best friends (and still do). Thanks to our relationship, I wasn't leaving my best friends behind with every move. When my dad retired from the Navy, we made a final move from Florida to Virginia after my freshman year in high school. This final move was a true uprooting because we had lived in Florida for seven years. We had thus established strong friendships and were comfortable in our home, school, church, and community environment.

The move to northern Virginia entailed many dramatic changes in our lives, both as individuals and as a family. For instance, I went from a small Catholic high school in Jacksonville to one of the largest public schools in Virginia. The hectic, fast-paced lifestyle of northern Virginia contrasted significantly with the slower, calmer, family-oriented lifestyle in Florida. It was a difficult move for our family, demanding many changes in a short period of time: a different lifestyle, new schools with academic and social adjustments, job demands, time demands, the first sister off to college, and mom returning to work. Some of the transitions went smoothly while, with others, the adaptation took much longer.

I learned a lot from the move and the transitions that evolved because the move impacted my life and affected decisions I made in the years to come. One example relates to education. After a year of adjustment, I enjoyed my high school experience. I made new and strong friendships, became actively involved in school activities, and took advantage of the excellent education provided at W.T. Woodson High School. Unfortunately, I missed one important element from my previous experience in Florida, the integration of my faith in the overall environment of the school. When it came time to choose a college, I looked for colleges with a religious affiliation. My decision to attend Loyola University New Orleans, a Jesuit Catholic university, was one of the best choices I have made. Loyola provided me an opportunity to pursue my desire to teach in a faith-filled environment. I also did not find my transition into college life to be as difficult as it was for many other students. I believe the move in high school provided me invaluable insight into how to handle a new situation where one needs to adjust to a new lifestyle in addition to new academic and social demands. Moreover, the upheaval in high school made me more aware of what was important to me as an individual and how I should go about achieving my dreams.

For better and for worse, all of these experiences, as well as my experiences prior to high school, I brought with me to my relationship with Joe. Even today my relationships with my mom, my dad, and with each of my sisters impact me. I realize how my reactions to different comments, situations, and events may still be influenced by a comment, a situation, or an event from my past. I have a much better understanding of that influence now than I did twenty-six years ago when Joe and I got married. I likewise have a much better understanding of the difference in my reaction to situations from his reaction to the same situations.

About a year into our marriage, Joe's parents visited us on their way home from his brother's medical school graduation in New Orleans. We had a wonderful visit and were glad to have the chance to show them where we lived and some of Houston's sights. Not long after they returned home, we received a letter from his parents thanking us for the visit. The letter's contents also contained strong comments on our way of life. They were extremely disappointed in where we lived and how we lived, especially since Joe was a doctor. I was very hurt by the criticism and the insinuation that we were not living appropriately. I was amazed at Joe's lackadaisical reaction; he just took the comments in stride and told me not to worry about them. It was the first time I truly understood how different my background was from his—my parents would not have handled the concern in the same way. I realized, too, that the expectations held by our respective parents were quite different. Joe pointed out that his parents' expectations were unrealistic, not only for our stage in life but for what we wanted as a couple. He explained that they didn't understand that, as an intern, his income only permitted us to get by financially from week to week. We were happy, though, with where we were living and our simple lifestyle. **We knew we didn't have a lot of "things" and that our home wasn't lavish, but we were living within our means and content with who we were and the choices we were making.**

(Joe): It took me many years of marriage and conflicts to understand how influential my family was in both positive and negative ways. To this day, I continue to discover why I deal with some of the situations in my life the way I do. Likewise, Cathy has shared some of her own experiences. **We are both convinced that each of our approaches to finances, discipline, household responsibilities, communication, and conflict are influenced by our family's approaches and experiences; some good and some not so good. The recognition and understanding of these influences has helped us to deal with the conflicts that may have been generated by our past.** *We have been amazed at how these influences pop up in our relationship, even today.*

92

In retrospect, I should not have been surprised that my dad and mom expected to remain very influential in my life regarding the many issues of my new marital and my new family relationships. I now realize how much both my parents were affected in a similar fashion by their parents. My parents felt the powerful influence of their mothers throughout most of their adult lives. I remember both my grandmothers being the matriarchs of their families. I knew neither of my grandfathers since they both died before I was born. My memories of my grandmothers are sketchy other than impressions of how they were both respected and well-treated in their homes. (My maternal and paternal grandmothers lived with one of their daughters.) I also remember they were both rather cold toward my brother, sister, and me. We lived and attended school in El Paso. Our first language was English and, although we spoke some Spanish, my grandmothers often scolded my parents because we were not bilingual. As a result, relating well to either grandmother was severely limited.

I am convinced that both grandmothers influenced my parents' lives as they parented and managed their family. I do not believe this is uncommon in many cultures where the grandparents and older relatives are held in great esteem. Such an influence may be helpful when wisdom is imparted but can also be negative when such influence stifles the new relationship which is trying to find its own way. Keeping the elders revered and appreciated can be a difficult challenge while building a new relationship with your spouse and then your children.

The Traditions of Our Families of Origins

Another area of expectations and assumptions that often causes conflict or dissension in a marriage is the practice of traditions, especially traditions associated with holidays and special events. We very often expect and assume our spouse will want to share the traditions of our specific family, yet that is not always the case. How quickly we become territorial when it comes to long-standing traditions that we have held for many years. We remember the story of a couple who almost didn't spend their first Christmas together because they could not resolve when to decorate their Christmas tree. The tradition in the husband's family of origin was to decorate the tree shortly after Thanksgiving. The wife's tradition was to decorate the tree on Christmas Eve. Neither the husband nor wife could understand the other's position, and neither wanted to change his or her special family tradition. Eventually, with the help of a friend, they reached a compromise that sort of satisfied them both: they decorated the tree the weekend before Christmas.

Blending the traditions of both families is important. **We feel we have enriched our lives and the lives of our children by blending our family cultures and practices just as our parents did for us.** Joe's mother is Spanish, his father is Mexican; Cathy's father is Italian, her mother is Irish. What rich cultures and traditions to bring to our children!

The other issue couples find themselves dealing with is where to spend holidays and vacations. Usually, both sets of parents expect and want their children to spend time with them. Couples often feel a tug-of-war between families and between having some time to themselves, whether they live in the same city or not. It can cause a lot of stress for couples when they need and want the time to relax. We felt that pull too. We wanted to spend time with family, so we tried to establish a rotating schedule: one Christmas with one family in El Paso, the next Christmas with the other in Virginia. What then happens is, if you have other siblings and their families to coordinate with, you are out of sync with their schedules. Plus, in our situation, we were working with Joe's call schedule and the possibility he would have only a couple of days off. When the children arrived, the tugs increased because both sets of grandparents understandably wanted to be with their grandchildren.

We finally decided to spend the major holidays at home and begin our own traditions. As our family quickly grew, logistics and expense also entered into our decision. We realized, too, that when we visited during the holidays (although a lot of fun), we usually didn't have time to sit and talk the way we wanted to as there were so many other things to do. When we visited then, we tended to choose an off time to make the trip, especially when the boys were younger. As the boys got older, we had to work around their school schedules. It actually became easier for our parents to visit us. Having babies on a regular basis was also an incentive to visit. Cathy's mom came to Houston to help after the birth of each boy. Cathy's dad used to tease us that we didn't have to have a child for Mom to come visit. To this day, they "find" wonderful reasons to visit: First Communions, graduations, baptisms, Grandparents' Day (a special day to honor grandparents at the boy's elementary school on the Tuesday before Thanksgiving), when we're taking one of the boys to college, or when we have the opportunity to attend an out-of-town meeting. Their willingness to be flexible and to accept the fact that it is easier for them to travel here than for us to travel there has been a blessing for us and the boys—and relieved some of the stress associated with the infamous tug-of-wars.

Understanding Our Influence on Our Children

When we consider the influence our families of origin have had on us in our marriage and in our family, we realize the tremendous responsibility we have as parents to provide our sons with a loving, secure, healthy environment where each of them is respected and appreciated for who he is and for the gifts God has so graciously given him. It is through our example that we teach our children how to be loving, caring, respectful, compassionate, understanding, forgiving, responsible, well-educated, and faith-filled individuals. We must show them in our daily interactions how to deal with conflict and the unexpected events that inevitably enter our lives. We demonstrate our values, our priorities, and our faith by the choices we make and how we live our lives. It is a challenge each and every day to maintain a home that incorporates all our individual needs into one family. A family where each of us can share our individual dreams, a family where our expectations are realistic of each other, and a family where we provide opportunities for each son to find his wings and fly.

*There can be no happiness equal to
the joy of finding a heart that understands.*
—Victor Robinson

*Never let evil talk pass your lips;
say only the good things that men need to hear,
things that will really help them.*
—Ephesians 4:29

*Be consistent in your thought; steadfast be your words.
Be swift to hear, but slow to answer.
If you have the knowledge, answer your neighbor;
If not, put your hand over your mouth.*
—Sirach 5:12–14

Chapter Five

Healthy Communication—
A Reflection of Our Love

*W*e are both convinced that the way a couple communicates is a reflection of the quality of their relationship. Good communication skills must be learned and then practiced if they are to become second nature to both spouses. When communicating with our spouse, we need to use positive, uplifting words and maintain a respectful tone of voice. We should listen with our heart, share our feelings, and understand the moment. Most importantly, we must accept our spouse for who he or she is—every day and in every situation, not just when we find it convenient and easy to do so.

Our relationship is a joy or a struggle depending upon how well we are communicating. We all know how to talk, but we don't all know how to communicate. You would think talking and communicating with your spouse would be one of the simpler elements of the marital relationship. However, the inability to communicate and to resolve conflicts in a healthy, positive manner generates much stress in a marriage. Words spoken, words left unsaid, a disrespectful tone of voice, crossed wires, misunderstandings caused by assumptions or expectations, and selfish attitudes may all undermine our ability to grow closer together as a couple. And may ruin many a day! Kind, carefully chosen words, a respectful tone of voice, attentive listening, and a compassionate and understanding attitude build up our relationship while fostering a positive, secure environment in which to live.

Our Early Communication Skills

During the time we dated and were engaged, we were comfortable talking with each other about almost anything. That was one of the attractions of the relationship for both of us. We were able to resolve any differences that crept up quite smoothly, but then we didn't have any major disagreements during this time period either. Since we lived in separate cities the year before we got married, we didn't encounter the day-to-day squabbles that we witnessed in other relationships. We assumed any differences that arose once we were married would be resolved in a straightforward manner. We were both reasonable and sensitive people committed to making each other happy and determined to make our marriage strong. We weren't naïve enough to think we would never disagree or have a conflict, but we were unaware of the impact our families of origin would have on our style of communicating and resolving day-to-day issues, concerns, and, yes, conflicts.

We went through many growing pains redeveloping our communication skills as a couple. Initially, we found it difficult to express our frustrations with each other. We fell into the trap of not telling the other how we felt, either because we assumed the other knew how we were feeling or because we were uncertain of the other's reaction to our feelings. With both of us being sensitive individuals, we also consciously avoided saying anything that might hurt the other. This style of communication—avoidance—hindered rather than strengthened our relationship. What would often happen is that the frustrations mounted until some insignificant incident set off the fireworks. So much for healthy communication skills! How much better to just release the steam from the pot as it accrues. We had a lot to learn.

The development of healthy communication skills is an ongoing process. Because the relationship is constantly changing, we continue to learn and understand more about ourselves and each other. Likewise, our communication skills evolve along with our relationship's development. **We continue to remind ourselves that good communication skills require patience, constant effort, a determined spirit, understanding, acceptance, trust, and the willingness to change what is ineffective.**

Striving to build healthy communication skills strengthens our relationship. The mutual commitment we share to continually work on our communication skills reaps day-to-day rewards for us. We have not eliminated all conflicts and disagreements, but we are able to deal with them in a much healthier way than we did the first years of our marriage.

Give your spouse and yourself a gift by learning how to better communicate with each other. This is not always easy to accomplish because, like other areas of our relationship, it demands change; however, when we are committed as a couple to the principles of love, respect, trust, and faith, then we can truly appreciate the benefits the change will bring.

(Joe): The first assumption Cathy and I make about marital communication is that both spouses want to share and communicate in order to further develop themselves and their relationship. If either spouse does not value communication or is unwilling to strive for it, then the relationship will stagnate and fail to achieve its full potential. This is true in any situation where two parties need to relate.

When I first joined the Section of Neonatology as a new faculty member, I eagerly awaited my first opportunity to teach as well as manage the Newborn Intensive Care Unit (NICU); I had always enjoyed teaching and clinical care. My first NICU rotation, however, was less than fulfilling or positive. Each day on rounds, as I tried to impart my clinical experience and knowledge, the pediatric residents assigned to the NICU responded with one syllable answers and indifference. After rounds each day, I felt empty and spent. I tried to find ways to make the experience of taking care of critically ill infants positive and interesting for our pediatric residents, yet I was continuously confronted with apathy. In short, I was frustrated and discouraged. I decided to discuss the situation with the neonatology fellow who was part of the team. I asked him to honestly tell me what I was doing wrong. Why couldn't I effectively communicate with these young resident physicians? His answer was honest. There wasn't anything necessarily wrong with what I was doing or saying. The group just wanted to finish rounds, complete their responsibilities, and be ready to go home at the end of their shift. They had no interest in taking the teacher-student relationship beyond the "minimum needed" to complete the monthly rotation through the NICU. So, too, is communication in our spousal relationship often relegated to the bare minimum. **In order for the marriage to be mutually fulfilling, we must both commit ourselves to making our communication better—far beyond the "minimum needed."**

Inherited Communication Skills

In the previous chapter, we discussed the influence our families of origin have on who we are today. That influence is strongly evident in the communication skills we learned and developed over the years. **It is important for a couple to recognize the communication skills of their respective families and how they, as products of their families, may be using the same techniques.** Regretfully, many of these skills are poor and may actually hinder the growth of a relationship: avoiding or ignoring a problem, pouting, withdrawing, giving in, ranting and raving, manipulating, and verbally or physically fighting. If a couple dislikes the way their families of origin communicated, then they must be determined to change that pattern. **Each spouse needs to examine his or her own individual communication skills and then work to strengthen the healthy ones and to develop new**

ones where necessary. Reflecting on your communication skills is one more component in the process of learning, understanding, and knowing who you are.

When considering your family of origin's communication skills, recognize that each parent and sibling probably shares some of these communication skills and differs in others. Just as each parent brings with him or her the skills learned in his or her family of origin, so too do we. Siblings likewise develop communication skills unique to their personality, birth order, family events, and other individual circumstances. In short, many experiences from our families of origin enter into the way we communicate.

> *(Cathy): Each of my parents has his or her own style of communicating. My mom is a soft-spoken person gifted with listening skills. I remember coming home from school as a child and sharing all the day's events; my mom would patiently listen not only to me but to all five of her daughters. When mom disciplined, it was in a loving, gentle manner. Yelling and screaming were not her style. Often my mom's "look" was enough for me and my sisters to stop whatever we were doing wrong or considering doing wrong. While my mom will share her opinions, she is not argumentative. Rather, she is uncomfortable with conflict and dissension and tries to maintain a calm, peaceful environment.*
>
> *My dad would never be described as soft-spoken. He is vociferous and emotionally expressive. He has definite opinions and enjoys being argumentative, even if only for the sake of being argumentative. Dad's discipline style was more forthright and to the point. He did not like his authority questioned, so most of my sisters and I accepted the rules and responsibilities he established and the subsequent consequences when they were not followed. One sister, also argumentative and emotionally expressive, questioned the validity of different rules and tested Dad's rules often. Her dissension made for some less than quiet evenings, especially when the "test" revolved around curfew or telephone usage. The conflicts affected all of us, and I can remember many activities that were*

"altered" because of their communication style. I didn't enjoy being around when the conflicts started, so I learned ways to distance myself from them.

The way I communicated with each of my sisters varied. I was closer to certain sisters while growing up, depending upon personalities, activities, what was happening at that period in my life, and each sister's understanding and acceptance of who I was. For the most part, we were comfortable together and I don't remember having major confrontations with any of them. I was more like my mom; I didn't enjoy being around or involved with conflict, and my shyness did not lead me to be argumentative or divisive at that point in my life. Today, I am more "expressive" and willing to question policies that I sense are unfair or unjust.

I have brought all the communication styles of my family of origin with me to my relationship with Joe. I may not practice them all, but they do affect the choices I make in how I communicate. Different situations will demand different skills. *I am usually calm and easy-going, but when I deem it necessary to get involved or confront someone, especially regarding one of our sons, I will do so. I also learned to talk to Joe about an issue that is bothering me earlier rather than later in order to avoid the fireworks we experienced early in our marriage.*

(Joe): My father was the head of our household and set the rules and tone of the house when he was home. He was the "law-giver" and his decisions were rarely questioned. He was unapproachable when my brother, sister, and I thought that some of his decisions were unfair. My sister was the bravest and questioned his authority on a few occasions, thereby prompting an impassioned but short discussion. Most situations reminded me of the scene in the movie The Ten Commandments *when Pharaoh would proclaim, "So let it be written—so let it be done." There were very few instances of conflict resolution through direct communication with my father. Loving and caring as my father was of us all, he was still the authority and so unapproachable.*

On the other hand, my mom was easy to talk to and usually more sensitive about communicating criticism or praise to us. She was always available to listen to her children. She relished the opportunities to hear our stories as well as our complaints and concerns. This often meant listening to the times we disagreed with my father. We learned that we could get our concerns to my father through my mom. There were quite a few "decision reversals" after my dad's "supreme high counselor" had a chance to plead our case.

And so, although I was brought up in a loving and caring home, the communication styles of my mom and dad were very different. **I wanted to communicate more like my mom than my dad, but I did bring some of my dad's ways with me to our marriage.** Interestingly, I consider my sister the best communicator in our family as she is very open and willing to make her feelings known. By contrast, this continues to be a struggle for my brother and me although we are both getting better at opening up and expressing our feelings.

Developing Healthy Communication Skills

The marriage preparation program we use with engaged couples, *For Better and For Ever,* by Robert Ruhnke, C.SS.R., presents four major skills needed for effective marital communication: sharing, listening, acceptance of myself and my spouse, and speaking my mind and heart with love. Since, more often than not, we did not learn all these skills and practice them growing up, we need to learn and use them as adults. As we learn and practice these skills, we experience the positive difference that healthy communication makes both in our marital relationship and in our relationship with our children.

Sharing Our Feelings with Our Spouse

While we may feel comfortable sharing our opinions or knowledge with our spouse, we often feel uncomfortable sharing our thoughts and feelings. Our ability to honestly share our feelings is influenced by how we communicated growing up. In many families, expressing feelings and emotions is frowned upon as an inferior characteristic, especially for boys. If we express ourselves, we are reprimanded or demeaned for our feelings. Thus, we learn to keep our feelings inside. In a marital relationship, hiding our feelings undermines the growth process because we do not allow ourselves to be known by either our spouse or ourselves.

(Cathy): I remember the many times I assumed Joe understood why I was upset or angry. As I eventually realized, he did not understand where I was coming from. Although Joe is a multi-talented individual, he cannot read my mind. Often my expectations and assumptions of him were not in sync with what he assumed was expected of him. I also did not know how to handle the pent-up anger that surfaced from the accumulated frustrations. If only I had realized the importance of sharing my feelings, concerns, and anxieties with Joe as they occurred instead of hiding them from him or ignoring them, then we could have avoided many heartaches.

Avoiding or ignoring problems won't make them go away. In my case, it often led to my being "quiet" because I didn't know what to say that wouldn't create more problems or hurt Joe's feelings. Joe, though, reminded me that he couldn't read my mind and encouraged me to open up so he could understand what I was thinking and feeling. I realized that for change to happen, I needed to share with Joe what was on my mind—for better and for worse.

Joe's gifts of listening and understanding made this initial step easier for me to undertake. Although I grew up in a family where my sisters and I shared our innermost thoughts, I felt more vulnerable sharing some feelings with Joe. Would he think less of me because I needed him emotionally more than he had expected? Would he love me less because I had admitted my weaknesses? Would he think me too demanding because I wanted changes in our routine? Would I be more trouble than he felt I was worth? Joe gave me no reason to feel intimidated or anxious, but opening up inner thoughts and feelings can be risky and scary for any of us, even confident, independent people.

Sharing my frustrations with Joe regarding the amount of time he watched television, the need to spend more time together, and the division of household responsibilities enabled us to move forward in our relationship. I became more comfortable talking to Joe about the things that bothered me, about our relationship and other areas of my life. He teases that he wasn't prepared for my eventual forthrightness; he will tell you I "express" myself very well today. He sometimes wonders if he didn't open Pandora's box.

As new areas of differences arose, we were more readily able to talk about our concerns although we didn't alleviate our old habits completely. They just manifested themselves for different reasons. I found I still would keep feelings to myself because, at times, Joe's reactions made me uncomfortable. He would feel bad about a situation, which was not my intention, and then respond in a manner that took me many years to understand. Because I was upset, he felt he had to do things that would earn back my love and respect. What he didn't understand was that he had never lost my love and respect and so he didn't need to earn it back.

It took many years of getting to know Joe and his family for me to understand what was happening, how he was feeling, and why he was reacting the way he did. I used an analogy with our sons to help Joe understand that my love was always with him, even if I disagreed with him or was disappointed in something that had happened. I explained to him that when the boys do something wrong or make a poor choice, I may be upset and disappointed with them, but I never stop loving them. They do not have to earn my love back because they never lose it. Although I may be upset with him, my feelings do not equate to not loving him. I believe this helped Joe understand what he was uncon-sciously doing—and his knowledge of it propelled our communication and our relationship to a new and higher level. I was able to talk to him without worrying about him feeling like a martyr or struggling to find ways to reestablish our bonds. He was able to listen with the knowledge that I loved him in spite of whatever had happened.

(Joe): I felt very confident when we got married about our ability to communicate well with each other. Our time together was spent talking about many areas of our lives and sharing our feelings. We were both extremely happy. When our first conflict arose, I was surprised that it was my behavior that had caused the problem. Of course, I was also hurt that it was me—my self-perception of being a good husband was shaken. As I asked Cathy to open up more, I became more shaken in my ability to be a good spouse. My insecurity caused me to withdraw and not share my feelings with Cathy. Instead of talking about the issues, the conflict, the causes of the conflict, my feelings and Cathy's feelings, I set about "to fix" the problem and to do what I could to "earn" Cathy's love again. In retrospect, I understand my solution to resolving the conflict only made matters worse. Yet, how could I talk about my feelings to Cathy and further unveil to her any more of my shortcomings. I thought, "I've hurt her again! How can I further jeopardize her vision of me by telling her how I feel? I just can't risk it." Instead, I looked for ways to make things better. I would try to change my behavior and try to assume more responsibilities around the house since time was often the issue of conflict.

Although these actions may have had some benefit for Cathy and the boys, they left her and our relationship hanging. I know this was very disheartening to Cathy. In the past, I could always deal with conflict by never placing myself in such a position or by working harder at reducing or solving the problem, such as when I tackled schoolwork or sports. I didn't know what else to do. When conflict arose in my family of origin, it usually meant acceding to whatever my dad wanted us to do. To voice my feelings or opinions would have been considered disrespectful and have only created more conflict.

It took many years for me to understand my difficulty in dealing with my feelings. Today, it is only by understanding Cathy's unconditional love for me that I am able to risk showing

more of myself to her. What a difference this understanding has made in our relationship. What a difference this has made in our daily approach to the boys, our challenges, our interests, and our physical relationship. All aspects of our relationship have benefited from this new level of communication between us, not to mention the peace it has brought to me. I still have much to learn about myself, but I feel better prepared to further develop our communication.

Developing the Art of Listening

The art of listening, truly listening, is so important in a marriage. We must learn to listen to what our spouse has to say, even if we don't like what we're hearing or disagree with what is being said. We demonstrate that we care about what our spouse is saying by giving him or her our full attention as well as maintaining eye contact. Nothing undermines communication more quickly than when one person appears disinterested in what the other has to say. In addition, allowing the other person to speak without interrupting to offer our opinion or a solution exemplifies respect for our spouse's concerns. Cutting someone off when they are speaking is not only disrespectful but also implies to the speaker that what he or she is saying is not valid or important.

(Cathy): I become very annoyed and hurt when I am talking to Joe and he doesn't seem to be listening. I'm convinced it is not a conscious act on his part, but all the same I am annoyed and hurt. If I'm talking to him and he walks away before I finish telling him what I have to say, I am extremely irritated. In response, I react— immaturely and inappropriately I might add—by clamming up. I tell myself, "If he's not going to listen to what I have to say, why say anything at all." His actions, in my mind, negate the value of my words. With all the responsibilities to fulfill in our home, I know it is easy to become distracted. But for me, who may have been home all day with children and little or no adult conversation, I

need for Joe to listen to me and in listening make me feel good about myself. I may not have an earth-shattering comment to make or a Nobel prize winning story to tell but, nonetheless, I need him to listen to me.

And, if I am voicing my frustrations about my day, I just want and need him to listen to me. What I don't need him to do, unless I ask for it, is to offer advice or try to "fix" the problem. When Joe would call from the hospital and I would "unload" on him the stresses of raising three, five, or seven children, he felt bad because he couldn't be there to help share the responsibilities with me. I knew he couldn't rush home and change a diaper or two or give me a much needed break; that was not what I expected. But having the opportunity to share the stresses of the day with him was often the release I needed to move on. Just knowing he was there, emotionally supporting me, gave me the lift I needed. I learned to listen to him, too, and not offer my opinion about a situation at work unless he asked for it. **Listening, we learned, is truly an art!**

(Joe): Cathy loves to share her day with me, and I enjoy listening to the events of her and the boys' day. There is always plenty to tell me; as you might guess, no two days are alike in our household. However, I was not always a good "listener." When I arrived home in the early years of our marriage, I still had the hospital or related activities on my mind. I wasn't "ready" to listen. By not truly listening, I missed so much. This "hearing block" on my part hurt Cathy, and gradually she shared less and less with me about the happenings of our home. My lack of attention took its toll on Cathy and the boys and, eventually, on me. My bad habit of not listening led to Cathy's "explosions" from time to time.

Little by little, I began to listen, truly listen. I had to make a conscious effort to tell myself to "switch gears" and open my ears—and my heart. By listening I became more aware of so many facets of Cathy and her day as well as the occurrences and facets of our boys' day. I am able to more capably respond to what I am hearing because I am truly listening. That response may only be a hug or an *"I understand and I am sorry,"* but Cathy and the boys know that it is a response that is uttered after I truly listened. My listening is appreciated by us all.

The art of listening also goes beyond hearing the words that are spoken to what is said between the lines. **"Listening" to the silent message is a communication skill worth developing. The words may make a statement, but the emotion, the tone of voice, and the body language of the speaker may all be conveying a different message.** In his book *Will the Real Me Please Stand Up?* John Powell, S.J., describes the good listener as someone who not only understands the "content" of the sharing but also listens for the "context" of the sharing. He encourages us to walk in the other person's shoes.

As we shared more and understood more about ourselves and our families of origins, we grew in our ability to listen with our hearts as well as with our ears. We more often understand now what is behind the words and emotions than we did in the early years of our marriage. By "listening" to all that is being communicated, we can determine what the other may need from us —a hug, a laugh, an empathetic word.

(Cathy): When Joe walks in the door at the end of his day, I can tell he's had a good day if there's a bounce in his step, a lilt in his voice. If his movements are slow, his voice tired, I discern, even though he says he's okay, that it's been a long day. What I say and do in response to what I'm "hearing" depends on how well I "listened" to what Joe is revealing, consciously or unconsciously, to me. If it has been a less than stellar day for him, I won't bombard him with minor problems or concerns that may have developed over the course of the day. I communicate to him my love and understanding by being sensitive to his mood and needs.

Likewise, Joe listens to my verbal and nonverbal expressions. They convey whether I'm up or I'm down. Many evenings he understood from my body movement, energy level, or a sigh or two, how tired I was from taking care of the boys all day as well as coping with the physical and emotional demands of a pregnancy. His willingness to provide extra emotional and physical support reassured me that he was "listening," even when we weren't actually conversing. Often Joe is more able to determine from my voice than from my words what my frame of mind is.

The art of listening is essential, too, when raising children. For example, I hear much more than two simple words when the boys say "Hi, Mom" on returning home from school. In their own ways, they appreciate my ability to read their true emotions because then my response in what I say, do, or expect from them takes their feelings into account. When the older boys call from college, their tone of voice indicates their mood. One of the hardest sounds for me to hear is the homesickness behind the voice. The boys are all very close, so being away from the constant interaction and support of their brothers has been difficult, to different degrees, for each one of them. I learned rather quickly to tell them stories about their brothers and the activities of home. Rather than the tales making them miss us more, the day-to-day escapades actually made them feel closer and a part of what we were doing. Having the opportunity to talk with their brothers also provided an extra touch of home. By the time we hung up, the voice on the other end sounded uplifted and less homesick.

Accepting Our Spouse with Love

"Love is patient; love is kind. Love is not jealous, it does not put on airs, it is not snobbish. Love is never rude, it is not self seeking, it is not prone to anger; neither does it brood over injuries. Love does not rejoice in what is wrong but rejoices with the truth. There is no limit to love's forbearance, to its trust, its hope, its power to endure" (1 Corinthians 13:4–7).

In order to accept each other, we need to strive to live the characteristics of love described by St. Paul in his letter to the Corinthians. It is in loving that we are able to accept the qualities we have in common with each other as well as those traits in which we differ. We refer back to the principle of love and the understanding that love is a choice we make each and every day to accept and respect each other in our uniqueness. **Our common interests and values may have brought us together, but appreciating our differences will enable us to grow and develop as a couple.**

In marital communication, accepting our differences in style and content is a difficult task at times. We want and expect our spouse to agree with us on most issues, so when we find out this is not the case, we may feel as if we made a wrong choice in a life-mate. "How can I live with someone who feels that way? I didn't expect him or her to think or act in that manner." Our willingness to accept these differences is an important process in developing our relationship. We reiterate that it takes patience, a constant effort, and a determined spirit to develop effective communication in a marriage. At the first sign of differences, even after a period of time, we cannot simply pack up and run from our differences; rather, we need to dig in and work through them.

(Cathy): Although we didn't realize it before our involvement, our decision to be a sponsor couple in our church's marriage preparation program was probably one of the best choices we made for our own marriage. The program provided us with information that enriched our relationship, information that had never been concretely presented to us before. After working with the first engaged couple, we garnered many insights into why some areas of our relationship were strong and why we struggled in other areas. The session on communication offered us the most significant awareness of what we were doing right and what we needed to work on, individually and as a couple, especially in regards to accepting each other with our similarities and our differences. Outwardly I feigned acceptance of Joe, but inside I harbored feelings of dissatisfaction or disapproval concerning some of his choices and behavior. At the same time, I was hopeful that Joe would change, ignoring the fact that he probably felt the same

way regarding my own need to change certain attitudes and modus operandi.

After answering the questions presented by the program, I realized that, although I thought I was listening to Joe and being accepting, in reality I was not. I expected him, for example, to want to spend our off time (which wasn't very often while he was in training) going places and doing things. He preferred to stay home and watch sports. He enjoyed the social get-togethers organized by the nurses and residents; I found them distasteful. I was a morning person; he struggled to get out of bed each day. I preferred to complete a task promptly; Joe chose to take the time allotted. I insisted on balancing the check book monthly; balancing the checkbook was not a priority in Joe's life. At times even our day-to-day priorities were different.

Answering the questions provided by the marriage preparation program allowed me to realize how "unfair" and unaccepting I was of Joe. I couldn't expect him to be a carbon copy of me—and I knew in my heart I didn't want him to be. **In his book** Romancing the Home, **Ed Young suggests a married couple will benefit from each spouse asking themselves, "What is it like being married to me?" I find the answer to the question humbling. The answer helps put the differences between Joe and me in perspective. I am able to accept our differences and use them to strengthen our relationship.** We learned that, along with our different talents, strengths and weaknesses, our attitudes and styles provide us greater opportunities to achieve our mutual goals. In Joe's words during one preparation session: "I like to think of our differences not necessarily as an example of how opposites attract or that they are couple divisors but, rather, that our differences help us create 'a good fit' as a couple." I believe our ability to accept each other for who we are, with all our pluses and minuses, is one of our greatest strengths as a couple. **As an added benefit, our ability to accept each other enables us to more readily accept our sons with their strengths and weaknesses and to build on the wonderful gifts each one of them brings to our family.**

As we discover new "differences" in our attitudes or approach, we acknowledge our feelings, accept our differences, and then decide which direction we need to follow. The differences may revolve around discipline of the boys, an activity to attend for us or the boys, financial matters, educational concerns, medical decisions, or time commitments. Practically anything that involves family life can be a source of difference for a couple. We just need to remember that those differences do not have to divide or pull us apart, or create a confrontational atmosphere in our homes. As we've said over and over again, take advantage of each spouse's uniqueness to enrich and fortify your relationship. We've discovered new and exciting qualities belonging to each other in the process.

Speaking My Mind and Heart with Love

How often do we hear the words "I'll give you a piece of my mind"? While some of us are quite capable of speaking our minds, others have difficulty sharing what's on our minds and in our hearts at all. We are uncertain of the reaction to our thoughts and feelings. Yet speaking our minds and hearts with love is another communication skill that we need to learn and practice. This skill is closely tied to the previous skill of accepting our spouse with love, because it is easier to share your thoughts and feelings when you know you will be loved and accepted in spite of them.

Over the course of our marriage, we have experienced many changes. Our lives today, as a couple and as individuals, are significantly different than they were twenty-six years ago, fifteen years ago, or even five years ago. Each stage of our marriage and family life offered new challenges and opportunities, some exciting and others disconcerting. Both of us faced struggles along the way, as individuals and/or as a couple, in adapting to the new experiences we encountered. **Our ability to share our feelings, fears, needs, and dreams became critical because those feelings, fears, needs, and dreams changed as we faced these new challenges and opportunities. For our relationship to continue to grow, we**

realized how essential it is for us to be able and willing to share with the other what is in our hearts and minds with love.

Commitment and trust play an essential role in our willingness to share our hearts and minds with love. When we share our thoughts and feelings with our spouse, we need to feel confident that our spouse will accept and love us, even though he or she may not like or is uncomfortable with what is being said. Often, a husband or wife won't share what is on their mind because they don't want to change the status quo or they are unsure or afraid of how the other will react. How vulnerable we feel at times, and the fear of the unknown all too often holds us back from moving forward in our relationship.

(Cathy): I can think of many instances when I held back from discussing a concern, a need, or a dream with Joe. I refrained from sharing with him for various reasons, depending on the circumstance. As our trust and commitment have grown, I am less inclined to withhold my thoughts and feelings because I am confident Joe loves and accepts me for who I am. I didn't always possess that confidence though.

During the early years of our marriage, I was afraid to say all that was on my mind because I was unsure how Joe would react: Would he be disappointed in me? Would he doubt my sincerity? Would he think me childish? Would he dismiss my concerns as trivial? I remember, for example, how excited I was during my first pregnancy, especially after the nausea subsided enough to enjoy the experience. Accompanying the joy of the pregnancy, though, were many questions, concerns, doubts, and fears about my role and ability to be a good mother. I was concerned as well with Joe's ability to be a good father, more from the standpoint of his time than his nature. Joe's hours were horrendous, and I didn't see the possibility of change in the near future. If his schedule played havoc with my life without children, how would his hours affect my life with children? Unfortunately, I didn't have the confidence to approach him with these thoughts and feelings. Instead, I pushed them aside and made plans for the baby.

We had two children before I finally built up the courage to voice my concerns and dismay about the amount of time and involvement he had with me and the boys. When I shared my feelings with Joe, I did not know if he would ignore my concerns, dismiss my feelings, consider me unreasonably demanding, decide to forego the marriage and family in favor of his medical career as I had witnessed other physicians do, or decide to make some changes in his time commitments to include us in his life. I knew, though, that our relationship was quickly growing stagnant from lack of time and attention and that it needed major adjusting before our marriage crashed. I did not expect or want to spend most of my life alone or raise the children alone. I'm not sure Joe truly understood how discouraged, distraught, and unhappy I was with the situation until I openly confronted him with my feelings and need for change in our relationship.

Joe didn't discount or ignore my feelings. He could tell they were from my heart, and I believe he could feel the love behind the words. I loved him but, at the same time, I needed and wanted a marriage where both partners were actively involved in the relationship. This experience, as difficult as it was at the time, was a turning point for our relationship: Our commitment to the marriage was reinforced, we greatly improved our communication skills, and we appreciated how a relationship grows through both the good times and the hard times. John Powell, S.J., reminds us: "Weathering the storms of the love process is the only way to find the rainbows of life."

(Joe): I have many memorable days in my life, but the saddest day was the evening when Cathy opened up her heart about the state of our relationship. She related with much sadness, frustration, and fear her concerns about how my time and my interests did not include her and our sons. She had come to the realization that she was a single parent in dealing with our sons, our home, and our relationship. She needed to know if I would be willing to make a change for their sake. How

115

devastated I was. *I realized I had not been listening to all the signs that were there. I had missed so much with my growing sons and my wonderful love, Cathy, who was holding our family together by herself. I had choices to make—hard choices, but choices that I knew would make a difference for all of us.*

How we could have avoided many of our heartaches if we had been better at communicating with each other. How I could have made our lives easier if I had looked for those verbal and non-verbal signs of Cathy's frustrations and joys. *Fortunately, I took advantage of this opportunity to refocus on what was important in my life and how we could pursue our goal of keeping our spousal relationship and our family a priority.*

Our communication skills continue to improve with each passing year. Our commitment to our marriage motivates us to work through the times when we aren't on the same page. We thought we were comfortable talking about almost anything when we got married but discovered we weren't. We now know we are comfortable sharing our thoughts and feelings with each other. This sharing enables us to grow more and more in love as the years go by—to come closer to "two becoming one." The communication skills we presently have were developed during our twenty-six years of marriage. We can honestly say from our experience that the progression of our communication skills required patience, constant effort, a determined spirit, understanding, acceptance, trust, and the willingness to change. Was it worth the time and energy as well as the ups and downs? Yes—many, many times over!

The Power of the Human Tongue

"By your words you will be justified, and by your words you will be condemned" (Matthew 12:37). The human tongue is a powerful muscle—not one of the largest muscles in the body, but one whose use has tremendous long-term impact on the people around us. We should never underestimate the power of the spoken word. The words we say and how we say them trigger a positive or negative response from the person(s) to whom the words are directed. The brain and the tongue need to work as a team—with the brain kicking in before the tongue wags. That means that before we speak we must consciously think about the effect of our words on others. Respect for the dignity of the person must be at the forefront behind the purpose of our words. We make that choice to be respectful every time we speak—to either build up the other person or tear him down. **When we love someone, especially our spouse, our speech conveys the presence of our love or the absence of it. Thus the choice of our words exemplifies to our spouse and to others the love, respect, and commitment we have for them.**

(Cathy): I'm sure we can all remember different instances when someone said something to us that made us feel special and unique. Likewise, I'm sure we can also remember those times when we were hurt by the words of another. From my own personal experiences as a wife, mother, teacher, and friend, I understand the effect my words and tone of voice have on Joe, my sons, my students, and my friends. My words can either motivate, encourage, strengthen them or else discourage, offend, and demean them. I can make them feel loved, or I can make them wish they were someone or somewhere else. The choice is mine.

The influence of our families of origin on our pattern of speech is significant. When a person grows up in a family where respectful, compassionate, positive language is spoken, he or she will learn to speak with respect, compassion, and uplifting words. Likewise, when a person experiences language filled with negativity, cold-heartedness, and disrespect, he or she learns to communicate in a similar way. Our understanding of the impact our families of origin had on our communication skills reinforced to us the responsibility we hold to teach our children, by our daily example, healthy and effective communication skills.

(Cathy): *I grew up in a positive environment where I was encouraged and praised. Even when I was disciplined, my parents were constructive and positive. I never remember being demeaned or harshly criticized. My sisters, too, were kind, respectful, and supportive in their words and actions, even to this day. For instance, I could always depend when I was growing up on my sister Patrice to say the right words to build me up when I was discouraged or to motivate me when I needed a boost in my confidence. She could have just as easily teased me about my shyness and insecurities or laughed at my failed attempts at new activities. Instead, she chose to be loving and supportive in her words and actions. Her positive example taught me lessons that have stayed with me all these years.*

Likewise, teachers provided me with countless examples of both positive and negative approaches and attitudes. When a teacher was encouraging, I felt confident in my ability to achieve. When I received negative criticism, my confidence was shaken, and I had to try even harder to overcome my difficulty with the subject matter or activity. These experiences guided my choices in how I dealt with my students when I taught first grade and, similarly, in my interactions with Joe and our sons. I knew the difference positive words and attitudes could make on an individual. There is no doubt in my mind that the words I say and how I say them impact the people around me.

The simple "thank you" I say can convey appreciation or, when spoken in a sarcastic tone, annoyance or ingratitude. I can bark orders at our sons and even Joe or respectfully and politely make a request: "Put your clothes away" versus "Please, put your clothes away for me." I see better results with the second statement. I can choose to concentrate on the strengths of Joe and the boys or constantly remind them of their weaknesses. What a difference it makes when I focus on encouraging them to develop to their full potential.

Many wives openly criticize their husbands for not participating at home with the children and/or with the responsibilities around the house. At the same time, when husbands do try to help, their wives find fault with how or what they did. No wonder more husbands don't eagerly offer to help—they can't do anything right! As wives, we must learn to step back and realize that our husbands may choose to handle the task in his own way—and it may not be our way. For instance, when Joe bathes the boys or reads stories to them, he follows a different routine than I do. It's actually good for the boys to see that there are various ways to handle the same situation. **Words of appreciation for your spouse's participation will more likely generate a positive response and a more willing attitude in the future, whereas nagging and bemoaning the fact that it wasn't done "appropriately" creates feelings of discouragement.** *Who wants to continue to do something when they are constantly criticized and reminded they are a failure? As wives and mothers, the words we speak can make a difference in the attitude of our husband and children and their subsequent willingness to accept responsibilities at home.*

(Joe): Attitude, attitude, attitude. Our attitude is a vital element in our approach to any situation. Our attitude is especially important in our approach to our spouse who ventures into "untrodden territory." When I took on some of the household responsibilities, Cathy and the boys experienced a different approach to bath time, story time, and bed time. They also sampled some "interesting" tasting cuisine. My ways were quite different from Cathy's approach. If she had berated me for my "style" in accomplishing the various activities, I might have given up or told her to do it herself and not ask for my help again. **A psychiatrist once told a medical audience that for every negative comment a child hears it takes seven positive ones to undo that single negative one. I assure you that this formula applies to adults as well.**

Remember a home filled with words of encouragement, love, and honest praise is a home environment where each member of

the family is able to feel loved and secure. Each and every one of us wants to live in that kind of an environment. We have the power through the spoken word to make our homes a peaceful and loving place to flourish.

Communicating When we think about communicating,
Without Words speech is usually the first method that
comes to mind. We communicate, though, in many different ways: through speech, touch, our eyes, the written word, and body language. They are all effective means of communicating, and they all play a role in marital communication. Consequently, they evoke similar reactions, positive or negative, as do spoken words.

Our body language, for example, conveys many messages. When someone slams a door or stomps around the house, that someone is obviously upset, even if the dissatisfaction is not voiced. Responding to a warm caress versus pulling away from our spouse's touch, a smile versus a scowl, an outstretched hand versus a clenched fist, accepting rather than rejecting a spouse's attention, listening to a spouse versus ignoring him or her are all ways we relate our feelings at the moment. Facial expressions and eye movements send messages, too. The longer we are married, the more capable we are in discerning the meaning of our spouse's body language. As related earlier, discerning each other's mood at the end of the day is an example of communicating/listening without words.

(Joe): I remember a lecture on communication given by a child psychiatrist one afternoon during my residency years. He told a story about the parent of one of his patients. The patient's father stated that his child was not communicating with him. The father related the scenario that he had refused to let his fourteen-year-old son go to the movies with a friend. His son turned, stomped up the stairs, slammed his door, and turned his music on full blast. The father wanted to know why his son was not communicating with

him. *The psychiatrist then explained to the father that his son had communicated with him very effectively.*

*(Cathy): As a parent, I've learned that the boys' body language or their moods transmit many messages that the boys usually don't realize they are sending. Observing and "listening" to our children even when they aren't speaking is a beneficial parenting skill. An incident that immediately comes to mind regarding observing a child who has something on his mind is our son Tommy three years ago. It was the middle of June after a week of emotional events in our family's life: I miscarried our eleventh pregnancy on a Wednesday and then on Saturday Timmy, three years old at the time, was rushed to the emergency room with a ruptured appendix. Because the appendix had ruptured, Timmy needed to remain in the hospital to receive several days of antibiotic treatment. The family routine was significantly disrupted since I spent the majority of the day at the hospital with Timmy. When I was home I noticed Tommy was unusually quiet. At first I assumed it was due to the different routine, but after a day or two of similar behavior, I felt something else must be bothering him. I made the time to sit and talk with him to try to determine what was on his mind. After a few minutes of sharing and talking about the events and routine of the past week as well as their effects on each of us, Tommy looked at me and said, "I know this is a hard time, but do you remember my birthday is next week?" Tommy was afraid that with everything else going on in our lives that Joe and I had forgotten about his upcoming birthday. After some reassurance that we had not forgotten his special day, a relieved Tommy reverted back to his peppy self. **Even in the midst of our busy days, we must be cognizant, as parents and as spouses, of the messages family members are sending to us.***

The Importance of Touch

We both feel strongly about the power of touch in our lives.

Many messages are conveyed through touch. The way we touch our newborn, for example, gently or roughly, telegraphs our feelings to the baby. Research bears out the importance of touch. Children deprived of physical contact manifest slower rates of physical, mental, and social development. Touch stimulates the child and lets him know he is loved. With our belief in the importance of touch, our younger children have truly been blessed because their older brothers, in addition to us, held and rocked them endlessly. Touch and physical contact shouldn't stop at a certain age. The hugs and kisses we continue to bestow on our sons reflect our love for them and foster an unspoken sense of security.

(Joe): Fortunately, we both grew up in families where physical expressions of love were acceptable. When we see our parents, brothers, sisters, aunts, uncles, and cousins, we are comfortable with the exchange of hugs and kisses. This continues in our home with each other and in our relationship with our sons. My good-bye kiss to Cathy in the morning before I set out for the day, and the little touches and caresses in the evening when we are together, mean so much to both of us. Our touch when we are close, no matter where we are, brings us a sense of peace and assurance of our fidelity, commitment, and love. Those little touches add to our day and reasserts our love for each other. I am continually amazed at the difference that simple hug makes to our sons, too, no matter what age they are. The hug is like a recharge for each son and an affirmation that Dad and Mom are here for me and love me for who I am.

It would be difficult for me to not share my touch with Cathy. When I am on call at the hospital and unable to be home for thirty-six hours, we both miss that physical presence that has become so much a part of our relationship.

(Cathy): Spoken expressions of love and affection are necessary and wonderful, but the messages sent and received through a gentle

touch, a hug, and/or a kiss are irreplaceable. Joe and I have always been comfortable sharing physical expressions of our love. We both grew up in homes where that was an integral part of our lives. It still is. I appreciate the kiss Joe gives me when he arrives at one of the boy's soccer games or the hug and kiss when he arrives home in the evening. There's a comfort in our holding hands. Nothing fancy, nothing expensive, just the touch that says you're special.

Our sons are comfortable, too, sharing their feelings through touch. When I am visiting the schools, they will come over and give me a peck on the cheek. Talk about warming a mother's heart. I love their hugs and kisses when they return home from school or work each day. Moreover, both of us are moved by their expressions of affection to each other. When Tony comes over for dinner, his brothers still run over and give him tackling hugs as they did when he returned home for breaks during college. I always remember Timmy's comment one Thanksgiving when Tony and David arrived home from college: "I love it when my brothers are all home. We can fight." His definition of "fight" was ending up in a pile on the den floor.

I had a book signing in Dallas a couple years ago for our first book, Good Families Don't Just Happen. *A former first grade student of mine, Kim, attended the book signing. We had a few minutes to reminisce about our experience that year. She shared with me that, of all the things I did that year, her fondest memories are of the hugs I gave the students when they arrived in the morning and left in the afternoon. It wasn't the science lessons I so painfully prepared or the writing sessions I attempted to make fun and creative. Instead, it was my hugs and simple expressions of affection that she carried with her.*

We all need to feel loved and secure. With a simple hug, we can show our spouse and children how much they mean to us. We encourage families to demonstrate their love and affection with each other on a daily basis. Those simple touches can soothe many hurts and melt many a heart. We know how quickly the days go by, so don't miss one opportunity to show your spouse and children how much they mean to you. So hug, hug, and hug some more!

The Written Word

Since we lived in different cities the year before we were married, letter writing was our primary method of communication. (Long-distance calls quickly became cost prohibitive.) We found writing to be a very different, yet rewarding, form of communication from the spoken word. Writing provided us an avenue to relate experiences and/or express feelings that were sometimes harder to share face-to-face. We gained an insight into each other through our written words that we probably would not have attained otherwise.

We still find writing to each other a helpful means of communication, both for expressions of content or discontent. For the first nineteen years of our marriage, we used this method of communication sparingly. Once in a while, usually when we were having a difficult time with an issue and were distant in spirit rather than in miles, we resorted to writing our thoughts and feelings down for the other to read. Reading our spouse's thoughts and feelings provided both of us the opportunity and the time to absorb the words in a way talking to each other didn't allow. It wasn't until we attended a Marriage Encounter weekend that we fully understood the potential and effectiveness of the written word.

Marriage Encounter is a program for couples who want to strengthen and enrich their marriage. Marriage Encounter stresses the importance of healthy, effective communication. The method of communication they recommend is called "dialogue"—a combination of writing and talking about our individual feelings on the same topic or emotion. The four communication skills recommended earlier by the marriage preparation program *For Better and For Ever* are necessary for "dialogue" to be effective: sharing, listening, acceptance, and speaking our minds and hearts with love.

(Cathy): Although Joe and I don't "dialogue" on a daily basis using the process recommended by Marriage Encounter, we do utilize the technique of writing our thoughts and feelings down whenever it will prove helpful. Writing sometimes helps us resolve an issue when other methods of communication have not been effective. I can express my emotions and thoughts on paper in a nonthreatening way to Joe, yet still be honest and open. He can read my words and digest them, as I do his, before we come together to talk about the issue. We resolve many issues through this process of communication.

When I write down my thoughts, I am able to sort through my emotions in a more constructive manner, even when the writing is just a release of my emotions rather than an opportunity to share with Joe. I clear my mind and feel better after "unloading" on a piece of paper.

We recommend the "dialogue" technique to the couples we sponsor in our church's marriage preparation program. We feel it is another useful method of sharing with each other. The week after we had discussed with one couple how we benefited from writing down our thoughts and feelings, especially when we hit a stalemate, they told us how they took advantage of their newfound knowledge in resolving a conflict. The young man decided he and his fiancee weren't moving forward talking about a particular issue, so he wrote down what he was thinking and feeling for her to read. They were able to calmly come together and talk about the problem and resolve it in a healthy and effective manner. They were excited, and pleased, to tell us the technique works.

We believe you will find some communication approaches more effective at different times, depending on the issue and the emotions involved. The important thing to remember is that you want to be able to share with your spouse your thoughts

and feelings in a way that will enable you to grow as individuals and as a couple. .

Gender-Based Differences in Communication The ability to accept our differences is a theme that has followed us throughout the book. The chapter on communication would be incomplete if we didn't mention the topic of gender-based communication differences. The subject of male-female communication styles is explored in depth in books dedicated solely to the subject. Therefore, we will not reiterate the findings by those authors. Rather, we want to share with you the effect gender differences have on our communication skills and thus on our relationship. We realized that we communicated differently, but we didn't initially connect our communication styles with our genders.

(Cathy): I was raised in a family of five girls and no brothers. I remind you of this fact because communicating with primarily girls while growing up determined my understanding of effective communication. Being married to Joe for twenty-six years as well as raising ten sons, I can profoundly attest that there are gender differences in the way males and females communicate. My understanding, appreciation, and acceptance of these differences promotes better communication with Joe and the boys. (And it behooves me to do so, since I am living in a male dominant household.) There are still those times, though, when they can't figure me out and I don't have a clue as to where they're coming from.

I gradually learned that Joe and I shared different views on the same situation. Similarly, our responses differed. We approached and resolved conflicts, problems, and concerns, whether at home or outside the home, in our own unique ways. In the first years of our marriage, this lack of understanding of each other's mind-set caused confusion and additional disagreements. We literally could not understand where the other person was coming from or why.

Even when we wrote business letters, our focus and approach differed: Joe's letters were factual and to the point, whereas mine stated the facts but with a touch of emotion thrown in.

As Joe and I developed our communication skills, we became more cognizant of gender-based differences. And as our sons grew older, I realized even more how differently men and women communicate. *Boys talk about sports, significant events, and activities, while girls share feelings, attitudes, and happenings. The content of Joe's conversations with the boys when they are away at college are different from my conversations with them. They will go into detail with Joe about a soccer game they played, whereas with me the conversation will revolve around the whole experience. The boys' phone calls with friends revolve around the details of what's happening: which movie they are going to, what time, where, and with whom. They discuss the latest sports events and scores. They can tell me how many points a friend scored in the basketball game but probably not where he's applied to college.*

When young girls are visiting our home, I become even more aware of how differently men and women communicate. One spring break a group of girls visited Houston from St. Louis University, where Tony attended undergraduate school. They stayed in Galveston most of the week but came to Houston one day to shop at the Galleria. After shopping, they stopped by the house to visit and have supper with us. As soon as they walked in the door, they showed me their latest purchases and bargains. They shared stories of people they had met and the funny experiences of their day. My sons do not walk in the door after shopping—when they do go shopping—and show me their purchases; I have to ask to see what they've bought. And it is the rare occasion that they would want to sit and talk about the experiences of the day. They are ready to move on to the next activity.

I remember reading an article that related how, even at a very young age, girls and boys communicate differently. The article mentioned that when you listen to girls interacting you usually hear words, whereas with boys, more often than not, you hear just sounds—*sirens, car sounds, random noises, etc. I started observing whether or not this was true. I was amazed when I listened to Timmy and Jamie playing, for that is exactly what I heard—sounds.*

I realize, too, that when I call my parents, I primarily talk with my mother. If Dad answers the phone, he will usually make a few casual remarks before handing the phone over to my mother. If my mother is not home when I call, Dad spends considerably more time talking and sharing with me. He'll tell me about his experiences umpiring Little League baseball; my dad continues to umpire at seventy-four years of age. He relates stories about some of the players and their families; I can feel the satisfaction he garners from his interaction with them. I also enjoy the Santa Claus stories he shares. (My dad became Santa Claus several years ago when my sister Michele asked him to play Santa Claus for her daughter Erica's preschool. He now is Santa Claus for several organizations each December.) The stories he tells range from the comical to the sensitive. One afternoon a family with six daughters came to visit Santa Claus. He told the girls that he knew a family in Houston with ten boys. When the oldest daughter's turn arrived to make her request, my dad asked her what she wanted for Christmas. She smiled and answered, "The address of that family in Houston." Another time, a little boy told Santa that all he wanted for Christmas was for his mommy and daddy to get back together.

I believe that my dad relinquishes the phone when my mom is home because he appreciates and respects our need to talk with each other in a mother-daughter way. With five daughters, he grew to understand, as I have with ten sons, that men and women have their own way of communicating. My parents now have fourteen grandsons and two granddaughters. They can verify that the communication styles of girls and boys are very different.

(Joe): *The gender differences in the method and content of our communication are obvious in our day-to-day interactions. Our differences become very evident when Cathy and I sit down at the computer to accomplish a joint project. How and what she wants to* *see on the screen and how and what I want to see on the screen are incredibly different. It takes constraint on both our parts to work through the differences and compromise on what eventually we produce. While both of us know what needs to be done and that we will eventually accomplish our goal, we are continually amazed at how differently we approach the process. Yes, God knew what He was doing!*

Acceptance of our gender-based communication styles is important to the growth of a couple's relationship. We encourage you to read one or more of the books on male-female communication. We think you will recognize yourself and your spouse in many of the scenarios. You will also gain a greater understanding of the communication skills each spouse brings to the relationship in addition to how your relationship can benefit from this understanding.

Healthy, effective communication skills reap many rewards in a marriage and for a family. Remember that developing these skills is an ongoing process. At times it may seem like a roller coaster ride, up one minute and down the next. We still experience those days when we are not on the same page. We wonder how we can be so alike and, at the same time, so different. Yet, because of our acceptance, understanding, and trust of each other, as well as our willingness to change and adapt to improve our relationship, we are better able to handle the conflicts, disagreements, and uncomfortable situations that inevitably face a married couple, whether married two years or twenty years. When we look back at where our communication skills were twenty-six years ago and realize where they are now, we know that we have learned a lot over the years. We have had our growing pains, but we are definitely reaping the rewards of our patience, determined spirit, and efforts as individuals, as a couple, and as a family.

My lover belongs to me and I to him.
—*Song of Songs 2:16*

Set me as a seal on your heart, as a seal on your arm;
For stern as death is love, relentless as the nether world is
devotion; its flames are a blazing fire. Deep waters cannot
quench love, nor floods sweep it away.
—*Song of Songs 8:6–7*

Chapter Six

Intimacy and Sexuality

The marital relationship enjoys many different facets. Finding an equilibrium among these facets that is mutually acceptable and satisfying for both spouses is more often than not a challenge. We have found, though, that the rewards that often result from the constant struggles are worth the time and effort we have invested over the years. Intimacy and sexuality are two facets of our relationship that often create a disequilibrium. However, when they are understood and balanced, they generate much peace and happiness in a marriage.

In his book *The Mystic,* David Torkington beautifully describes what most of us dream of for our marriage on our wedding day: "The most sacred moment of that sacrament (marriage) is when the couple are bonded together to one another, in every way possible here on earth. They give to each other their hearts, their minds, and their bodies as a means of giving their inner selves, through a union that will grow deeper and deeper, and bond them ever more fully to each other in their mutual journey into the perfect love that will have no end this side of eternity."

We wanted a marriage that grew deeper and deeper and bonded us together forever. We wanted to love with our hearts, minds, and bodies. We didn't know, though, that it would be so difficult at times to achieve our goal. As with all areas of our relationship, we had to grow in our understanding of the role played by intimacy and sexuality in the marital relationship. The growing season for this dimension of our relationship encompassed periods of blue skies and sunshine, periods of drought, periods of thunderstorms, and periods of wonderful fertility. We now realize that we needed to experience all these seasons in order to appreciate the fullness of our commitment to each other and our love for each other. We don't understand why we have to go through the challenges and struggles to attain joy, peace, and happiness—but we do. Kahlil Gibran reminds us: "The deeper that sorrow carves into your being, the more joy you can contain."

Understanding Intimacy and Sexuality

Intimacy and sexuality are often equated in meaning, but they are genuinely distinct in and of themselves. You can have an intimate relationship with someone without it also being a sexual relationship. Similarly, you can be involved sexually with someone without experiencing an intimate, loving relationship. Yet, as we have learned in our marriage, both intimacy and sexuality are inseparable "partners" in the growth and richness of the marital relationship.

Intimacy and sexuality take on a significant meaning in a marriage. Both are integral in a couple's striving for "two to become one." The marriage is no longer viewed as needing intimacy or sexuality but, rather, needing a blending of the two. The physical, sexual dimension of the relationship is understood as only one component, a necessary and fulfilling component, of the process of a husband and wife becoming one. Intimacy is a couple's sharing of their thoughts, dreams, goals, and fears. Intimacy in a marriage is different from the intimacy in other relationships because, in a marriage, intimacy also includes the sharing of oneself physically. That is why the marital relationship is unique in and of itself. **We**

become complete in the total, committed giving of ourselves: emotionally, intellectually, and spiritually as well as physically.

The physical and sexual dimensions of a marital relationship are natural and important for the relationship's continual growth. Physical attraction and physical desires are part of God's plan for us. In most relationships, it is physical attraction that initially brings us together and keeps us interested in the other person. We are "romantically" in love. As we spend more time with our new love getting to know him or her better, hopefully we move from just physical attraction to appreciating other qualities in that person. We feel good being with this individual and want to be with him or her more often. The progression of a healthy relationship begins with this physical attraction but cannot end there because a good marriage requires both sexuality and intimacy.

Society places an excessive emphasis on the physical attributes we are endowed with: height, weight, and physical features such as the shape and size of our nose, our breast size, our muscular development, our hair texture and amount, and the color of our skin. The media bombards us with the physical qualities we "need" in order to be attractive, not just physically attractive but also sexually attractive. Individuals become defined by their sexuality as if that were the most important characteristic of a person. Cosmetic surgical procedures are being performed in continuously greater numbers in order to "perfect" our image. More and more teenage girls, as well as adult women, are having breast augmentations and lipo-suctions. Teenage boys and young men are taking steroids and other muscle enhancing products to build up their muscle mass and strength. Increasingly dissatisfied with our physical characteristics and who we are, we try to change ourselves into someone else. We are unaccepting of the features God has bestowed on us and seek to improve on His handiwork.

As we become more enamored with physical appearance and characteristics, we become less and less concerned with the interior characteristics of a person—the characteristics that truly define who we are. Too often relationships are built on the outward appearance of a person while the interior qualities are ignored. We do not deny that appearance is relevant in a relationship. As mentioned previously, most of us are initially attracted to someone because of his or her physical attributes. We must move forward, though, from the physical characteristics to learning more about the person as a whole. A relationship based solely on the physical will not develop into a long-lasting, mutually satisfying, and loving relationship.

Fostering an intimate and sexually fulfilling relationship where both persons are loved and respected in *all* aspects of their lives requires maturity and a willingness to love outside of oneself. Relationships based solely or primarily on the physical or sexual dimension of the relationship focus on self and fulfilling the needs of "me." The needs of the other are irrelevant or secondary to one's own.

While it may have been the physical characteristics that initially attracted us to each other, the relationship moved forward only as we learned more about each other. Sharing our thoughts, feelings, dreams, and fears enabled us to become intimate in non-sexual ways. It is essential to a healthy relationship that couples first gain a sense of closeness in nonsexual ways before expressing their love through sexual intercourse. In their article "Sexuality and Intimacy in a Marriage," Evelyn and James Whitehead explain that "a well developed capacity for intimacy enables a person to sustain the adjustments and compromises of life with others, without jeopardy to one's own integrity. A flexible identity, an empathetic awareness of others, an openness to continued develop-ment of the self—these strengths of intimacy make possible the creative commitment of marriage." We strongly believe that for sexual intercourse to be fully appreciated as it was meant to be, we need commitment—commitment made through the vows of marriage.

Society questions this concept. The media bombards us with propaganda that tries to convince us of our right to engage in sex whenever we want and with whomever we want. The media distorts sex and makes it an end unto itself. Sexual pleasure becomes a right for the individual, and the needs of the sexual partner are secondary or nonexistent.

What a shame so many people have been deceived into thinking that sex void of commitment is the ultimate pleasure! We give away one of our most treasured gifts so cheaply, often with serious consequences: AIDS and other sexually transmitted diseases as well as unplanned pregnancies, infertility, and/or psychological and emotional stress. Many couples feel that living together can resolve relationship problems, both sexual and non-sexual, before they get married. Yet statistics do not bear that out. Couples who live together before marriage have a significantly higher rate of divorce than couples who do not live together. We wonder whether that happens because sex and the physical relationship took precedence over the development of intimacy in the relationship. The Whiteheads in their article support that concept: "In most relationships, even most sexual relationships, sex is not enough. Lovers want to and need to have more in common. An inability to develop this broader deposit of common interests can lead to the deterioration of the quality of the sexual experience as well."

Whereas commitment may be voiced between a couple who live together, *total* commitment happens when you commit unconditionally to someone for better and for worse, in sickness and in health, for richer and for poorer until death do you part. The marriage vows are not just words to be spoken but a commitment to be made to your spouse, a commitment that provides the opportunity to grow together in all areas of your lives—a process that leads to "two becoming one."

The sexual relationship is a significant part of that process and commitment. The sexual dimension of a relationship is meant to enhance and enrich the marriage. "Sexual intercourse celebrated in a context of total commitment has the power to make two people a 'couple' not only in their bodies, but also in their hearts and souls" (*For Better and For Ever*).

(Cathy): *If there is one area of our relationship that has grown in appreciation and understanding, it is the sexual dimension of our marriage. (By no means does that mean that I am the next Dr. Ruth, or care to be.) My initial understanding of the importance and the integration of sexuality in our relationship was naïve. While sexual intercourse itself was not hard to figure out, understanding all that enters into that one sexual act took time to appreciate. Likewise, the appreciation of the totality of the giving of myself to Joe and vice versa in the sexual act developed over time.*

Assumptions and expectations play a significant role in our sexuality, as they do in all areas of our relationship. And as was the case in the other areas of our lives, our assumptions and expectations about sexuality sometimes differed. When we married, I felt ignorant of what to expect sexually from myself or from Joe. I assumed, since Joe was a physician, he understood this aspect of our relationship better than I did. I depended on him to show me the way. I initially questioned my ability to please Joe and fulfill his needs, whatever those needs might be. I was also unprepared for the significant importance of the sexual dimension for Joe as well as the impact it would have on our relationship. Sexual intercourse enabled us to express our love in a new, exciting, and complete way. At the same time, I found that while we expressed our love more physically, we shared less nonsexually. Intimacy outside of sexual intercourse was pushed back several notches, and not for the better.

Although I enjoyed and understood the need for the sexual side of our relationship, I began to realize that I missed the other sharing we had done before we were married. All of a sudden, I didn't feel that Joe found talking and sharing important anymore, whereas I did. I still wanted and needed to share my thoughts and feelings, dreams and fears, with him. There seemed to be time for love-making but not time for sharing in any other way. I felt his needs were being met but mine weren't. I also began to realize that the sexual relationship was more fulfilling for me when I felt closer to Joe in other areas of our relationship as well. That "intimacy," *while of less importance to Joe's sexual fulfillment, definitely enhanced the quality of my own sexual fulfillment because it provided a sharing and caring that included and transcended the physical realm of matrimony. When I didn't feel appreciated outside the sexual dimension of our relationship, I didn't feel special, unique, or loved. Instead, I felt like just another "thing" in Joe's life. I needed more from our relationship than that. I didn't want to replace or eliminate our love-making but, rather, blend my needs with his. **Over the years we've learned that sexual intercourse isn't really love-making when one or both spouses don't feel loved and respected in all areas of his or her life.***

We both recognized that we had a lot of learning to do regarding our sexual relationship. While you can read about the "how to" of sexual performance, no one can teach you about your spouse's needs or how to specifically please your spouse. Each couple's sexual relationship is unique. Spouses must be willing to share their sexual needs, wants, fears, and insecurities with each other no matter how uncomfortable doing so can be at times. We can't read each other's minds, though, so in order to learn the "how to's" for our relationship, we must be open, trusting, accepting, and loving. That is, we must be intimate. To quote again from *For Better and For Ever:* "The ultimate measure of intimacy in Christian marriage is not the frequency or quality of orgasm, but rather the degree to which each person feels more safe, whole and accepted through the couple's experiences of making love."

We learned how important communication is to enhancing the love we physically express to each other. We know that when we are communicating well, all areas of our marriage are enhanced—especially the physical. To quote the Whiteheads: "Communication may not be the whole of intimacy, but—as both theology and psychology show us—it is at love's heart."

We gradually gained an understanding and appreciation of each other's needs in our relationship, both sexually and nonsexually. In his book *Romancing the Home,* Dr. Ed Young points out very

emphatically that the number one need of a wife in the marital relationship is affection, while the number one need of a husband is
sexual fulfillment. Many couples are unaware of that major difference. While we may begin to understand our wants and needs in
the relationship, we may not understand that they differ from those
of our spouse. As a matter of fact, Dr. Young apprises us that *none*
of the top five needs of the wife coincide with the top five needs of
the husband. That should tell us something about the importance of
understanding the needs of each other. If we don't understand the
needs of each other, then it is difficult to meet those needs.

(Cathy): *If I appreciate and respect Joe's need for sexual fulfillment and its relationship to his self-esteem, then I will consciously
choose to fulfill that need for him, not because it is my "duty" to do
so but, rather, because I love him. Likewise, Joe will meet my needs
for intimacy out of love for me. In our giving we receive. As I share
my love physically with Joe through love-making, he showers me
with the affection and love I emotionally need. As he provides for
my needs, I lovingly attempt to meet his needs.* **We are both
enriched and become better lovers from our mutual giving, Our
differences, instead of tearing us apart, once again become our
strengths. The differences in our needs actually enhance the
total giving of ourselves to each other.**

*Respect, trust, commitment, and our mutual desire to make our
relationship a strong and healthy one provides us with the means
to make the physical sharing of our love mutually satisfying and
mutually beneficial. I don't see it as another chore to perform but as
a gift I, and only I, intend to give to Joe. As a wife, I need to understand that if I want to ensure as much as possible that I am the only
woman to share Joe's sexuality, then I will lovingly meet his need
for sexual fulfillment. Likewise, if Joe wants me to remain faithful
in mind and body, he will recognize and lovingly fulfill my need for
intimacy. The big "I's" become little "i's" once again as we selflessly
strive to "bond ever more fully to each other in our mutual journey
into the perfect love that will have no end this side of eternity."*

(Joe): *It took me many years to understand that the progression and development of all aspects of our relationship go hand in hand. In order for the physical relationship to grow and flower, I needed to attend to the other facets of our marriage. In the early years of our marriage, I believed that our physical relationship was healthy since we both seemed to enjoy our love-making. Indeed, it was a new experience that brought pleasure to both Cathy and me. As time brought about different changes and challenges to our marriage, however, we reached a plateau in the progression and development of our marital relationship. This plateau concerned Cathy because she knew that our relationship had the potential to develop into a stronger and more meaningful relationship.*

After many years of trying, Cathy convinced me that we needed to attend a Marriage Encounter weekend. Cathy's parents were in town and willingly agreed to watch the boys for us so we could attend worry-free. The weekend proved enlightening for me and fostered a new appreciation of our relationship. ***I "relearned" the importance of communication in our marriage and that all aspects of the relationship (emotional, physical, intellectual, and spiritual) develop together. I was reminded that the physical part of the marriage will not grow unless the other aspects of our marriage are growing along with it.*** *Likewise, the weekend pointed out that the physical dimension of our relationship would help the development of the other facets of our relationship. They go hand in hand. Prior to the weekend, I naïvely believed that the different facets of our marriage existed separately and were not intertwined.*

Although I still had a lot to learn about communication and understanding Cathy's needs, I had at least made an important step. As our communication skills improved, our physical relationship also improved, thereby affirming what the Marriage Encounter weekend had articulated. It made me want to strive to be a better spouse by being a better communicator with Cathy, developing both the emotional and intellectual dimensions of our marriage.

I came to realize that one reason for the differences in our approach to the sexual aspects of our relationship was due to the difference in how men and women perceive sex. Women's approach to sex has both a physical side and an emotional side; the emotional dimension is paramount. On the other hand, men emphasize the physical nature of sex yet often neglect the emotional dimension. This difference is further widened by the media's compartmentalization of sex. The media portrays sex as solely an act that exists to bring us pleasure with no implications or repercussions beyond the act itself. Therefore, the media supports the approach that our goal toward sex is to make ourselves more sexually attractive—work out, look pretty/handsome/sexy/appealing, smell great, drive the right car, vacation in the right spot, and wear sensual clothes—all in order to find the "best" partner who will bring me the greatest pleasure. There is no mention of the effects the sexual encounter will have on the partner. Self-gratification through self-love as well as pleasure through sex is what is important.

I truly believe that such an approach is both destructive and self-limiting. This self-centered approach, destructive to the individual and the spouse, ultimately, leads to the stagnation of the marriage. Since the relationship is focused on the self, it is self-limiting and does not allow the individual, the spouse, and the marriage to grow. When I consider the needs and perspectives of my spouse, I open many avenues of emotional and physical growth in our marriage.

Love-making is no longer limited to sexual intercourse. We both realize the importance of nonsexual expressions of love to the strengthening and affirming of our relationship. Our simple kiss good-bye in the morning, our love pats, hand holding, hugs, and arms wrapped around each other are all part of our physical relationship. They are physical expressions of our commitment, love, and respect for each other.

A couple must also realize that each and every sexual experience need not be a passionate "10" for it to be loving, fulfilling, and "right." When over time the level of passion, intensity, and even frequency of sex changes, a couple should not worry and be concerned that they are a poor "fit" sexually. Change, even in the sexual dimension of our relationship, is normal in the growth of the marital relationship. Change does not have to be interpreted as a couple's sex life becoming dysfunctional or worse. Rather, when a couple grows to understand the physical and emotional needs of each other and attains a new level of intimacy, the changes should improve their sexual relationship and enable it to be more fulfilling.

(Cathy): I gradually learned that each of our sexual experiences is unique unto itself. Sometimes we both feel passionate and our sex unfolds accordingly. Other times we may both be addressing different emotions or responding to different highs and lows during the day. The stresses and fatigue of our days factor into our love-making. These feelings and experiences affect our responses to each other and our approach to love-making. It doesn't mean we aren't loving, rather, we are just expressing our love according to the moment. If I am exhausted physically and emotionally at the end of the day, I may make love to Joe, but he has to realize I may not be a "10" on the passionate scale. A "tired" response is different from one conveying lack of desire and/or disinterest.

Children and Their Effect on Our Sexual Relationship

Many changes accompany the arrival of children to a family. We can allow these inevitable changes to cause stress in our sexual relationship, or we can choose to look at the changes as an opportunity for growth in the physical dimension of our relationship. Children do not have to be an impairment to the continuation of a satisfying sexual relationship. As a couple, though, we have to recognize that we need to adapt our sexual relationship to fit the changes that are taking place.

(Joe): When children become part of the marriage, our perceptions concerning our role and identity within the new family structure may likewise change. I am now not just a husband but also a father with the additional responsibilities that that entails. Financial demands increase with medical bills, additional food and milk, education, and juvenile paraphernalia. Time demands change: attending early and late meetings are harder, planning outside activities with friends involves more effort, coordinating routine day-to-day tasks may require additional time and attention. The physical responsibilities alone that children necessitate are significant—diapering, bathing, and feeding. A child's total dependence on us can be taxing and fatiguing. How can we deal with these changes and maintain a mutually satisfying and loving sexual relationship?

Maintain your priorities and goals. Make the time you do have with each other as a couple a priority, maybe by turning off the television and/or computer. Recognize that the sexual dimension of your relationship is one of those priorities. Couples with healthy spousal relationships make better parents. Be flexible. Since prior routines of time spent together may be harder to keep with children around, learn to adapt. Learn to deal with fatigue. I've jokingly always said that good parents are chronically fatigued parents. Men, be understanding of how tired your wife may be at night, especially in the first months after the birth of a child. Women, understand the physical needs of your spouses as well. Respect of each other's needs at this time is essential. Couples, understand that on some evenings love-making is just what two very tired parents need at the end of a long day. Although you may be tired, the sexual experience will bring you closer together physically and emotionally.

Healthy, effective communication skills are definitely an asset during this transition from couple to family. If you're in the early years of your marriage, you may still be working on developing these necessary skills. If so, recognize the importance of sharing your joys, concerns, fears, and insecurities with your spouse during this time. Many of the feelings and fears we experience as new parents are similar. Yet there are many feelings and fears that are indigenous to us specifically as a mother or a father. Being able to express to our spouse these feelings and fears will ease you as a couple through this adaptation period from couple to parents.

(Cathy): I remember changes occurring in our sexual relationship beginning with our first pregnancy. I experienced severe nausea and fatigue during the first trimester of each pregnancy, but during my first pregnancy the nausea and fatigue were significantly more pronounced. Mornings were a disaster. Joe tried not to be around, if he could help it. His leaving early was okay with me since nothing he had tried to do to relieve or reduce the nausea made a difference. In the evenings, he would call from the hospital and, more often than not, wake me to come pick him up. (We only had one car in the first four years of our marriage.) I would pick Joe up, fix dinner, and then head back to bed where I slept until the next morning. I assure you I was not a lot of company or fun during that time.

I was also amazed at the changes my body was going through, and I was definitely unprepared for the degree of nausea and fatigue I had. It had to take a toll on Joe; I was too sick and uncomfortable, though, to even recognize it at that point in time. After the first months, I felt better and our relationship resumed, for the most part, its prepregnancy state. The pregnancy progressed normally so there were no restrictions on our sexual activity. We did have to accept the fact, though, that my body was shaped differently and so required some adaptations in our love-making.

What helped me through this period was Joe's understanding and patience. Those first months of my pregnancy were not easy for me, and they were quite contrary to what I expected a pregnancy to be like. In addition, I had to face the fact that my body was beginning to look very different from anything I had experienced before. From never having a "stomach" or "breasts" to having both took some getting used to. Clothes I had thought I'd be able to wear for several more months quickly became too tight and uncomfortable. Since most women want to look pleasing to their husbands, and I am no different, I wondered if Joe would find the changes unappealing. Fortunately, for both of us, that wasn't the case. Joe made me feel beautiful and desirable during each pregnancy. Those feelings of love, respect, and appreciation, in spite of my changing appearance, helped us enjoy our physical relationship during our pregnancies. My appreciation of Joe's needs, admittedly after those first months, also had a positive effect on our relationship.

Once the children were born, we had to work hard to focus on our relationship. We still do. I was amazed at how much time and energy one eight-pound baby required. (If someone had told me at that point in my life that I would have ten children, I might have collapsed from the thought.) I remember expecting to bounce back to my normal energy level and routine after Tony, our first son, was born. How wrong I was! Again, Joe and I had to blindly adapt to the changes we encountered.

With the birth of each of our sons, we had to make adjustments in our relationship. We realized, though, that our relationship had to remain a priority in spite of the challenges, demands, and constancy of parenting. *Thank goodness we did realize it, too, because the ability to deal with all that family encompasses necessitates that the marital relationship remain strong and healthy. I believe, too, that as husband and wife we need to know and feel we are still the "one and only" in the eyes of our spouse.*

We recognized that what may have worked for us in our sexual relationship before we had children may not necessarily work with children. If we are too tired to respond to each other's needs in the evening, for example, maybe we need to try the morning when we're better rested. We're convinced hugs, kisses, and some loving in the morning are more warming and invigorating than any cup of coffee for getting the day off to a good start. When children are napping on a weekend, we "nap" too. If we could get away for a night or weekend, we took advantage of that time to reconnect as a couple. We didn't have family in town but traded off with another couple or two at watching each other's children so we could have a night or weekend alone. (At least we could do that when we had two or three children. Our family grew to where the odds were not in the other family's favor.) Get inspired, be creative, and stay connected as a couple! You both deserve it!

Fertility—Gift or Burden?

Society encourages us to compartmentalize the different aspects of our lives. In keeping with that approach, we are encouraged to compartmentalize our sexuality and our fertility. Unfortunately, couples want to reap the pleasures of their sexuality but hesitate to appreciate their God-given gift of fertility. Likewise, society separates the spiritual nature of our fertility and the physical nature of our fertility. Our sexuality and fertility, though, encompass both.

In the Bible, fertility is continuously presented as a gift. A shift has definitely evolved over the centuries from the appreciation of fertility as a treasured gift to the notion of fertility being a burden that complicates our busy lives. Generally, couples want children and want to be family. Unfortunately, many couples struggle with infertility and seek ways to enrich their homes with children. Yet we witness contradictory messages being conveyed. On one hand, infertility procedures are on an increase as are multiple births. On the other hand, abortion and contraception proliferate. A couple may appreciate their fertility when they want children but consider it a burden once their family is complete.

We do not advocate that couples should throw their fertility to the wind and let what happens happen. We do not advocate that couples have ten children. Rather, we advocate that couples view their fertility and their sexuality as one integrated gift from God.

Our church, the Catholic Church, is criticized by Catholics and non-Catholics alike for her teachings on human sexuality. People want to believe that the church expects all couples to raise large families. On the contrary, the Catholic Church does not dictate how many children a couple should have to be a family; rather, the church asks us to be responsible parents. We are asked to appreciate and respect the sexual act as a gift given to a married couple to enrich their lives, and we are likewise asked to appreciate and respect the fertility that accompanies the sexual act—not as separate and distinct entities but as one.

(Cathy): When Joe and I mention responsible parenting, many people look at us with a look that says: "Who are you to talk about responsible parenting?"—as if having ten children denotes irresponsibility and lack of intelligence on our part. We assure you that responsible parenting is not defined by the number of children a couple has but, rather, by how a couple raises the children they have, whether they have one, two, four, or ten children. If responsible parenting were defined by the number of children we have (1.8 children per family in the United States), then we should have the most responsible society that has ever existed. Sadly, we know that is not the case.

Responsible parents determine whether they, as a couple, are physically, emotionally, spiritually, and financially capable of fulfilling the needs of a child or children. (Notice the emphasis is on needs not wants.) A couple must honestly and consciously discern whether they are capable of meeting the physical, emotional, intellectual, and spiritual needs of each of their children. I underline capable because the issue that usually determines the answer to that question is a couple's willingness to accept the responsibility of parenting and the self-giving it entails.

Societal values usually enter into the decision making. We are told that children will inhibit our lives financially, physically, and emotionally. Yet Joe and I have found that the financial, physical, and emotional investments and "sacrifices" we make for our family reap innumerable dividends. We don't deny that society is right when they tell us we won't have as many material possessions as families with fewer or no children. What we do have as a family, though, is more rewarding and longer lasting than any "thing."

Nothing—not a more expensive home, fancier and newer cars, exciting vacations, the latest fashions, a 54" television set, exquisite jewelry, freedom to come and go as we please—could enrich and satisfy our lives more than watching our children grow up together—learning, loving, and being family.

(Joe): As I would tell colleagues and friends about each new pregnancy, responses varied from: "Hey, you're a physician, don't you know how that happens?" to "Don't you two have a TV set?" They were the true friends and understanding colleagues who expressed their joy to accompany Cathy's and mine. Initially, the tacky comments did sting but later on were easier to weather as I acknowledged to myself the shortsightedness of the individuals making them. In reality, it was none of their business whether we were having another child, especially since Cathy and I were the ones who were ultimately responsible for caring for them. **Cathy and I had developed a good "track record" raising our boys— they were well behaved and caring of each other. However, each time we were blessed with another child, people were quick to question our sanity, our good judgment, and our impulse control.**

The other "interesting" comment we often hear is that we must be "good Catholics"—as though having a large family is one of the criteria of determining whether or not one is a good Catholic. We assume these comments imply that there are more "bad Catholics" than "good Catholics" in our community and that this can be readily determined by simply counting the number of children a family has when each family leaves church after Sunday Mass.

Indeed, it is our mutual love and support during each pregnancy as well as that of our family and true friends that adds so much to the appreciation that each child is a unique gift.

Since we are Catholic, many people assume, correctly, that we practice natural family planning, a nonartificial method of regulating the spacing of children. They may also assume, incorrectly this time, that because we have ten children, natural family planning (NFP) is noneffective. We assure you our sons are not mistakes or a continued effort to have a daughter or two. The truth is we prayed God would bless us with children. We know people have an extremely hard time understanding why an educated couple would choose in today's world to have a large family. Yet, choosing to have our children, all ten of them, is right for us and a blessing in our relationship. We believe, too, that as we practiced NFP our appreciation of its role in our marriage grew. The periods of abstinence provided us opportunities to communicate and share our love—to be intimate—in nonsexual ways. When we did make love again after a period of abstinence, we found the sexual experience was usually very fulfilling. Maybe there is some truth to the saying, "Abstinence makes the heart grow fonder." We also learn to better appreciate what we don't have readily available all the time.

Many misconceptions regarding NFP abound. For one, NFP is not rhythm. Rhythm was a method couples used decades ago to space their children based solely on calendar days. Women were told to abstain from sexual intercourse a certain number of days following their monthly period if they wanted to avoid conception. The assumption was that all women ovulated on the same day of their menstrual cycles. After much research on ovulation and the observation that the "rhythm" method was ineffective, it was determined that each woman has her own "rhythm" of ovulation. While one woman may ovulate on day 10 of her cycle, another woman may ovulate on day 17. No wonder the rhythm method was ineffective; it was based on "one size fits all." Yet each woman's fertility is unique. The knowledge now available regarding a woman's menstrual cycle makes it possible for any woman to determine when she is ovulating. A couple can then choose to abstain during the fertile period of their cycle or attempt to conceive. We use the NFP method for both purposes.

(Cathy): Joe was initially skeptical of my ability to accurately pinpoint my time of ovulation. Natural family planning and the science supporting it is not taught in medical schools, although the validity of the science is recognized today and promoted for couples

experiencing infertility. As the months went by, Joe was more and more convinced that I could determine the phases of my menstrual cycle. At the same time, I appreciated the increased knowledge I gained of my body and the interconnectedness of the various systems. I also enjoyed the freedom this knowledge provided me.

We will not deny that practicing NFP in our marriage has at times been a struggle. We enjoy our sexual relationship, for it is an integral part of our marriage. Using artificial contraception would reduce the need for us to keep track of our fertility and would give us the freedom to have sex anytime we wanted without the need to consciously think about conceiving a child. Society continues to try to convince us that to refrain from sexual intercourse when you're married is absurd. Society questions the whole concept and practice of chastity or abstinence, not only before marriage, but especially once a couple is married. Self-denial in any area of our lives is not encouraged, especially regarding sexuality. Yet, we find that practicing self-denial in all the different aspects of our marriage, even the sexual component, strengthens the whole relationship. Our love, respect, and commitment to each other enables us to say "yes" when we need to express our love physically and to accept the "no" when we strongly feel it is not an appropriate time to conceive another child. We understand the value of not turning our fertility on and off at whim but, instead, participating with God in His plan for us.

Appreciating the relationship between intimacy and sexuality enables us to continue to grow in our marriage. The intimate side of our relationship provides us the ability to deal with the ever changing facets of our sexuality. The sexual side of our relationship continues to develop as an outgrowth of our intimacy and continues to be a source of pleasure and fulfillment in our marriage.

We encourage couples to recognize the importance of developing both their intimacy and their sexuality, and then blending the two together. When that happens, a couple begins to fully appreciate the sexual dimension of their relationship and how it bonds them closer together in hearts, minds, and bodies.

Endeavor to be patient in bearing the defects
and infirmities of others, of what sort soever they be:
for thou thyself also hast many failings
which must be borne with by others.
                              —Thomas A. Kempis

Remove the plank from your own eye first;
then you will see clearly to take the
speck from your brother's eye.
                              —Matthew 7:5

Weathering the storms of the love process
is the only way to find the rainbows of life.
                              —John Powell, S.J.

Chapter Seven

Building Blocks or Stumbling Blocks?

*E*very facet of our lives presents opportunities to strengthen our relationship as a couple. Our attitude and the choices we make regarding these facets determine whether they evolve into building blocks or fragment into stumbling blocks. Each couple differs on which issues and to what degree these issues cause dissension and friction in their relationship. Differences and conflicts are inevitable in a marriage. No married couple is immune from them. The factors that influences whether the differences or conflicts create building blocks or stumbling blocks are the attitude and commitment each spouse embraces in making the necessary choices and changes that will place the couple back on track and then propel them forward in their relationship.

Before a conflict or problem can be resolved, it must be identified and acknowledged. In many relationships, couples either deny there is a problem, hope the issue will work itself out, or simply pray the conflict will disappear. In some situations, only one spouse feels there is a problem while the other spouse is unaware that anything is awry. Whichever the case might be, the problem or issue must be brought to the forefront if a couple is to determine the best course of action to follow in resolving the difference.

Resolving conflicts and differences requires practicing the four essential components of a relationship: love, respect, commitment, and faith. The quality of a couple's communication skills affects their ability to resolve differences in a healthy, effective manner. Likewise, the techniques that the families of origin used to resolve conflicts and problems influence a couple's expectations and assumptions concerning the methodology of conflict resolution. Learning the "how to's" of conflict resolution reveals how intricately the various facets of our relationship intertwine with each other. We recognize that if we practice mutual love and respect, developing healthy and effective communication skills as well as recognizing the pattern of conflict resolution in our families of origin, then we are better capable of maturely and lovingly resolving conflicts and differences in our own marriage. We have stated that the marital relationship is an ongoing process. As each area of our relationship changes, so too are other areas of the relationship affected. The choices we continue to make determine whether the changes and growth are positive or negative—building blocks or stumbling blocks.

The Rules and Tools of Conflict Resolution

As witnessed by our experiences in this book, our relationship has had its share of ups and downs. Many of our difficulties resulted from differences in each spouse's assumptions and expectations as well as variations in our backgrounds and families of origin. Our lack of selfless love, respect, commitment, and faith coupled with poor communication skills also complicated our struggle to resolve differences and misunderstandings. As we made positive advances in addressing these situations, we improved our ability to resolve our simple day-to-day differences as well as the deeper conflicts that still arise. We have not eliminated all conflict, since our relationship continues to change with time. We have learned positive ways, though, to remedy the conflicts so we can resume the closeness we both enjoy.

We truly miss the closeness of our relationship when we are at odds about an issue. Neither of us has a good day. We may be testy with colleagues at work and with the children at home. The absence of that internal peace is noticeable. Fortunately, the absence of this intimacy motivates us to resolve the misunderstanding in a timely manner. In addition, we are both uncomfortable with conflict. Therefore, we strive not only to reconcile our differences when they arise but to avoid the situations that create them in the first place.

As we worked with engaged couples in our church's marriage preparation program, especially the first few years, we learned many helpful techniques to employ in resolving conflicts and differences in our relationship. Moreover, we read articles and books on the marital relationship that also recommended the same conflict resolution "rules and tools." Some of the rules and tools we were already using; others we weren't (especially those related to effective communication). As we incorporated some of the recommended techniques into the process of handling our misunderstandings, we were pleasantly pleased with the results. Furthermore, as we used the new "rules and tools" on a regular basis, they gradually replaced our old techniques.

One of the first things we learned in our own relationship was the importance of acknowledging that we had a conflict or difference. We know that sounds extremely simple, yet we cannot overemphasize the importance of admitting that there is a misunderstanding. Frequently, only one of us realized that a problem even existed. Therefore, the disgruntled partner was responsible for bringing his or her concern to the attention of the other. Old habits of ignoring or avoiding the situation or praying the problem would rectify itself had to change. The old ways didn't resolve the conflict anyway. By not letting a problem brew for any period of time, we learned that we lessened the chance of the conflict festering to the point of a massive explosion. Even at those times when we both knew we were in disagreement regarding an issue, we needed to discuss the matter in a timely manner. Delaying the discussion of an issue for any length of time only fueled further resentments.

Dealing with conflict was difficult for both of us in the early months and years of our marriage. The main reason for our difficulty was a lack of understanding on how to effectively and compassionately resolve our differences. Our problem wasn't in the desire to resolve a misunderstanding but, rather, in the dynamics of constructively discussing an issue and creating a positive change that was mutually beneficial and satisfying. Having had few disagreements before we got married, we suffered from a lack of experience with resolving difficulties. In addition, neither of us had developed effective conflict resolution skills in our family of origin. Ironically, both of us constructively dealt with differences or conflicts in other relationships with friends or colleagues.

Why was dealing with conflict in our marriage so much harder? One factor in our reluctance to face our conflicts and maturely deal with them was the uncertainty of the other's reaction to our feelings of disappointment or anger. We are both sensitive individuals. As such we avoided talking about an issue that could possibly hurt the feelings of the other, even at those times when we ourselves were hurting. At other times, we assumed and expected the other person to understand our moods or feelings, even when we had not expressed them.

(Cathy): I plead guilty to assuming and expecting that Joe knew what I was thinking and feeling. I can laugh about it now but it wasn't always funny. I couldn't believe he wouldn't know and understand that I would be upset when he arrived home much later than he had indicated he would or that I would be annoyed if he changed the evening's plans without my knowledge. He honestly didn't realize his watching television in the evenings increasingly frustrated me. He was truly "clueless."

In retrospect, the transition from being single, with little accountability to anyone but oneself, to being married, with new responsibilities and accountabilities, to a spouse, was harder for Joe

154

to make than for me. Having lived in Houston before we married, he continued following the routine he had developed since he started his pediatric training. I was the new kid on the block. While I understood that Joe had established a pattern of living, I also felt that his way of life was not conducive to the development of our relationship. I was unsure, though, how to "fix" what I saw as a problem.

(Joe): One of the benefits of dealing with conflict promptly is that it allows the relationship to get back on track. When we don't move quickly, the delay may cause either party to "stew" and "ruminate" about the problem. As we have both learned the hard way, to delay confronting the issue may add yet another stumbling block before the issues at hand. Believe me, we don't need another obstacle in the way of resolving the conflict!

Why didn't I always deal with conflicts sooner? There is a risk, a personal risk, in dealing with a problem or conflict. Dealing with the conflict may mean that one or both of us might have to face our own weakness, selfishness, shortcoming, disrespect, poor choice, or unhappiness. The conflict that I produced may mean that I have to realistically assess the person in the mirror, the person/spouse/parent that I think I am. Maybe I'm not as caring as I thought I was. Maybe I'm not as considerate as I thought I was. Maybe I'm not as loving as I thought I was. Maybe I'm not as good a father as I thought I was. Maybe I made a bad choice without really thinking. Dealing with the conflict then, may mean that one or both of us will have to change for the success and growth of the relationship (spousal and/or family) to continue. That prospect may not be easy to confront or deal with. To paraphrase an old adage: "I have found the enemy and the enemy is me."

How can I learn to successfully deal with areas of conflict in my life while building up myself and our relationship? My willingness to face these conflicts, although still not easy, was brought about by my understanding, acknowledgment, and trust of Cathy's love and forgiveness as well as knowing that she accepts me for who I am. She may be mad at me about something that I did but

*we can deal with it, make the changes or simple compromises
necessary for the betterment of our marriage, and move on to accept
the rewards of those decisions. Without Cathy's willingness to be
open, loving, and accepting of me, any willingness on my part to
deal with these conflicts would have been squelched. **There has to
be a bigger carrot at the end of the stick for each of us to willingly
travel the road of conflict resolution. That carrot for me is the
peace of heart and the intimacy of the relationship in its emotional
and physical facets that make it all worth doing. Ultimately, the
growth it brings and the maturity it fosters benefit both spouses.***

We recognized that our conflict resolution skills were ineffective when the same issues continued to cause dissension. Were we
just slow learners? Were we not choosing to change our behavior?
Were we unrealistic in our expectations? Were we not being
completely honest in unveiling our feelings or in our commitment
to resolve the misunderstandings? Were the conflicts due to situations out of our control? Were we not clear on what we needed to
do individually and as a couple to produce concrete results? Our
desire for change motivated us to seek the answers to the questions.

We recognized that similar skills and guidelines (rules and tools)
are needed to resolve every misunderstanding, whether the
disagreement revolves around time commitments, family commitments, financial matters, or careers. We heartily encourage couples
to learn and adapt the conflict resolution skills recommended by
marriage counselors.

∾Acknowledge that there is a misunderstanding or an issue of
conflict. Lack of communication or crossed wires cause many
misunderstandings that can be resolved quickly. Gender differences
alone account for many minor misunderstandings.

∾Choose an appropriate time (appropriate for both of you) to
discuss the issue.

∾Use "I" sentences that reflect your feelings and understanding
of the situation instead of using "you" statements that are
inflammatory and blame the other person for the problem.

∽Be understanding and accepting, not judgmental.

∽Stick to the issue at hand. Leave past disagreements in the past and place irrelevant issues aside.

∽Be respectful in the tone of voice and the choice of words you use. Yelling and screaming, demeaning or disparaging comments, and name-calling all create additional resentments. Remember that unkind and bitter words spoken with a harsh tongue cannot be erased and are not easily forgotten.

∽Listen to your spouse with your ears and your heart. We need to feel that our spouse cares about our thoughts and feelings.

∽Accept and admit your responsibility for the misunderstanding if you are at fault.

∽Take a mutually agreed upon "time out" if tempers begin to flare. Resolve to finish the discussion after a short time out. Do not postpone resolving the problem indefinitely.

∽Avoid all physical and verbal abuse.

∽Reassure your spouse of your love and commitment. We need to feel loved in spite of our weaknesses and failings.

∽Offer forgiveness, seek forgiveness, and accept forgiveness for any hurt or wrongdoing, whether intentional or unintentional. Then let bygones be bygones. Realize that some hurts require longer to heal. On the other hand, understand that holding a grudge or continually harping on a past offense is counterproductive to improving a relationship.

∽Pray for God's loving guidance in resolving your differences. He wants us to be at peace in our marriage.

∽Keep misunderstandings and disagreements private. The thoughts, feelings, doubts, fears, and concerns of your spouse are not for public airing. Family, friends, and coworkers do not need to know your intimate affairs. Your spouse deserves your trust, understanding, and confidentiality.

∽Choose to make the necessary changes in your own behavior and attitudes to avoid misunderstandings and conflicts in the future. Recognize the fact that you can change only yourself and not your spouse. Your sincere attitudes and actions, though, can evoke positive change in your spouse.

ﾟﾟRecognize when you need outside help in resolving your conflicts. Be willing to seek professional assistance before either of you reach the irreconcilable point in your relationship.

Once we became aware of the rules and tools of resolving misunderstandings and conflicts, we needed to take the next step and apply them to the reconciliation of differences. This is an ongoing process that requires the committed effort and unconditional love of both. When we learn to resolve our differences, though, in a healthy and effective manner, we create a home environment that enables us to grow stronger as individuals and as a couple. Likewise, we foster a home of peace and happiness.

(Cathy): I wish every married couple was required to attend a marriage follow-up class on their first anniversary and again after they have children. Many of the topics presented and discussed during the marriage preparation program would be more relevant after experiencing the daily challenges and joys of marriage and family life. Concerns specific to each couple could then be addressed. As a sponsor couple, Joe and I could determine which areas we effectively covered and which ones missed the mark. (The areas might differ from couple to couple according to each couple's unique strengths and weaknesses.)

The reason we would like to see a follow-up class is because we learned many relevant, effective skills during our sessions with engaged couples. Although we attended an engaged weekend before we married, the conflicts that arose were conflicts in areas of our relationship that we didn't expect to create problems. The time spent answering questions and then sharing our answers with each other a few years into our marriage addressed our specific needs. We filled in the gaps that were holding us back from reaching our full potential as a couple. As a result, we strongly recommend that every couple avail themselves of a class, seminar, or retreat on a regular basis to reaffirm why they married each other and to recommit to their marriage vows.

At the end of a marriage and family seminar Joe and I gave in Calgary, the parish priest provided the couples in attendance the opportunity to renew their marriage vows and receive a marital blessing. What a wonderful way to end the day as well as invigorate the couples as they continue their life's journey together! The vows evoke so much more meaning after you experience the joys and challenges of married life. Whereas a couple may not fully understand the commitment being made on their wedding day, a couple grows to appreciate the full commitment expressed by their words after living the vows. **Each time Joe and I renew our vows, my eyes water and my voice chokes, for I realize how much he loves me and the commitment he continues to make to me as conveyed by his love and respect. Likewise, I know how much I love him and how strong my commitment is to fulfilling my vows and to making our marriage a source of peace and happiness for us and our children.**

When our son David was twelve years old, he wrote an essay entitled: "A Happy Family." One line reads: "A happy family is but an early heaven." He later writes: "Why should I wait until I die to reach heaven when I can have it now?" David, at only twelve years old, was clearer on the concept of experiencing heaven on earth through love of each other than many adults. If our differences and conflicts are unaddressed or ineffectively resolved, they interfere with our ability to attain heaven on earth. On the other hand, when we lovingly strive to reconcile our differences, married and family life provide us "an early heaven."

The Issues at Hand Each married couple struggles with their own unique set of problems. What may cause dissension for one couple may not necessarily be a source of conflict for another couple.

Marriage counselors have identified, though, the most common areas of conflict for couples: time commitment, finances, career, family, religion, sex, roles and responsibilities, extended families, and inappropriate and/or unhealthy behavior. In our marriage, we experienced significant conflicts in some areas while, in other areas, the disagreements were minor or nonexistent.

Conflicts, whether revolving around religion or financial matters, can be effectively resolved if a couple chooses to practice the conflict resolution tools and rules presented. Both spouses must be willing to work on a problem, though. When one spouse won't even agree to listen to the concerns of the other or isn't willing to attempt to rectify their differences, the marriage will continue to struggle. On the other hand, the willingness and ability to compromise and change enriches a relationship. **In a marital relationship, there is the constant need for giving and taking—not giving in.** When one spouse feels he or she is always "giving in," resentment builds up, a sign that effective communication skills are not being practiced, and that the essential components of love and respect are lacking. Our commitment to work through our problems and differences together enables us to "weather the storms" in order to enjoy the "rainbows of life."

A parent is often encouraged to "pick their battles" when dealing with their children. Married couples need to pick their battles, too. If spouses prefer different brands of toothpaste, buy both brands rather than argue about which brand to buy. If your spouse has never enjoyed going to the ballet or a football game, don't expect or demand him or her to develop a sudden love of the ballet or football once you're married. Instead, attend that activity once in a while with a sibling or friend. Too many couples argue about insignificant issues and let them grow out of proportion. A friend of ours and mother of eight, Mary, shared some words of wisdom with us years ago. She said to ask yourself when a "crisis" hits: "How significant is this issue or problem in the scheme of life?" **Keeping a healthy perspective on day-to-day issues makes a difference. Maintaining a positive attitude and approach in the**

160

way we speak as well as the way we handle a crisis or conflict makes a difference. Choosing to compromise and alter our ways because we love our spouse makes a difference.

(Cathy): How easy it is to get bogged down by the negative! Instead of considering the possibility that a mistake was made unintentionally, we often react by being accusatory. We can quickly talk our minds into considering all the negative qualities in our spouse rather than concentrating on the positive, loving qualities. All too often we allow one minor infraction to transform our spouse into an evil monster. Instead, we should reverse the process by giving our spouse the benefit of the doubt by thinking of all the good qualities he or she possesses rather than dwelling on his or her inadequacies. We restate the question that was posed by Dr. Ed Young: "What is it like to be married to me?" Honestly answering that question reminds me of my own imperfections and selfishness. Neither of us is perfect.

When negative thoughts start infiltrating my mind, I can either sit back and let them take over or I can decide to reverse the trend. We need to learn and practice ways to maintain positive thinking. *For me, listening to upbeat or spiritual music helps change my mood and thought process. If I am really annoyed and can feel my frustrations mounting, whether with Joe, our sons, or a situation, a pause to say a prayer or two (or three or four, if I'm really upset) opens my heart and my mind to peaceful thoughts rather than vindictive ones. Joe and I keep saying "love is a choice." If we accept and believe that love is a choice, then we will work hard to keep our minds and hearts thinking kind and loving thoughts, despite the difficult conflicts all married couples inevitably face.*

We want to touch on the different areas that cause dissension in many relationships. We advise couples, though, that if one area is causing them significant difficulty, then they need to find additional materials to read about those specific problems or seek help from someone outside the relationship.

Roles and Responsibilities

Our assumptions and expectations of spousal roles and responsibilities evolved from our families of origin as well as societal and cultural values. During our engagement, we discussed sharing responsibilities around the house, so we thought roles and responsibilities would be a "nonissue" in our relationship. How quickly we discovered otherwise as our daily routine began.

(Cathy): As we shared earlier, we initially modeled the roles of our parents. Once the school year started and I began teaching, the distribution of responsibilities required adjustments. Adjustments continued to take place as changes occurred in both our home life and careers. A major adjustment was needed when I returned to school to attain my master's degree. Another major adjustment in our roles and responsibilities took place when we started our family. Additional minor tune-ups have taken place on and off over the years.

Gradually, what we found worked for us was linking our individual interests and strengths with various household and family responsibilities. Time availability was also a major consideration. We did not consider any responsibility gender specific but, rather, we determined who did what, when, and how depending on the availability of time and one's ability and interest. *With Joe's schedule demanding that he be away for thirty-six hours at a time, I accepted the fact that I would need to perform nontraditional roles and responsibilities. I didn't have a problem with that since I grew up in a family of all girls where there was no distinction between "male" and "female" chores.*

Although today we tend to fulfill the same responsibilities on a regular basis, we willingly adjust responsibilities or accept additional responsibilities when one of us has outside commitments or is not feeling well. Joe usually oversees repair work unless the repair needs to be completed at a time he is unavailable. Then I will handle the repair. Similarly, if I am nauseated during a pregnancy, Joe will prepare the evening's meal. Couples who tend to assign responsibilities according to traditional husband-father and wife-mother roles struggle with this issue more than couples who blend their home responsibilities. When a working spouse does not respect and appreciate the energy and demands required by his or her spouse to care for children and maintain a household, resentments and frustrations build up. For the working spouse to come home and expect to be finished with his or her day while expecting the other spouse to continue to fulfill home responsibilities is selfish, demoralizing, and choosing not to love. Likewise, if both spouses are working outside the home, each spouse needs to understand the importance of sharing responsibilities at home. When St. Paul wrote that "wives should be submissive to their husbands," he never implied that husbands, as head of the home, are allowed to treat their wives as maids or inferior individuals. He tells husbands to "love your wives, as Christ loved the Church." The love Christ had for His Church was not demeaning or disrespectful but, rather, enriching and nourishing. When a husband loves his wife, the choices he makes reflect that love. Joe's willingness to help me out at home is a sign of his love for me and the boys. Likewise, I willingly accept those responsibilities that need to be fulfilled because our situation and home deem it necessary for me to do so. **When couples choose to unselfishly work together, they will experience less friction and tension regarding roles and responsibilities.**

Another issue that necessitated resolution involved the completion of certain responsibilities. I grew increasingly annoyed and frustrated when Joe agreed to fulfill a responsibility or complete a task but didn't. For years I would "rescue" him by completing the task or fulfilling the responsibility. One day I realized that I was doing with Joe what I wouldn't do for the boys: rescue them when they didn't do what they needed to do. I was "parenting" Joe instead of being his wife. I decided—and it was very difficult at first—to not rescue him. If he didn't want to repair the leaking shower and the leak caused additional problems, so be it. I thought I would not be able to follow through with the process because the additional problems along with the original one would make me mad.

Surprisingly, that didn't happen. As Joe realized that I wouldn't rescue him, not to mention the consequences of a task unfulfilled, he more readily accomplished what needed to be done in a timely fashion. We must be spouses to each other and not parents. (There is a difference in rescuing and the willingness to help each other out. If he asks for me to help, I am there for him.)

It is important to reemphasize that we cannot change someone else. A change, though, in the behavior and approach to a situation by one spouse can create positive change for the relationship. It doesn't even require yelling and screaming, belittling, or temper tantrums.

Careers

We both knew at a young age what we wanted to be when we grew up. Joe wanted to be a doctor; Cathy wanted to be a teacher. We worked hard to attain our dreams: jobs at college and during the summers, scholarships, dorm resident assistantships, and student loans. Our investment of time and energy was worth it because it enabled us to achieve our goals.

(Cathy): We shared our career goals with each other as well as the road we wanted our careers to follow. We understood that I wanted to teach a few years, pursue my master's degree, and then, hopefully, start our family as Joe neared the completion of his pediatric training. We weren't sure where Joe's medical career would finally lead us, but we felt confident that we would be prepared to tackle that decision when the time arrived. As with many other situations that occurred in our relationship, these unknowns threw us a curve.

The first curve hit when I decided I was ready to return to school for my master's degree. I intended to teach first grade during the day and attend graduate school in the evenings. I felt diminished support and encouragement from Joe when he told me that he felt I should either teach or attend school. He didn't see how I could do both since I was extremely busy already. I knew that he needed to accept more responsibilities at home in order for me to successfully handle both. Joe's willingness to accept those responsibilities allowed me to continue pursuing my dreams. (I never did complete my master's degree since we had five sons in rapid succession, and the time allotted to complete the program ran out. My dream is still alive though!)

I was unprepared for the next curve thrown me. Joe came home from the hospital toward the end of his pediatric training to inform me he wanted to do a fellowship in neonatology. I cried! The fellowship meant two additional years of medical training. The hours would continue to be horrendous and the pay insignificant. I was definitely ready for his hours to decrease and the income to increase. In addition, we were ready to begin our family.

While I knew the hours would continue to be dreadful and the compensation minimal, Joe deserved the opportunity to pursue his dreams. It wasn't an easy time for me—not during the process of making the decision or during the two years of training. Yet Joe needed to feel my support on this decision just as I had needed his support when I wanted to return to school.

In the section on "roles and responsibilities," I touched on "submission" in the spousal relationship. My support of Joe's choice to continue his medical training in neonatology is an appropriate example of my understanding of what St. Paul means by "submission." The support I offered Joe didn't involve a loss of dignity on my part. I wasn't being relegated to a lower status. It wasn't as though what I thought or felt didn't matter to Joe. My acceptance and support of Joe's decision to specialize in neonatology, although difficult, was accepting God's plan for our marriage.

We expected the neonatology fellowship to be arduous on both of us. Fortunately, we knew there was light at the end of this tunnel. Or so I thought! When Joe completed his training, he was invited to join the faculty at Baylor College of Medicine. Joe made the choice to remain in an academic setting versus a private practice because he felt the demands on our family would be lessened. Initially, that did not happen. Joe's hours continued to be long. He rarely made it home in time for dinner or to play with the boys before they went to bed. This was a difficult time for me personally and for our marriage. I saw the mutual goals we established as a couple slipping away to Joe's medical career.

(Joe): I loved taking care of patients and teaching when I was a pediatric intern and still do even after practicing medicine and teaching different levels of students and residents for over twenty-eight years, twenty-five of those specifically in neonatology. It is still a joy and great source of gratification for me. However, as a generalization, those talents are not enough to be successful in an academic setting. There is much pressure to do research and successfully compete for grants. Likewise, it is imperative to publish the results from those research efforts so that academic promotion can be achieved as well as prestige for your medical school and department. The fruits of these accomplishments are touted frequently in one's academic environment, and those who are successful in this venue deserve every accolade they receive. These fruits are powerfully seductive, especially when you are in a successful academician's office and see the plaques, the photographs with dignitaries, and the title of "professor" before his or her name. I chased that dream when I began my fellowship and in the early years after joining the faculty. I wanted to be invited to speak at national meetings, present my research, and see my name at the front of scientific articles published in prestigious journals. I wanted to be able to have my name mentioned with those of the great physicians in the field of neonatology. However, I realized that those were not realistic goals for me because of some of my intellectual limitations and, more realistically, because my talents lay elsewhere. More importantly, the pursuit of my dream was leaving little time for Cathy and the boys. **When Cathy told me that she felt as though she were a single parent trying her best to raise our two sons all by herself, I knew I had better reassess my**

career dreams and goals and refocus on those family and marital dreams and goals that Cathy and I shared. It finally was becoming obvious that my spousal and family goals were always taking second place to my career goals, a position that I had vowed would never happen. So I sat down and did some serious reassessment. It reminded me very fondly of a story of assessment that the sister of a close friend once told us. Lynn was a very pretty and intelligent girl who had always been an activist in everything she had done. She was also very slender. As she was about to embark for college and the challenges that awaited her, she recalls getting up early to shower on the morning of her departure. Drying off in front of the mirror in her bathroom, she took stock of herself and then vowed: "It will have to be my brains and personality that will help me achieve the successes that await me." We all laughed at her story, especially knowing what a fantastic individual she is and all that she has accomplished, not to mention knowing the wonderful man she married. So it was my turn to take stock of my talents and shortcomings and the truly important persons in my life. I managed over the next several years to refocus my efforts on my academic strengths that would let me be in more control of my career commitments and time as well as still be an academic success although in a different venue than I had originally chosen. Fortunately for me, I had a loving, supportive, and forgiving wife and sons who were glad to have me back. The hours are still challenging for me, Cathy, and the boys (they will always be), but I know that my family supports my career because of the time that I have been able to commit to them. Likewise, I had an understanding, supportive, and nurturing boss, professionally and personally, who allowed me to fulfill some of my dreams in a different area than I had originally chosen. Oh, to have known then what I know now!

As happens all too often in marriages, career goals may take precedence over marriage and family goals, whether one or both spouses are working. Commitments change—and not always for the better. There is tremendous pressure in society to be financially successful and renowned in one's field of expertise. The cost to attain this level of success is often at the expensive of one's marriage and family. Career and family are not necessarily incompatible. We need to work in order to support ourselves and our families. The incompatibility develops when the priorities and commitments are inconsistent with or destructive to the fulfillment of family responsibilities.

We must decide what our priorities are and how our career fits into those priorities—not the other way around. We have to ask ourselves: What are my career goals? Where does my spouse and family fit in with my career goals? Is the price I have to pay to attain my career goals worth it? Have I taken into consideration my family when making decisions regarding career choices and changes, whether involving more responsibilities and time commitments or moving to a new location?

(Cathy): When I chose to stay home and raise our sons, I did so knowing I would miss the students and challenges of teaching. We realized, too, that we would struggle financially with only Joe's fellowship salary. Yet I felt strongly that it was in the best interest of our family for me to stay home. I had observed how stressful and difficult it was for families, parents, and children when both parents worked outside the home. I do not regret my decision. I am most grateful that I have been able to be home with our children in spite of the fact that my career was put on hold for the last twenty-five years. My teaching, instead of in the classroom with twenty-five to thirty students, has been at home with our ten sons. (Teaching is defined as my total interaction with them. I am not officially home schooling.)

When I began speaking to groups on parenting and family, I experienced the stresses and choices that many parents continuously make when they both work outside the home. At least I am able to decide when and where I speak so I am able to coordinate my presentations around Joe's and the boys' schedules, thereby minimizing my time away from family. Unfortunately, too many parents don't have that luxury. When work schedules and demands conflict with the schedules and demands of family and children, the stresses and pressures mount.

We have created a society where more and more families need both parents to work to meet their financial responsibilities. On the other hand, many families in which both spouses are working do not need the money. It is a true choice to work outside the home versus a necessity. Society has tried to convince us that we can successfully have our careers and raise our children. I know it can be done because Joe is a competent physician as well as a committed father in word and deed. At the same time, I am home to fulfill many of the needs of our family so that Joe does not have to worry about them. If we were both working, the stress to fulfill these responsibilities would significantly increase. **In addition, society does not value the mother or father who chooses to stay home with his or her children. The "job" of parenting is looked down upon as if the mopping of floors and the washing of clothes is all I do all day. I assure you it is not the household responsibilities that kept me home all these years but the interaction with my children.**

Our career choices must take second fiddle to the needs of our families. Only then will we see a change in our society—a society where the needs of family and children are again valued.

Time Commitments

Before we get married, we spend a lot of time together fostering the relationship. We make the other person feel loved and unique. It is such a wonderful feeling to have someone appreciate us in our uniqueness. After a couple marries, other priorities may begin to get in the way of the time and attention we formerly devoted to each other. We have to decide what our priorities are and how we will balance our individual needs.

(Cathy): *The discretionary use of time has been a major source of conflict for us during our marriage, especially for me. I knew Joe's hours would be demanding during his pediatric training and was prepared to accept that. It was his off hours that created frustrations for me during this period of our marriage. We seemed to resolve one issue only to have another one appear, similar yet different. Joe assured me that his hours would improve once he finished his training. I didn't notice any difference. His call nights, commitments, and responsibilities were still taking him away from me and the boys for an excessive amount of time. I was beginning to feel like a single parent.*

In addition, I also felt a lack of respect for my time and the effect his schedule had on what I could do. I didn't appreciate the last-minute phone call to inform me about a meeting he had forgotten to inform me about or write on our calendar. I called it the "by the way" syndrome. "Cathy, by the way, I have a 6 P.M. meeting tonight. I'll be home late." "By the way, I switched call with someone for next weekend."

Although Joe knew I would most likely be home (Where would I be going at night with babies?), I resented the assumption and expectation that his last-minute change in schedule didn't affect me. I resented, too, that he took for granted that because I would be home, he was free to come and go.

Change in the "by the way" syndrome took time for us to resolve. As I became more involved in church and school activities and had commitments of my own, the need and importance of writing meeting dates, appointments, etc., on the calendar took on real significance. I worked my commitments around Joe's meetings and call schedule. If that wasn't possible, I arranged for a baby-sitter. The "by the way" phone calls continued until the afternoon Joe called to tell me he forgot he had a meeting that evening. I had one too—and mine was written on the calendar. I was willing to change my commitment that evening with the distinct understanding that I wouldn't do it again. I deserved respect for my time and commitments, even if they were not an income source.

Resolving this issue took time but paid big dividends for both of us: because I was less frustrated and angry, Joe didn't have to come home to a frustrated and irate wife. Today before either of us schedules an activity outside the normal routine, whether Joe has a dinner engagement or meeting or I am scheduling a presentation, we check with each other. I still receive a phone call, but now it's in advance of the activity to determine whether we have other commitments scheduled on that day.

As our family grew, respect of each family member's time and needs became extremely important. Our kitchen calendar helps us stay organized and meet our individual and family obligations, significantly reducing the stress and conflicts in our relationship.

Finances

While we need sufficient money to meet our financial responsibilities, we also need to responsibly manage the money we have. Money and the management of it are sources of many disagreements in marriages. The conflicts cross all economic levels, although they may revolve around different financial issues.

Our society has become very materialistic and consumeristic. We define ourselves and our success by what we have, what we do, and where we go. Instead of money being a tool to meet our needs, money has become the mode to fill our wants. We grew up hearing the adage "Money won't buy happiness," but people still seem to want to try. People are convinced that if they have more money, all their problems will disappear. We just have to look at the lives of the "rich and famous" to know that doesn't happen. The media bombard us with the constant message that we need "this" and we need "that." They want to convince us that we'll be happy if we have more, bigger, and better things. The truth is that the media's message is a lie!

For a couple to minimize financial disagreements in their marriage, they must set financial goals and determine how they will meet those goals. Most of us receive very little education regarding financial matters. With credit cards so readily available, a couple can quickly accrue significant debt if they don't know how to manage their finances as well as their desires. Financial management requires discipline and the willingness to establish long-term goals at the expense of short-term pleasures.

We discussed finances a little before we were married, but we did not sit down and establish financial goals for ourselves, although we wished we had. Once we were married and had an idea of our financial commitments and income, we formulated a budget and tried hard to stick to it. Neither of us was interested in accruing debt. We made the decision early in our marriage that we would live within our means. That decision and practice continues to this day.

The first rule of thumb is for couples to live within their means. When a couple begins spending more than they are bringing in, the debt accumulates and becomes more and more of a struggle and source of conflict. Realize it is okay to gradually furnish your home. We bought a new piece of furniture when we had saved enough to pay for it. As a society, we have become inpatient in our demand for instant gratification. "If I want it now, I should have it now." It's almost as if the "want" becomes a "right." Couples aren't interested in "starter" homes anymore. They want the home similar to the home that took their parents decades to purchase. In the process of filling our wants, we lose focus on what is really important in our lives. Our priorities shift from what our spouse and family needs to how to fulfill our wants.

(Cathy): It is so easy to get caught up in our materialistic society. The wants are advertised everywhere. When you don't drive the fancy car, live in the elegant home, wear the name brand clothes, and take exotic vacations, you are made to feel inferior. How unfortunate that society determines our self-worth and success by our material accumulation.

I personally know that's not true from my experience teaching first grade in a small Catholic school where my salary was barely more than the tuition I had paid the previous year at Loyola University. I measured my success by the students I taught—not by the paycheck I received. Even today, Joe and I are not surrounded by the many material trappings that denote "success." Our choices and priorities over the years have focused on meeting the needs of our sons, all ten of them. In order to meet those needs (defined as their physical, emotional, spiritual, and intellectual needs), we had to establish financial goals and priorities early on in our parenting years. If you don't establish goals, you don't know where you're heading or how you're going to get there. Only by establishing our goals early have we been able to reach these goals.

One of our goals was to educate our sons in the Jesuit high school here in Houston. Once we realized the financial commitment it would require, we established a "Strake Jesuit Education Fund"—and this was when Tony and David were just starting school. Only because we established a long-term goal of educating our children and both remained committed to fulfilling that goal have we been able to send our sons to Strake Jesuit College Preparatory. Our fifth son, Matthew, graduated in the year 2000—only five more to go! Families with similar incomes and less financial commitments can't understand how we do it year after year. How? We drive our cars many miles past their warranties, we choose a simpler lifestyle, we hand down clothes, we buy non-name brand clothes, we rarely eat out as a family, and we take simple vacations to Galveston or to visit family. We often tell people that having our large family helped us to keep our priorities in the right place. We are more interested in seeing our children well-educated and faith-filled individuals than we are in having our sons drive their own cars, wear the latest fashions, or play with the latest gadgets.

Both spouses must be on the same page financially. Goals must be mutually agreed upon and committed to. How often do we see couples say they are saving for a home and then the husband decides he wants a new computer or the wife goes on a shopping spree, thereby frustrating the other spouse and causing problems.

(Cathy): Several months after I had given a presentation at a neighboring preschool, a mom who attended the talk stopped me in the grocery store. She shared with me a personal story. She and her husband had been having a difficult time in their relationship because she wanted to build a new and elaborate home in one of the new up and coming prestigious areas of Houston. He preferred to remain in the home that he had purchased before they were married. The issue was driving a wedge into their relationship.

In my talk, I shared my views on chasing the American dream—wanting the more, the bigger, and the better, often at the expense of what is truly best for our family. I stressed how we have become so entangled in society's materialistic values instead of focusing on long-term values. The words hit home for this mom. She realized she was placing her desire to have "the acceptable home in the acceptable neighborhood" above her desire to have a good marriage and family. When she approached her husband with the idea of staying in their present home but remodeling it, he was most agreeable. She had tears in her eyes when she said, "Our relationship has never been better and we have never been happier. To think I almost threw this away for a house!"

We need to remember that we each bring into our marriage the financial styles of our family of origin or maybe one parent in particular. We need to ask ourselves what role money and finances played in our family of origin and what role it plays in our life now. Were money matters a source of dissension in your family of origin or a nonissue? Was money considered a source of power or status? Was there sufficient income to cover needs, or was there never enough to meet expenses? Were your parents spenders or savers or one parent a saver and the other a spender? Am I a spender or a saver? Do I understand financial matters? Am I financially disciplined or financially irresponsible? It is important to recognize which financial traits and attitudes you and your spouse possess.

(Joe): Financial matters in my family of origin were handled by my father. Mom was provided a budget for groceries and incidentals while both of my parents handled the general needs (clothing, etc.,) for my brother, sister, and me. We kids thought that we were "well off" compared to many people around us and never felt that we went without. We wore decent clothes and were well fed. We all thought that Dad and Mom were good providers.

Stretching the paycheck for what we needed was often a struggle. As my dad looked at the ledger each month, he worried and worried since he knew he had Catholic school tuition to pay on top of other expenses. When finances grew very tight, my dad often dealt with this tension by worrying out loud about how stretched our finances were. I know that this was his way of dealing with the pressure. He often directed his worries to my mother, but as kids you hear everything. It upset me when he was so worried.

I promised myself that whatever I did in the future, I would work hard enough so that money would not be a major issue in my family's life. I did not want my family to have to listen to financial worries similar to those expressed by my dad.

Cathy and I both work hard to provide for our family. We have managed to keep our financial worries (which are part of managing a family) under control. We accomplish this by living within our means (which both of our parents did) and by planning ahead (Cathy brought that to our marriage). After doing that and keeping our priorities in place, we place great trust that God will provide— He always has. Cathy and I find ourselves playing different roles at different times regarding our concerns and ability to handle the financial demands of the family. I will find myself overwhelmed by financial demands only to have Cathy remind me that God will take care of us and that I shouldn't worry. When Cathy worries, I remind her about the last time that we were financially stretched.

God managed to find a way to help us meet our financial commitments.

(Cathy): In my family of origin, money was a nonissue as far as causing disagreements or conflict. I know that my parents struggled with the financial demands of raising five children, but I never remember them arguing about money or making us feel as if we were "poor." We had what we needed and were happy. It was obvious that I didn't have as many clothes or things as some of my friends, but at the same time, I had more than others and was content.

My parents set a good example of living within their means. Mom handled the day-to-day financial matters as far as writing the checks and paying bills. I also had the impression that she was instrumental in saving and planning ahead for long-term expenses. She instilled in me a sense of financial responsibility, not from book knowledge but from her own example.

I tend to follow her style of handling financial matters. When we got married, I realized that if I wanted the checkbook balanced on a monthly basis, then I better accept the responsibility myself. Balancing a checkbook was not one of Joe's priorities. Not knowing whether our checking account was balanced or not didn't bother Joe, whereas I was uncomfortable not knowing. I gradually realized that I had more of a knack and understanding of the financial side of maintaining a home. Although Joe remains intricately involved in our financial decision making, I tend to be the one who handles the day-to-day financial matters, the income tax preparation, the boys' college financial aid forms, and finagling our financial resources to meet our expenses. We're both comfortable with this arrangement.

One of the reasons the arrangement works is because we both understand our financial commitments and goals and what we have to do to achieve them. Just because one of us is writing the checks doesn't mean he or she has the freedom to buy or do anything he

or she wants. **We always make large purchases together. One of us isn't out buying what the other isn't aware of or will resent. We sit down every year to determine our short-term goals and long-term goals in all areas of our marriage, not just the financial side.**

People assume that because Joe is a physician, financial concerns are not an issue. We assure you that if we had not established goals years ago, committed ourselves to them, prioritized and accepted a simpler lifestyle, then the choices we are now able to make would not be possible. We're both willing to make these "sacrifices" because we know what we want for our family and know what it takes to get there. By mutually establishing goals, being committed to them, prioritizing our financial decisions, and living within our means, we substantially reduce the stress, tensions, and conflicts that arise from money and the management of it.

Religion

Our faith as individuals and a couple should inspire, strengthen, and guide us in our relationship. It is hard to believe that religion and one's faith can be a source of conflict in a marriage when spirituality is understood as a source of peace. Whether a couple shares the same faith or are of different religious denominations, disagreements and misunderstandings arise when there is a difference in each spouse's beliefs and/or understanding of the role faith will play in their individual and marital lives.

Each spouse, whether the couple shares the same faith or different faiths, may practice his or her spirituality in his or her own unique way. Beliefs, teachings, and traditions may be understood and practiced differently. Faith may be an integral part of one spouse's life while, for the other, it is more a matter of heritage, meaning you are a Catholic or Baptist in name only but are not actively practicing the faith. One spouse may feel the importance of attending church regularly, while the other may only feel obligated to attend services occasionally. One spouse may want to pray as a couple and family. The other spouse is uncomfortable or uninterested in praying together. The level of participation in church life may be a source of problems when one spouse wants to be actively involved but the other doesn't care to be.

Religion is often not discussed at length before a couple marries, even when a church wedding is planned. **It is important, though, for couples to discuss their religious beliefs and practices and the role they will play in their marriage. Assumptions and expectations may differ for each spouse.** If your faith is an integral part of your life and you want it to be in the life of your spouse, then it is important to know and understand the faith commitment of your spouse. The issue does not go away once you are married.

(Cathy): The faith life of the person I married was of importance to me. In a previous relationship, the individual was not understanding of the role faith played in my life. He did not appreciate that my faith was a big part of what made me who I am. When I began dating Joe and we could share in that dimension of our relationship, I realized how significant attending church together and talking about faith issues was to me. We shared a mutual appreciation and understanding of the integration of faith in our lives.

The quality of a couple's faith life affects their marriage. A marriage preparation leader in Helena, Montana, told us that statistics show that couples who practice their faith together and share a mutual commitment to their spirituality only have a 1 in 1,000 chance of divorcing. Not bad odds when you consider the divorce statistics in the United States. Faith does strengthen, inspire, and guide couples through the decisions and choices they make in their marriages.

Working in our church's marriage preparation program, we've noticed that the level of faith commitment is reflected in the total relationship of a couple, even when the couple practices different religions. Their level of intimacy is stronger and they seem confident on most facets of their relationship. When we begin to discuss with engaged couples the role of faith in their marriage, in many instances one partner is uniquely surprised and often dismayed by the responses to the questions regarding spirituality by his or her partner. We can tell that they have not discussed the topic before and that the assumptions they made regarding their partner's faith were not on target.

We believe that when God is an integral part of the individual lives of each spouse, then as a couple they will make Him an integral part of their relationship. **When choices and decisions are made in the context of one's faith, the choices are more likely made with a loving, respectful, and giving heart. If a spouse compartmentalizes the different dimensions of his or her life, faith is viewed as a separate entity or a nonessential and may not enter into the way he or she treats the spouse or the decisions he or she makes.**

Faith provides the foundation for the marital relationship. All the other facets of the relationship revolve around the faith commitment we either have or don't have: financial, career, family, behavior, sex, and time commitments. Our mutual commitment to our faith helps keep us on the right track and moving in the right direction.

The Extended Family

Our families of origin influence the many facets of our married life. We previously stated that you marry not only your spouse but also your spouse's family. As we have learned, there may be both positive and negative influences derived from our families. Likewise, our extended families can be a source of harmony or dissension in our marriage, depending on the type of influence they continue to bear on us.

When extended families are there to offer their support and not to interfere or continue to parent, then the relationship between the couple and the spouse's family will more likely develop harmoniously. When the extended family makes unrealistic demands on a married couple or expects to still make decisions for their son or daughter, the extended family relationship may become strained.

Sometimes it is one or both of the spouses who cannot cut the strings from their parents. When a spouse remains dependent on his or her parents rather than shifting the focus of her needs to her spouse, the neglected spouse will begin to resent the time and involvement the wife or husband spends with family. Priorities change once you marry. Your spouse becomes your number one priority. Parents and siblings aren't discarded from your life but, instead, take a back seat to the needs and responsibilities of married life. Not all parents want to understand that shift in priority status, and so cause stress in the extended family relationship.

Likewise, if a spouse's parents do not like the partner their child has married, they may not be accepting and loving in their words and actions toward him or her. This type of behavior drives couples away from family instead of bringing them closer together. As difficult as it is in dealing with this issue, couples need to discuss their concerns with their parents and siblings in order for family time to be rewarding and not tension filled. If this is a source of conflict in your relationship, we recommend reading *Going Home Grown Up*, subtitled *A Relationship Handbook for Family Visits* by Anne F. Grizzle, LMSW-ACP. She offers guidelines for making visits home positive experiences, whether in town or across the country.

Another issue that we want to mention is one we touched on previously. It is essential that couples keep their disagreements and misunderstandings to themselves. Sharing intimate discussions or problems with parents and/or siblings can influence their opinion of your spouse once the misunderstanding has passed. Remember, your spouse deserves your trust, understanding, and confidentiality.

(Cathy): In spite of the fact that neither of our families lives in Houston, our families have played a role in our marriage over the years. Joe and I have appreciated the continued support my family has offered us and the space allowing us to grow in our own way without interference or criticism. Joe is comfortable calling my dad and asking for his advice on various issues. My mom and Joe have a relaxing and comfortable relationship. Both my parents treat Joe

with such love, respect, and admiration that there is no doubt in my mind that they are pleased with whom I married.

My family's support is emotional, but over the years, they also demonstrated their love for us by physically helping us when we needed them. When I needed surgery to repair a detached retina, my mother flew from Virginia to help us out even though being away would be an inconvenience for my dad and younger sister. She took care of Tony and David (who were fifteen months old and three months old at the time) during the two weeks I was in the hospital. Following the surgery, I flew to Virginia where my family continued to help us during a very difficult time. My sisters rotated vacations and schedules to look after me, Tony, and David. They were a true blessing in our lives.

My mom (and dad as his job permitted) has been here either before or after we have delivered each of our sons. What wonderful memories we have of Grandma and Papa sharing in the birth of our children! We laugh at the pink outfits and feminine baptismal garments my mom would faithfully bring. Each time she would declare, "There's no way Cathy can have another boy!"—only to take the outfits back to Virginia to await the next try.

My sisters, too, are a source of joy in our lives. I was thrilled and touched when Michele and Paula drove to Baltimore to spend the day with me prior to the National Catholic Education Association's annual meeting. We laughed and talked—girl talk—all afternoon. On my visits to Virginia, Patty will drive up from Richmond so we can share some precious time together. Telephones and e-mail are wonderful, but there's nothing like sitting there in person with your sister. Linda, in spite of her many commitments, coordinated speaking engagements and media coverage for me while I was in Florida promoting our first book. We share unique memories of "interesting" radio interviews and book signings.

Family's love and support can be such a blessing in a marriage when roles are appreciated by everyone. Joe and I hope we will provide similar support and love to our sons' families when they are started. It will be as much our decision to make it a positive experience as it will be for our sons and daughters-in-law.

(Joe): In retrospect, I realize that I was the first of the Prats children and the Garcia children to leave home for college and not return after graduation to settle in either El Paso or its sister city across the border, Ciudad Juarez. Although I had often stated my desire to return home when I went off to Loyola University and then Tulane Medical School, the attraction and opportunities that were afforded me outside of El Paso were too enticing.

In this respect, I think I disappointed my parents. I believe that they wanted me to marry a Hispanic lady, return to El Paso as a respected physician, and become a proud member of El Paso society. When I decided to do my training in pediatrics and neonatology in Houston and then accepted a position at Baylor College of Medicine, my parents realized that I would most likely not return to El Paso, at least not any time soon. When I married someone from Rhode Island, I think that their dreams and expectations about my future in El Paso came crashing down. Even after being in Houston for many years, they would still mention that I would do well in El Paso if I ever wanted to return. It was difficult for them to accept the fact that I had not fulfilled their expectations. Yes, they were proud of what I had accomplished, but the future was not turning out as they had hoped it would.

This disappointment probably inserted a bit of a wedge in the relationship that we as a couple felt with my dad and mom. Cathy experienced the major brunt of this, but she has weathered the ups and downs with great patience and love. More often that not, it was Cathy who sent our second set of photographs of the boys to my dad and mom or reminded me of my mother's or father's birthday. The fact that we were in Houston provided a comfortable cushion.

Difficulties in the Sexual Relationship

In the chapter on sexuality, we discussed many aspects of the sexual relationship. The sexual dimension of the relationship is meant to enrich the entire marital relationship. Couples struggle with this part of their relationship when they view their sexuality and sexual intercourse as entities separate and distinct from the whole of their relationship.

Assumptions and expectations as well as each spouse's attitudes on sexuality affect the role sex plays in the marriage. Open communication is critical if a couple is to understand and appreciate the individual needs and feelings of each other: the husband's need for sexual fulfillment and the wife's need for affection. The media present an unrealistic view of sexuality. If a couple depends on the media to provide them direction in this area of their marriage, they are bound to have difficulties. **A couple needs to realize that their sexual relationship is unique to them.**

Problems arise in the sexual relationship when couples use sex as a means of exerting power or control over the other spouse. Refusing to have sex is a type of control used to punish a spouse. **Whenever respect is not an integral part of the sexual experience, the sexual act is not an expression of love.** It becomes no different than animals copulating.

One issue that causes great pain in a relationship is infidelity. The expression of a couple's love through sexual intercourse is the one area of the relationship that is unique to that couple. Someone else can take care of the emotional, spiritual, and intellectual needs of a person, but the sexual dimension of the relationship is specifically intended to be an expression of love between a husband and wife only. It is a commitment and giving of one's whole self. When that commitment is broken, the pain flows deep. The breakdown is not only on a physical level but permeates the entire relationship.

We have witnessed the pain a couple experiences when a spouse has been unfaithful. We have also seen the healing process that enables the relationship to continue and grow stronger. The process of healing as well as the rebuilding of trust and commitment takes time and a tremendous amount of love and forgiveness.

(Joe): One of the most disheartening aspects that we have observed when a situation of infidelity has surfaced is the impact it

has on the "other" members of the couple's circle of family and friends. Although we understand that the problem may lie with the dynamics of the couple's relationship, the impact reaches far beyond the husband and wife. The maelstrom is deeply felt throughout the immediate family, and, sadly, the ripples of hurt even pierce the couple's friends, acquaintances, and colleagues far beyond what one would expect. So often that aspect is forgotten when such a problem arises. Likewise, when the couple is able to reconcile, the joy is felt far beyond the love rekindled in that home.

Remember, the sexual experience takes on a deeper, more fulfilling meaning when love, respect, and commitment are woven into the sexual act. We encourage you to value the sexual component of your marriage.

Children

A future chapter is dedicated to the issue of children and their impact on the marriage. There are a few issues we want to address at this time.

We are amazed at how many couples do not discuss the role children will have in their marriage. We know a couple who divorced after the husband found out his wife had no intention of having children. He assumed they would have three or four. We can't imagine such an important part of the relationship not being a topic of conversation before they married.

Children are gifts in our marriage. Albeit challenging and demanding gifts at times, these gifts require our constant love and attention. Because of these constant and challenging demands, children may create tension in a marriage. A couple must consider the place their children will have in their home. Moreover, a couple must be willing to provide them with the love and attention they need, not just when feel like it, but every day. Children need to be a priority in your lives as a couple. **At the same time, spouses must understand that their spouse and their marital relationship is the**

number one priority. The marriage provides the foundation for the children. When it is strong, it provides an unspoken sense of security for the children.

One of the reasons children create tension in a marriage is because we can lose sight of each other while focusing on meeting our children's needs. A couple must learn to take time for each other and to continue to foster their love. If the wife is neglecting the needs of her husband because she is giving all of herself to the children, she needs to reevaluate her priorities. Her husband may begin to resent the attention she is providing the children at his expense. Similarly, the wife feels resentful when her husband is primarily focused on work or extracurricular activities. We must always remember our spouse is number one.

Both spouses must recognize the need to be responsible parents. When the responsibility to care for the children falls on one spouse's shoulders, the demands become overwhelming for that spouse as any single parent will tell you. We all come into parenting at different levels of ability, depending upon an individual's previous involvement with children. We assure you none of us has all the answers or all the expertise, even with lots of experience. For those unsure of their parenting ability, begin by providing lots of love and attention to your child as you diaper, bathe, rock, and walk him.

Discipline is another area that causes disagreements when raising children. The style of parenting you adapt will mirror your own parents. You tend to parent the way you were parented.

The parenting style of each spouse is probably different in certain ways, thereby necessitating a couple to blend the two styles. Providing structure and limits for your children is part of responsible parenting, so spouses need to work on their parenting style, which may or may not differ from one or both families of origins.

The different developmental stages of our children may also cause tension between parents. We have found that when couples work together to determine what is beneficial for the child, the difficulties lessen. The child knows what to expect, as do both parents.

Parenting is challenging but it doesn't have to tear parents apart. By working together and practicing responsible parenting, stress in the family and between spouses can be minimized.

Inappropriate or Unhealthy Behavior

Alcohol and drugs deeply affect marriages and families. If one spouse recognizes there is a problem, he or she must not hide from the problem but honestly discuss the situation with the other spouse. When alcoholism or drug abuse is not controlled, it can lead to abuse, suicide, auto accidents, and divorce. Couples must realize that they need professional help and cannot get through the alcoholism or drug abuse alone. There are many assistance programs available. When someone we love is involved in unhealthy or inappropriate behavior, it is our love for them that should drive us to seek the assistance he or she needs. At the same time, the individual that is living this unhealthy behavior must recognize he or she needs help and then be willing to seek it for positive change to occur.

Building blocks or stumbling blocks? Each facet of our relationship offers struggles and opportunities for growth. Conflicts when unresolved fester and, ultimately, destroy a marriage—if not on the outside then on the inside. In her book *Rules of Benedict*, Joan Chittister writes: "Destroy the axis, stop the heart, collapse the core of a world, and the world shrivels or shatters or disintegrates in space. That is what divergence between husband and wife does to the family."

Every relationship must deal with conflicts and misunderstandings. How we deal with them determines the long-term peace and happiness of the marriage. The effort is worth it! As we struggled through our difficulties, we grew to know, love, and appreciate each other more. Our love, respect, and commitment is much stronger today than it was two decades ago. We know conflict will not disappear from our marriage. As we continue to grow and change as individuals, a couple, and a family, we face the struggles that sometimes come with change. They may be different issues that cause problems for us in the future, but we know that we have learned constructive ways to deal with our disagreements. It took time and many heartaches to reach this point. We encourage you to dig in and accept the challenges that are inevitable in a marital relationship.

We know that if we really want to love
we must learn how to forgive.
                                    —Mother Teresa

Learn to forgive yourself for your faults,
for this is the first step in learning to forgive others.
                                    —S. H. Payer

You must forgive those who transgress against you
before you can look to forgiveness from Above.
                                    —The Talmud

Chapter Eight

Forgiveness

*T*hree small words—"I am sorry"—followed by three more words—"I forgive you"—are at the heart of a loving marriage. Forgiveness may be a noun in the dictionary, but it must be an action word in the marital relationship. A good marriage cannot exist without forgiveness.

The process of forgiving is difficult yet, at the same time, essential in the construction of a loving relationship. Both husband and wife need to learn how to ask for forgiveness and how to offer forgiveness with a loving heart, whether the hurt was intentional or unintentional, major or minor in nature. Forgiveness plays an important role in strengthening the marital relationship.

Forgiveness is one of the rules and tools of communication. Forgiveness is the final step in resolving the conflicts discussed in a previous chapter. We can discuss a problem, share our emotions, and say we're willing to move on, but if we don't forgive in both our heart and in our actions, the conflict will likely surface again. When we fail to forgive, resentment, bitterness, and anger result just as they do when we don't confront a conflict. In an article in *Faith and Family*, Philip Mango, Ph.D., states that "the number one threat to marriage is resentment and bitterness that generate anger." Resolving our differences and forgiving each other for the misunderstandings and hurts allows us to move forward in our relationship.

Forgiving isn't always easy, however, especially when the hurt is significant or reoccurring. When one spouse feels as if the problem just keeps resurfacing, the resolve of the other spouse to change may be questioned as well as one's own ability to repeatedly forgive. When that happens, it is important to remember the dialogue between Christ and St. Peter: "Lord, when my brother wrongs me, how often must I forgive him? Seven times?" "No," Jesus replied, "not seven times: I say, seventy times seven times" (Matthew 19:21–22). We're convinced Jesus was thinking of marriage when he answered Peter, because the need to ask for and offer forgiveness in a marriage arises often.

(Cathy): During the early years of our marriage, I found it easier to ask Joe to forgive me for my failings than to be open to forgiving him for his. I would offer my forgiveness but it was often just words, not honest sentiments felt in my heart. For example, Joe would arrive home late—again—from the hospital and tell me that he was sorry. Although I would say his late arrival was okay, I really wasn't okay inside. The "I'm sorry's" seemed to come too frequently without any commitment to change. Because I wasn't truly forgiving him for continually arriving home late and because I hadn't expressed my growing frustrations with him regarding his time commitments, resentment and bitterness brewed. It wasn't until we sat down and shared our feelings and concerns with each other that we were able to move forward. The forgiveness still wasn't complete on my part. As Joe's work commitments continued to take priority over our relationship, I doubted whether his commitment to change was sincere. My inability to trust his efforts held me back from opening my heart to forgiveness. As with the other areas of our relationship, forgiveness took us time to learn and develop.

What we learned was that forgiveness requires a mature heart that loves unconditionally—the strengths, the weaknesses, the successes, the failures, the kindness, and the inconsiderateness of another. As we grew in all areas of our relationship, we grew in our understanding of true forgiveness—the asking for forgiveness from the heart and offering it in return from the heart.

The growth in self-knowledge was the biggest step forward for me in appreciating forgiveness. As I grew to understand myself more deeply and honestly, I was able to face the reality that I kept failing in the same ways over and over again. Therefore, I became more understanding of the "mistakes" of others, especially Joe's. As I accepted the fact that I had more than my share of sins of commission and omission, I was able to accept the repeated missteps of Joe. St. Matthew reminds us: "Remove the plank from your own eye first; then you will see clearly to take the speck from your brother's eye" (Matthew 7:5). Working on my own weaknesses and failures as well as understanding forgiveness in the context of my faith journey and relationship to God enabled me to be more understanding of the weaknesses of others.

I don't want anyone to think this is an easy process or that my understanding and ability to forgive happened overnight. I still deal with emotions that surface when Joe does or doesn't do something that triggers old doubts or memories of past hurts. He may not even be aware of the connection or the depth of the hurt of a past incident. I've learned to either move on with the emotion if I feel I can or should or, if I find it affecting our relationship, share my thoughts and feelings with Joe. We hear the phrase "forgive and forget," yet while we can forgive we can't always totally forget. I can remember those times when I know I was upset but can no longer remember why. There are other times, though, that I do remember the why but know we have moved on in our relationship since then. Forgiveness and healing occurred.

I'm convinced every marriage experiences deep hurts stemming from at least one event in the couple's relationship. Some hurts take longer to heal than others. The spouse asking for forgiveness should not expect a "quick fix" just because he or she has said "I'm sorry." Similar to a deep cut that requires stitches and a longer time to heal than a mere scrape on the knee, some hurts in a marriage take longer to heal than others. That does not mean that the wounded party has the right to continually resurrect the issue. Doing so will not facilitate healing but, instead, create new problems.

Becoming a mother was the second step in fostering an understanding of forgiveness in our marriage. When we talk about our sons enriching our relationship, forgiveness is one area where our ability to forgive them strengthened our ability to forgive each other. I have always found it easy to forgive the boys—at all ages. It was much easier to forgive them than to forgive Joe. I realized that I was able to forgive them so readily and yet struggled with offering Joe that same heartfelt forgiveness. "Why?" I would ask myself. There was no doubt that I loved Joe, so it was not a question of love. I believe that because the boys are children—my children—I could accept their actions or missteps more readily than those of Joe, an adult who should know better. I could voice my concerns, disappointments, and frustrations with the boys and move on. With Joe I had a harder time moving on. I finally realized that it was the moving on that made the difference in the forgiveness process in regards to the boys versus Joe. The boys knew I was upset, but they also knew I loved them even when they made a mistake or a poor choice. Even as the boys grow older and their poor choices and mistakes are of a more serious nature than those at four or six years of age, I believe they know that I love them and forgive them when they trip and fall. I had to develop this same level of forgiveness in my relationship with Joe. **The change had to begin with me demonstrating to Joe through my words and actions that I not only forgave him but loved him unconditionally.**

(Joe): I am not sure whether asking for forgiveness or forgiving is harder. In either case, the difficulty of either action probably depends on one's estimation of self-worth. When I am feeling right about who I am, either action surfaces more readily. Maybe it is because you feel closer to God because you understand the value He places on you. If He feels that way about you, one of His children, how can you not forgive or ask for forgiveness. Cathy has mentioned how important self-love is (again, not selfish love) and this becomes the basis for asking for forgiveness and forgiving. Although we may feel bad about hurting our spouse, we must have

a certain confidence in our self-worth to ask for forgiveness as well as being able to truly resolve to try harder so that this particular action does not recur. Likewise, our willingness to forgive is rooted in our own self-worth. The hurt that we have experienced may chip away at our estimation of how we feel about ourselves, so if we don't have self-love, it may be very difficult for us to forgive and heal our hurt and move on.

When things are going well at work and at home and my self-esteem is where it should be, what might otherwise be considered hurtful just doesn't have the same impact that it does when I am at a low. When Cathy and I are sharing as well as seeing and feeling each other's love, this serves as a sort of armor against the little things that are potentially hurtful. Consequently, we are both more ready to forgive—another reason to keep lines of communication open and flowing both ways.

Around our home when I am feeling like a good parent and spouse, I have noticed how more readily I deal with the boys and their little transgressions. I deal with them in a more heartfelt and fatherly fashion. When my self-esteem is "troubled," my readiness to forgive the boys is challenging.

Just as love is a choice we make, forgiveness is also a choice we make. There are days when choosing to love may be hard. Likewise, there are days when choosing to forgive may be hard. We've found, though, that similar to the times we don't confront a misunderstanding or conflict, the peace and happiness in our day-to-day life is missing when we haven't dealt with forgiveness. We don't feel right about ourselves and our marriage. We don't enjoy our days. In addition, the harbored feelings of anger and bitterness zap our energy and spirit. **Forgiveness allows us to free our spirit and feel the closeness that we both need, appreciate, and desire.**

(Joe): Asking forgiveness should also precipitate the question: "How did I manage to hurt my spouse?" These transgressions against the person I love should provide me an opportunity to

discern their causes. It may give me an insight into a part of our relationship that we need to address. Was today just a bad day for me or Cathy? Are we just a bit more sensitive or more testy than usual? Is this problem happening repeatedly? If this is the case, why? What does this say about me and Cathy? The questions and answers should prompt us both to reexamine why we are having a problem with this, especially if it is recurring.

For Cathy and me, respect for each other's time was a major issue, most especially my commitment to the responsibilities at work. Coming home late or not putting a commitment on the calendar so that Cathy and I could plan around the event caused many a conflict in our marriage. It did not seem like a big deal to me until I better understood what my delay in coming home meant to Cathy and the boys. Likewise, not writing the date and time of a meeting or commitment on our common calendar made for a makeshift schedule for Cathy, creating hectic evenings at a time when we all needed calm and routine, especially when the boys were young. On the other hand, with better communication before the meetings, Cathy could more easily understand, tolerate, and handle my attendance at these meetings. With advanced notice, we both had time to organize the evening for the boys and each other. We both tackled the problem. Though sometimes it is still hard for each of us when the other is away, we both understand that we have each other's respect for what we do for each other and the boys. We emphasize again that it is not a "me" that makes our marriage and family work; it is a "we."

Forgiveness in the Context of Our Faith

There are many references to forgiveness in the Bible. The prayer taught to us by Jesus Himself, the Our Father, admonishes us to forgive as we ask for forgiveness from God: "Forgive us our trespasses as we forgive those who trespass against us." We are asked to not be judgmental: "If you want to avoid judgment, stop passing judgment. Your verdict on others will be the verdict passed on you. The measure with which you measure will be used to measure you" (Matthew 7:1–2).

The ability—the grace—to forgive comes from God. Our faith enables us to each dig deep and accept our spouse, even when we've been hurt or wronged. If we accept the fact, too, that we ourselves are not perfect, then we are better prepared to forgive others. If in our pride we see only our own righteousness, then we are no better than the Pharisee in the parable on self-righteousness (Luke 18:9–14). We are called instead to acknowledge our own weaknesses with humility, as did the tax collector.

(Cathy): When we consider forgiveness, we usually consider it in the context of another person. Yet before we can forgive others we must be able to forgive ourselves. Acknowledging our failures is important, but then we must forgive ourselves despite them and strive to become a better person.

Wallowing in guilt and lacking self-respect are destructive and prohibit me from moving forward in my own life. I am harder on myself and less forgiving of my failures than anyone else; I am also more aware of my failures and shortcomings than anyone else. Fortunately, in our Catholic faith we have the sacrament of Reconciliation. I have the opportunity to confess my transgressions and experience the healing presence of God, His peace, and His grace to make the necessary changes in my life. Likewise I acknowledge that if God can forgive me, then I can forgive myself.

For the process of forgiveness to be mutually healing, both spouses must be involved in the forgiving. When one spouse won't ask for forgiveness or offer forgiveness in return, the marital relationship suffers. In her book *Blessing Your Enemies, Forgiving Your Friends,* Kristen Johnson Ingram reminds us that "God wants us to be whole people who participate in both sides of forgiveness: forgiving and being forgiven."

When asked why spouses refuse to forgive, Philip Mango, Ph.D., suggested that they see holding on to unforgiveness as a benefit. A spouse may use it as a defense mechanism or to foster self-pity or even to maintain an attitude of moral superiority. When a spouse won't enter into the forgiveness process, Dr. Mango provides a principle to follow: "If your spouse won't ask for or receive forgiveness, you still need to forgive them. Forgiving changes you; and, over time, this change can affect your spouse, too."

(Cathy): I am reminded of the story of St. Maria Goretti, who was stabbed to death at the age of eleven during an attempted rape. Before Maria died she prayed that Alessandro, the young man who had attacked her, would repent. Upon his release after twenty-seven years in prison, Alessandro went to St. Maria's mother to ask forgiveness for killing her daughter. Mrs. Goretti willingly forgave him. Alessandro changed his life and was in attendance with the Goretti family when St. Maria was canonized. As Woodene Koenig-Bricker points out in her book 365 Saints, *Maria's mother embraced saintliness in her willingness to forgive Alessandro. Forgiveness blessed both the person who asked forgiveness and the person who forgave. Koenig-Bricker also reminds us: "It doesn't take a saint to ask for forgiveness, but it can make one out of the person who gives it."*

Forgiveness has been an integral part of our relationship. To say "I'm sorry" and feel the other person's forgiveness provides such feelings of peace. One of the strengths of our marriage has been our ability and willingness to forgive and move on. The healing process can begin. Our love, trust, and respect for each other facilitates this process. We've learned, too, that as we understand and accept ourselves more and more, the ability to forgive ourselves and others improves.

(Cathy): I remember attending one of our parish missions during a time when Joe and I had had a disagreement. I can't remember what the disagreement was about so it couldn't have been too significant. The mission topic for the week related to relationships, specifically the marital relationship. When the issue of misunderstandings came up as well as how to deal with the hurt and healing in a relationship, the two visiting priests advised us to follow the

words and example of Jesus. First, forgive your spouse: *"Father, forgive them; they do not know what they are doing" (Luke 23:34).* Second, love your spouse and do good things for him or her: *"Love your enemies, do good to those who hate you" (Luke 6:27).* Third, bless and pray for your spouse: *"Bless those who curse you and pray for those who maltreat you" (Luke 6:28).* The priests told us it wouldn't be easy, but then they reminded us of the parable of the *"narrow door" (Luke 13:22–30).*

I also remember the Sunday morning we went to Mass with a little friction between us. The Psalm being sung that morning was: "If today you hear God's voice, harden not your heart." The words reminded me to not harden my heart but to open it to love. Later in the service a kiss of peace is shared among members of the congregation, reminding us to be at peace with our neighbor. The kiss of peace was truly a kiss of peace that morning, and both Joe and I felt the change. Another point to remember is that if we are not at peace with each other, then we cannot be at peace with God.

The lack of forgiveness generated from the hardening of one or both spouse's hearts keeps many couples from resolving their differences. We dig in and won't bend in our resolve. We let selfish pride and wounded hearts subjugate love and humility. How easy it is to start identifying all the inferior qualities of our spouse while ignoring the good qualities. With our love, respect, and commitment pushed aside, the conflicts escalate because we're looking for and expecting our spouse to fail. Only when we soften our hearts and emphasize the positive attributes of our spouse are we able to rebuild the relationship. A positive and uplifting attitude and approach heals a wounded heart, while negative and pride-filled revenge creates bitterness and hate. If the hearts remain hardened, the relationship begins to unravel.

I have a short prayer that I say if the negative feelings begin to enter into my mind-set: *"May the Lord be in my mind, on my lips, and in my heart." (These words are spoken before the Gospel reading during a Eucharistic celebration.)* If I stay true to these words, I will keep my thoughts, words, and actions positive and *loving toward Joe. I find myself saying these words not just during times that I am dealing with a situation involving forgiveness but almost anytime: first thing in the morning, interacting with the children, during a meeting, while writing, or even handling day-to-day activities. The important point to remember is to find a way to keep your heart from hardening toward your spouse or anyone else. We should imitate our children, who have such loving and forgiving hearts. If only we wouldn't lose those characteristics as we become adults!*

I was pleased when the Marriage Encounter weekend started off with each spouse identifying the positive qualities of the other. Our marriage would benefit from frequent reminders of why we married our spouse. Recognizing the qualities that first attracted us to our spouse helps us keep our spouse's lesser qualities in perspective. Just as we are constantly encouraging our sons, so too should we be each other's biggest cheerleader, building up our spouse instead of tearing him or her apart. In tearing the other apart, you fragment your relationship into pieces. If we are unforgiving with one another in our relationship, then our children grow confused about the process of forgiveness in their own lives. We must set the example for our children on how to forgive and be forgiving.

We are trying to teach our sons through our forgiving of their transgressions and our example of forgiveness with each other how important it is to forgive as well as resolve disagreements. We stress how useless it is to hold a grudge or be spiteful, hateful, and revengeful. We have shared stories of relatives who for years wouldn't talk to each other over a misunderstanding. We remind them that life is too short to waste time in anger and hate, especially with our spouse and family members.

A passage in *The Mystic* by David Torkington relates how over time in a marriage, we begin to see the faults in our spouse and let those faults negatively affect our relationship:

"When my parents entered into their night of the senses and all the wonderful feelings and emotions seemed to fade away, they had to face their own faults and failings as never before. Naturally they didn't like it, and they began to blame each other for what they didn't like in themselves, trying to highlight the splinter in the other's eye so they wouldn't notice the beam that was in their own. In the end, with the help they sought from prayer and the genuine love they had for one another, they were able to see themselves as they were and they confessed, not just to a priest but to each other, and received the mutual forgiveness that bonded them together more deeply than ever."

(Joe): Forgiveness is a blessing for all of us who are not divine. For me, forgiveness means another chance to get it right. It is like the radiant morning sun that brings the new day with all its potential to be so special. Every morning means another chance to get it right even if the day before had not been a particularly good one. If I knew that Cathy would not let me have that opportunity, it would be like the morning sun not rising for me. I admire and am grateful that Catherine has had the patience and love to give me so many chances. Remember, I am the slow learner. That's why I am always relieved and hopeful that I still have a chance when I hear Christ tell His disciples that we should forgive seventy times seven times. However, knowing this does not blunt my resolve to be a better spouse and father but, rather, acknowledges that I am human and must work and pray hard to be at my best. I believe that St. Ignatius Loyola became a saint and brought so many other souls to Christ because he had experienced what it meant to not do the right thing. He saw himself for the imperfect person he was and so was sympathetic to those who had to work just as hard as he did to do Christ's will.

During those times when our relationship has been in a desert (void of the enriching and peace-filled love we usually experience) due to the hurt we have caused each other, we appreciate the words of Mother Teresa: "We know that if we really want to love we must learn how to forgive." We learned that forgiveness and love go hand in hand. "I'm sorry" and "You're forgiven"—simple phrases with tremendous power to heal and enhance our love for one another.

A child is the greatest of God's gifts to a family,
because it is the fruit of the parents' love.
—Mother Teresa

I love little children, and it is not a slight thing
when they, who are fresh from God, love us.
—Charles Dickens

If you bungle raising your children,
I don't think whatever else you do well
matters very much.

—Jacqueline Kennedy Onassis

Chapter Nine

Richer by the Dozen:
The Joys and Challenges of
Children and Parenting

*W*e have been blessed with ten sons during our twenty-six years of marriage. As of this writing, the boys range from six to twenty-four years of age—kindergarten to medical school. Our sons undeniably changed our lives as individuals and a couple. They changed every facet of our marriage, enriching it in ways we could never have imagined possible on the day of our first son's birth. We say "enriched" because with the gift of our children came an even more profound understanding and appreciation of how important and integral to a relationship are the four components of love, respect, commitment, and one's faith. As we integrated these four components into our parenting, we strengthened them in our marriage. And, over time, we, the Garcia-Prats—dad, mom and ten sons—grew "richer by the dozen."

We learned that a child provides a unique opportunity to give of oneself—to truly give of oneself—selflessly and without counting the cost of that giving. This selfless giving (unconditional love) seems to come more naturally than the selfless giving of oneself to one's spouse, because a child is so totally dependent on his parents for all his needs. After all, our spouse is an adult and can take care of himself or herself. In addition, an adult's needs are different from those of a child. If we can learn to give this same selfless love to our spouse, our marital relationship will be enriched. David Torkington describes it as an adolescent love (self-centered love) "learning to grow up . . . learning to give time and time again, especially when they receive nothing in return." That's what we mean when we say that our children enriched our marriage because, as we strove to give selflessly to the boys, we learned to more consciously recognize the need to give selflessly to each other.

Parenting: Challenging, Demanding, Constant, and Rewarding

Our love and respect for children began for both of us long before we started our family, as reflected in Joe's decision to practice neonatology (a pediatrician who specializes in the care of the critically ill newborn) and Cathy's decision to teach first grade. Yet, parenting our own children proffered a different experience from both teaching and practicing medicine. Parenting, for one, was twenty-four hours a day, every day!

We acknowledge that parenting ten children—all boys—is challenging, demanding, constant, and exhausting! It didn't take having ten sons to realize that. We understood the challenges, demands, constancy, and fatigue after one child. We also learned, though, that parenting is extremely rewarding and fulfilling.

How challenging is our parenting? We had five of the boys in six years, and those same five boys were all teenagers at one time. Each of our sons is uniquely gifted as well, so we are challenged to recognize and appreciate their individuality as we help them to reach their full potential. It is challenging!

How demanding is our parenting? We changed diapers for twenty consecutive years! We have paid Catholic school tuition for twenty-one years, and with Timmy in kindergarten, we anticipate at least twelve more years. The demands are physical and emotional as well, often taxing our creativity and our spirituality. It is demanding!

How constant is our parenting? Like all families, we have the bills to pay, clothes to wash, groceries to buy, homework to oversee, practices to attend, school activities to participate in, and medical and dental appointments to make—just in greater number. We make several trips to the grocery store during the week to purchase the five gallons of milk the boys drink per day when they are all home. We may have seven or eight boys' schoolwork to oversee. We attend many practices and games, especially when seven of the boys are playing soccer. With the boys in several schools because of their ages, we are involved in different schools and many activities. It is constant!

How exhausting is our parenting? We assure you we are very tired at the end of our day. We try to watch the ten o'clock news in the evenings but invariably we both doze off. As the boys have gotten older, they wake us up and shoo us off to bed. During the summer Olympics a few years ago, we sat down as usual to try to make it through the evening news but quickly started dozing off. We were awake just enough to hear Matthew tell Joe Pat, "Look, Joe Pat, synchronized sleeping!" We are exhausted!

Importantly, we are also parents who love what we are doing in spite of the challenges, demands, constancy, and fatigue. **We have learned that it is the choices we make to love our sons, to respect our sons, to commit our time, energy, and resources to our sons, and to integrate our faith into all we do that enables us to make parenting rewarding.** We did not have our first child and innately become good parents. We got off to a good start with our love of children, but we developed our parenting skills as we observed other parents, reflected on our own parents' techniques, read books, asked questions, attended seminars, and did our share of praying.

We did know what we wanted for our children, though. We wanted them to grow up to be loving, caring, compassionate, forgiving, responsible, respectful, well-educated, and faith-filled individuals. We wanted them to understand that their self-worth and success would be measured in nonmonetary terms: by who they are, what they do with the gifts God has given them, and how they live their lives. Our goals for our children are the goals we set for ourselves. By establishing goals, like those in our marriage, we knew what we wanted for our children and then could determine the means to fulfill those goals. If you don't know what you want, you won't know how to get there. We realized that, in order for our children to develop these characteristics and to attain these goals, we had to strive to live them. Leo Buscaglia tells us: "Be what you want your children to be and watch them grow."

We, the parents, must set the example for our children in the choices we make and how we live our lives. It is an awesome responsibility, but when that responsibility is accepted and fulfilled, enjoying our children and our parenting years can become a reality.

We have learned many lessons over the years. We share these lessons with the belief that you can integrate and adapt them to your family, regardless of size, culture, or composition, thereby enriching your marital relationship in the process.

New Roles and Responsibilities

With the pregnancy and birth of Tony, our oldest son, we entered a new phase in our relationship. The roles and responsibilities we had become comfortable with took another shift. The change began with the pregnancy and continued after Tony's delivery as well as with the addition of each new child.

(Cathy): The first months of my pregnancy were extremely difficult because of the nausea and fatigue. The nausea persisted all day, with the mornings especially bothersome. We tried recommended remedies, but to no avail. As I eventually learned, nausea was to be part and parcel of all my pregnancies, varying only in degree with each one. Not only was it hard for me to eat food, but many nights I could not even look at food much less prepare a meal. It was probably to Joe's advantage at that point to be on call so often; he could at least get a reasonably tasty dinner at the hospital. In addition to the nausea, I was extremely tired the first months of the pregnancy. For a person blessed with excessive amounts of energy all her life, it was hard for me to feel so tired

most of the day. Most days I came home from teaching and fell asleep until Joe called to be picked up. After dinner, when there was one, I prepared my next day's lessons and fell back to sleep. It was an adjustment for both of us. Joe took on more responsibilities because I was either nauseated or tired. He also had to accept the change in our relationship, emotionally and physically; I'm sure I wasn't the most exciting person to be around. Once I moved into the second trimester of the pregnancy, the days grew easier and I was able to resume many of the simple day-to-day responsibilities that Joe had assumed.

The shifting back and forth of responsibilities is still how we manage our days. We do not have defined roles; rather, we fulfill our responsibilities according to whoever has the time, the ability. or the interest. So during the early months of a pregnancy, Joe fixes breakfast and dinner more often than at other times in our marriage. It meant with the first pregnancies he had to learn to prepare dinner since cooking was not his forte. Now after ten pregnancies, Joe is an excellent cook and capably prepares dinner whenever he needs to.

Joe's willingness to help me at home and not regard home responsibilities as solely my responsibility strengthened our relationship. **His help was also a sign that he understood that, although I was the one pregnant, we were both having this child.**

(Joe): Accepting and jumping into a different set of duties that I was unfamiliar with was at first uncomfortable for me. Unfamiliar duties? Yes, I had seen Cathy perform them and I had even done some of the duties myself when I was single, but now I had to perform them for someone really important—Cathy and the boys. When cooking just for myself, it wasn't a big deal if the food wasn't great since the audience (me) was easy to please. Now, however, I had to prepare food well enough so that other people would eat it.

The other challenge was having to follow Cathy, who had "set the bar high" for so many things she did so well for us at home. Expectations were high for mundane activities such as cleaning the *den and bedrooms as well as making sure the boys' diapers were put on tightly enough so the diapers wouldn't leak or fall off. We used cloth diapers for the first eight children, so learning to pin the diapers was fraught with risk for both the boys and Dad. As far as mastering the various activities that I needed to perform (cooking, bathing the boys, changing diapers), I tried to approach them with the same hard work and diligence as I had any other challenge. The real challenge, however, was to perform them with the same love and devotion as Cathy had.*

The mutual sharing of responsibilities eases the transition from being a couple to being parents. The day-to-day life of a couple changes dramatically once a child is born. There are new physical and emotional demands to fulfill for the baby as well as for the wife and husband. We confront new expectations and assumptions of who does what, when, and how once the baby is born. These expectations and assumptions initially derive from our families of origin. We need to consider what roles and responsibilities our parents assumed regarding child rearing. **The traditional roles we grew up with in our families of origin may not be conducive to the marriage and family you want. Women, whether they work outside the home or stay at home, expect and need their husbands to be an integral part in the raising of their children and accepting the responsibilities necessitated by having a family.**

(Cathy): My needs changed when I became a mother. Not only did I need Joe to physically help me with Tony and the other boys when they arrived, but I needed him emotionally in a different way than I had before the children. Whether a woman chooses to stay at home with the baby or decides to return to work, she faces new challenges, demands, and adjustments. I was no different. In addition, all women have to adjust to the changes in their bodies following a pregnancy and delivery. Since the pregnancy and child-bearing experience is so different for the husband, he may not

understand the emotional and physical changes of his wife. Each partner's assumptions and expectations concerning their new roles as mother and father most likely will differ.

(Joe): Many things changed after Tony was born. Not only were we happy and proud parents of a new child, but we also reveled in the potential for growth as parents and as individuals. But different needs arose that we were both unprepared for. For instance, the newborn with his own schedule unamenable to reason produces fatigue for mom and dad. Mom's "to-do list" and mom's energy for the next day go right out the window. Since baby can't read the night-call schedule, you go back to the hospital as tired as when you left. In addition to the changing physical demands were the emotional ones. It took me awhile to understand Cathy's emotional needs after Tony was born, most especially her need for sharing when I got home. In the past when we were both busy with our professions, we each had two avenues for sharing—at home and at work. When Cathy stayed home with Tony, she shifted her total dependence on sharing toward me. Unfortunately, I didn't figure out this need at first. A tearful spouse finally made me understand how Cathy's needs had changed and how I should be prepared to meet those needs. After all, she had certainly done the same for me innumerable times early in our marriage.

After the birth of a child, we encourage a couple to take the time to express their wants and needs as well as their expectations of themselves and each other as mother and father as well as wife and husband. We cannot assume our spouse knows exactly what our expectations and needs are. Since our family backgrounds and experiences vary, the involvement of each spouse's father in the responsibilities regarding the children will differ. A husband asking his wife, "How can I help? What do you need?" provides an opportunity for the wife to honestly share with her husband her feelings and her needs.

(Joe): After we started our family, the most important choice I made was to fulfill a promise that I had pledged to myself while still in high school. In El Paso, my fellow high school classmates were wonderful companions who worked very hard to succeed (at least most of them). What especially moved me were friends whose fathers were uninvolved in their lives. These young men seemed to lack something. It was something intangible, a shadow of doubt that permeated all that they did and thought of themselves. I sadly noted the absence of their fathers in their activities at school and at home. I told myself then that this would not be the case in my family. However, as I have said before, that is exactly what happened in the early part of my career. My boys had only a part-time father and Cathy a part-time husband. When I made the decision to change, one area involved my responsibilities at home after work. There was always much to do at home for Cathy and the boys. These valuable tasks included fixing dinner, giving the boys a bath, and getting the baby to bed. As the boys got older it meant attending their activities. It became very obvious that although I might take work home from the office, it would more often than not remain in the briefcase until the next morning. For the most part, work in the evening meant taking care of my family. A most worthy and wonderful endeavor which has reaped many dividends for the boys, Cathy, and me.

(Cathy): I was amazed at how dramatically my life changed after Tony was born. My entire day-to-day routine differed from what it had been the day before his birth. I was unprepared for the amount of time and energy a baby demanded and the adjustments I needed to make in my life.

The changes for Joe were significant, too. While his at-work hours remained similar to those before Tony's birth, his morning and evening routine entailed less "me" time and considerably more "we" time. A quiet, relaxing evening was rarely a given. Quiet time depended on what responsibilities needed to be fulfilled at home.

The first months after a child's birth, whether the first or the

tenth, are a time of adjustment for a couple and family. Since the demands and challenges were different for each of us, we needed to understand these new roles and responsibilities and how they affected us as individuals and a couple. How I appreciated that Joe would come home after a long day and help me with Tony—bathing, diapering, and feeding (once I wasn't breast-feeding). Beyond the physical assistance, though, I needed him to talk to after having been home without adult conversation most of the day—and sometimes two days when he had been on call. Most of my friends were the teachers I worked with; they were still teaching and unavailable during the day. Neither of our families lived in Houston, so they were not readily available for conversation and the emotional support you need as a new mom.

There were three major lessons I learned the first year of motherhood that have facilitated my transition after the birth of each of our other children: One, to be realistic of my time and expectations; two, to take care of my own needs; and three, to develop a support system.

Initially, I was very unrealistic about what I could reasonably accomplish in one day with a child around. Being an organized person, I would make my lists only to have nothing crossed off the list by the end of some days. Parenting was more time consuming than I had ever imagined. I made the mistake of trying to complete tasks when the baby was asleep so I could feel I had at least something to show for my day. I figured I could get something done and then rest. Inevitably, though, the baby woke up as soon as I finished what I "needed" to do. What I needed to do was rest right along with the baby. **I learned, and I emphasize learned, that it was more important for me to rest and get my energy back as well as refresh my mental outlook than to run around cleaning house and doing other asundry tasks.** It meant the house might not be as orderly as before the baby, but so what. A rested, pleasant mother and wife was more important than a clean kitchen or bathroom at that point in time. Taking the time to rest when the children rested made a huge difference for me over the years. In a *busy household with children, that rest time might be the only "me" time that I would scrounge up all day. Being "me" is important to being a mother and a wife.*

I learned to accept the fact that there were certain chores and activities I could do with the children around and others that were unrealistic. I could wash, dry, and fold clothes without a problem, but enter water into the equation and I knew a mess was in my future. The kitchen floor was mopped either before the boys woke up in the morning or after they were in bed. If I needed uninter-rupted time to complete something, then I planned accordingly. Otherwise, I became frustrated and testy with the boys for their constant questions and interruptions.

Just as I had to be realistic about what I could do, likewise, I had to be realistic about what I could expect from the boys. *To expect them to sit and be quiet for hours is unrealistic, but to expect a short quiet time was not. Children need to learn to respect our time and space as they grow older. A baby has no concept of respecting a parent's time, so consider that a totally unrealistic expectation.*

*As we had more children, I knew what was realistic to expect of myself and the boys. The boys gradually played with each other, and that allowed me time to accomplish a few extra things. **Ultimately, what I grew to understand was that taking care of the children was what I needed to be doing with my time and energy.** As a responsible parent, that was what I was being called to do. I felt satisfied that I was doing just that. By the time we had our seventh, eighth, ninth, and tenth sons, I completely understood the importance of maintaining realistic expectations of myself.*

I must emphasize, too, that it is important for the husband to be realistic of what his wife can accomplish with children around. What she might have been able to do before children is not realistic to expect now. *I highly recommend against walking in the door at the end of the day, looking around at the disorder, and asking your wife in a sarcastic tone of voice, "What did you do all day?" I assure you, from experience, your children are what she did all day!*

The second area of understanding that strengthened me as a mother is remembering that, although I am a wife and a mother, I am also "Cathy." That doesn't mean that I ignore the needs of Joe and the boys at my expense but, rather, that by recognizing my needs (the physical, emotional, intellectual, and spiritual dimensions of my life) and fulfilling them I am a better wife and mother. Neglecting my needs has the reverse effect.

I strive to meet my physical needs by eating and sleeping properly, although the latter is harder and harder to accomplish as a mother. Yet I know that when I am overly tired, my days are longer and harder. That's why it is essential for me to rest when the children do or catch a few extra hours at night instead of reading or catching up on another activity. Physically, I also need to have my annual checkups: mammograms, pap smears, blood pressure, and cholesterol counts as well as exercise. The time I spend walking or using the treadmill allows me time to think, pray, and release the stresses of the day (or anticipated stresses of the day) as well as keep my body functioning properly. The "power walk" invigorates your spirits, enabling you to handle the constant demands and commitments of parenting. Joe and the boys have grown to appreciate the difference a short walk can make for me.

Emotionally, I need to feel good about being me—all of the "me's" who make up who I am. Whereas meeting my physical needs came relatively easy, this side of my development took longer to interweave with being a mom and wife. **Joe and the boys added to my emotional strengths, but I eventually realized I needed friendships and activities that fostered my interests outside of being a mom and wife.** Teaching a Sunday preschool religion class gave me this first opportunity. The class was on Sunday mornings, a time when Joe was usually home. If he had to work, the boys were free to stay in the church nursery during the class. I realized that I enjoyed not only the teaching but also the positive effect it had on me. This one-hour commitment grew to encompass many other activities over the years. With Joe's and the boys' support, I am able to participate in church, school, and community activities. They all understand the benefit my involvements have for the family and appreciate that little time is taken away from my commitment to meet their needs.

Getting together with friends was another positive in my life. A couple of friends and I attended the ballet. The five or six performances were on Friday nights. Joe tried to work his schedule out so that he would be home. Ballet nights for me became "boys' nights" at home. The boys (including Joe) had fun while I was able to enjoy being with friends.

I didn't have to enroll in college classes to meet my intellectual needs. Reading, a big love of mine, was one way to meet this need. Since I am not a television watcher, whenever I have free time I spend it with a good book. When I don't have time to read a book, I read articles from Time, educational journals, religious magazines, or newspapers. I rarely go anywhere without some reading materials. Waiting for a soccer practice to end provides me a chance to catch up on my reading. I attend seminars or day retreats once in a while. With the boys a little older, I can attend events more frequently than when they were younger. But even when they were younger, I took advantage of lectures or programs, especially if baby-sitting was offered. With the advent of tapes, one can find various topics of interest to listen to during the day as you're folding clothes or preparing dinner.

Spiritual development can be incorporated into anything you do, so in a way this was the easiest of my needs to fulfill. How I enjoyed the quiet nights breastfeeding the boys and softly "singing" the rosary. (Breastfeeding at night when there were no distractions was so very peaceful!) Times of silence are needed for prayer, too, but was not an item in great supply in our home. Quiet time, as you can imagine, was harder and harder to come by as we had more children. I found my silence, though, and so much more.

Almost twenty years ago our parish church opened a perpetual adoration chapel, a chapel open twenty-four hours a day for people to pray in front of the Eucharist. Our pastor invited each parishioner to spend an hour with the Lord—a quiet, peaceful hour. I must admit, I heard "quiet and peaceful" more than any other words spoken that morning. We had just had our fourth son, Joe Pat, and he was feisty. The thought of one hour of peace and quiet was definitely enticing. I signed up for my weekly hour. I was drawn back each week, though, not for the silence of that hour but for the spiritual enrichment I gained week after week. I was strengthened over and over again to handle life's daily demands.

Although in a different parish now, Joe and I still visit the parish adoration chapel for one or more hours a week. **I learned that meeting my spiritual needs enabled me to meet the needs of Joe and our growing family and to appreciate being a wife, mother, and "me."**

The third area that made my parenting experience easier and more fulfilling was the development of a support system—friends. Many new moms have family in town or nearby. Unfortunately, we didn't. (My family continued to be supportive, but you need local support on hand.) Since I hadn't been in Houston for very long, my friendships were primarily the teachers I worked with, and they were still working when I had Tony. Many days I felt lonely and isolated. I was grateful for those times I could get together with Carol and Libby. We often arranged activities together and helped each other out when one had a doctor's appointment or other commitment.

Having other moms to laugh with, to share parenting experiences with, and to participate with in activities (with and without children) makes such a difference in one's day. I found that I wasn't depending on Joe to fulfill as many of my needs. In the mid 1970s, there were not many organized mother support groups around. We made our own. You found other moms and children at parks, in the library, even at the grocery store. I finally found a Mothers Day Out program a couple years after Tony was born which fulfilled dual needs for me: a few hours a week with fewer demands (I usually had an infant at home so I was never childless) and other mothers to interact with.

My friends still impact my life in a positive way. Joe may be my number one support system and our sons a close second, but having friends adds another level of support that I can't do without. With each new activity the boys participate in and as each child enters school, our circle of friends grows larger—another blessing of having ten children. They share in our good times and in our difficult times. We laugh together and cry together. In many ways our friends become the family we don't have here in town.

Jamie's First Communion celebration meant so much more by sharing the celebration with the Weavers and other close friends. Graduation dinners with teachers, coaches, friends, and family are a highlight for us on such a momentous occasion. Our last-minute summer barbeques with our neighbors, the Smiths, are a welcome treat. Our twenty-fifth anniversary Mass was so special not only because of the occasion itself but also because of the family and friends who shared in our joy.

Our friends are there in our difficult times, too. When we miscarried our eleventh child, our friends were there to shower us with loving care. The touching cards, the gentle words, the heartfelt phone calls surrounded us with much love and support. A few days later we were again touched by our friends when Timmy, three years old at the time, suffered a ruptured appendix. Due to the infection, he had to remain in the hospital for over a week. When our friends heard of the situation, they made sure the boys at home were taken care of with dinners, rides to soccer practices, and clean clothes. I remember the night I came home late from the hospital and opened the refrigerator. The refrigerator was packed with milk, juices, and all kinds of goodies. When I asked the boys where it came from, they told me Dr. Masera brought it. I felt my eyes water up. Then I opened the pantry door and the pantry was filled with food from top to bottom. I asked the boys where this food had come from. Again, they told me Dr. Masera. I sat down and cried. They went on to tell me how Mike had stopped by and unloaded bag after bag of groceries so Joe and I wouldn't have to worry about whether the boys had what they needed to eat. The boys were thrilled, too, because not only did Mike bring over what they needed, he provided them with what he thought they'd want to eat.

Whenever I think of the Masera's love and support of us as a family, I choke up and thank God for the gift of friends.

As a new mom and as a not-so-new mom, I need the support of family and friends. That need for support that strengthened me when the boys were little is still a need, just in a different way now because my needs are different. **Whether we're parenting a toddler or a teenager, we need to develop a support system that provides an additional source of guidance and strength in our lives.**

Understanding the roles and responsibilities we must undertake as a parent as well as being realistic in those role makes the parenting years run more smoothly. Parenting will remain challenging, demanding, constant, and exhausting, but, hopefully, many satisfying rewards will be part of the package.

Parents Set the Tone of the Home

The character of a home is determined by the character of the parents. Whether we live in a loving, peaceful home with disciplined children who are a joy to have around or we exist in a chaotic house with undisciplined children depends on the choices we, as parents, make about our own lives and the lives of our children.

We knew we wanted a home filled with Garcia-Prats, not a house occupied by Garcia-"Brats." We wanted to enjoy our children, not regret we had them. In order to achieve those goals, we had to choose to love and respect our children, to commit to them by prioritizing our time, energy, and resources, and to exemplify the integration of faith into all we do. We wanted them to know that they are gifts in our lives, not the burdens society tries to convince us they are.

(Cathy): Our attitude and approach to parenting communicates to our children whether they are gifts or burdens to us. We may say we love them, but if that is not the message being conveyed through

our actions, then the words mean nothing. **Children who feel loved are different from children who do not feel loved. I want my sons to feel my love from the minute they wake up in the morning until they fall asleep at night. The choice is mine.**

When I taught first grade, many of the children came to school full of life, eager to face the challenges of the day, while other children arrived with less zest and eagerness. As I observed the children and their families, I noticed a difference in the attitude and approach of the parents. The parents who displayed a true enjoyment of their children and appreciated the opportunities to be involved in their lives had children who were happy and excited about their days. On the other hand, the children who were less enthusiastic had parents who complained about every little thing they had to do for their children. Their parental responsibilities were obligations to fulfill, not acts of love to unconditionally provide. I noticed how similar responsibilities and challenges evoked different responses from different parents.

If I want my sons to feel loved and special, then I need to accept my parental responsibilities (the cooking, cleaning, laundry, homework, expenses, and so on) as part and parcel of family life and demonstrate that life with children is worthwhile. If children constantly hear us complaining about how much time, money, and energy they require, they assume that they are an inconvenience and burden in our lives—not gifts. Children "know" when something is done out of love.

(Joe): One morning I hustled to get Mark, Tommy, and Danny ready for school so that they could leave on time with their older brothers who drop them off at the grade school on their way to high school. As soon as the "first shift" was off to school, I hurriedly went about cleaning up so that I would be ready to go to work. As I was getting ready, Jamie and Timmy came into the bathroom to watch me shave. They were both still in preschool and did not need to go to school as early as their older brothers. Having some time on their hands before school, they elected to watch Dad shave. As I was

lathering my face with shaving cream, the two asked, "Can we shave too?" Cathy's mom and dad had given their brothers "Mutant Ninja Turtles" shaving kits with shaving cream and plastic shavers. After locating them for Jamie and Timmy, we all got our faces lathered up and "shaved" together that morning. I initially felt pressured that I would be late for work if I spent this extra time with the boys, yet I realized how special this time was for Jamie, Timmy, and even me. Cathy has a photograph of the three of us proudly brandishing our shavers, our faces lathered. What a classic! The boys knew that they were special because Dad spent some fun time with them.

The words come freely whereas the daily choices that give meaning to the words requires self-discipline and selfless love. Good families, like good marriages, don't just happen. People want to believe raising good children is all about luck, thereby releasing themselves from responsibility for their children's behavior. It doesn't work like that. If we want our children to grow up to be loving, responsible, respectful, well-educated, and faith-filled individuals whom we can enjoy being with, then we must make the choices and provide the means for them to develop accordingly.

Loving someone also entails making decisions that are in that person's best interest. One of those decisions is to provide a loving, secure home environment that enables them to develop to his or her full potential. There is the saying "The greatest gift a man can give his children is to love their mother." Conversely, the greatest gift a woman can give her children is to love their father. Our marriage is the foundation of our family, providing our sons with an unspoken sense of security.

*(Joe): After a long day at the office and the hospital, there is nothing more peaceful for me than going home. In fact, there is no more secure feeling for me than to be in our home. That may sound silly to some who wonder how, with ten boys at home, it can be peaceful and conducive of security. **Our home, hardly quiet and***

restful, is nonetheless a place of peace for me because it is where I am loved and appreciated for the person I am. It can be a place of refuge, especially after a particularly troubling day, as well as a great place to share triumphs. So it is with our children. We must make our home a place where one feels unconditionally loved and accepted for who they are. Can you imagine having suffered through a particularly tough day and then having to go home to an environment of more turmoil and unhappiness? Give me my dinner and let me go to my room.

We have all experienced very bad days. Fortunately, I cannot think of a better place for me after one of those days than to be with Cathy and my boys. Coming home after a stressful day is like coming home after being away for two weeks. Wow, is it good to be home!

(Cathy): When you love your children, you want what is best for them. Unfortunately, wanting what is "best" doesn't always translate into what is easy or convenient. Parents often don't make good decisions for their children because of the effort or sacrifice it entails for themselves. I am amazed, for example, at how many children are driving around the city of Houston not wearing seatbelts. A minor fender bender, and a child's life and the family's may be changed for years to come. When we had five of the boys under the age of six, we carefully planned any trip in the car— whether across town or across the country—because traveling anywhere was a major commitment just in getting them all seat-belted in the car. We can't imagine, though, any parent not loving their child enough to take the time to protect them from potential harm. Although it's an inconvenience and takes time, and the children may complain and resist, we do it because we love them. Likewise, we require the boys to wear helmets when riding bicycles or roller blading. (For children to understand that the need to wear seatbelts and helmets doesn't stop when you reach a certain age, parents must also wear them.) Parents need to set and maintain the *standards for all areas of their children's lives. Again, not because it's easy but because you love them and know the choice is best for them. In the long term, the best choice pays better dividends than the easy one.*

Along the same line, parents need to ensure that their children eat properly and sleep sufficiently. I'm convinced parents would avoid a lot of discipline problems or at least a lot of whining by assuring their children receive adequate sleep. From our experience the two go hand in hand, especially for younger children. What a difference in our sons' behavior at four o'clock in the afternoon when they had naps or quiet time versus when they didn't. I know that when I'm tired everything is a little harder for me to handle. Our children are no different. We need to be cognizant that many children are faced with very hectic days at very young ages. Assuring our children get adequate sleep affects their behavior, attitudes, and even their ability to learn. Although our children may resist going to bed, we choose to set a regular bedtime and maintain it for their benefit. Ultimately, it's a win-win situation. Our children are rested and better able to cope with the stresses of the day, especially at the end of the day when we're all tired, while we are more agreeable and less stressed because our children are more pleasant to have around.

Like love, respect is so important in a family. The way Mom and Dad talk and treat each other sets the stage for the way our children talk and treat us and each other. **Our children mirror what they see and hear. The atmosphere of a home is very much determined by the verbal interactions between family members. What we say to each other and how we say it makes a difference—and it begins with us, the parents.** We've learned that asking our children to complete a chore rather than demanding they do it gleans a different response. They deserve to hear "please" and "thank you" from us as well as words of appreciation and kindness. They also need to hear words of encouragement and praise instead of demeaning and negative comments.

Our home should be an oasis where all members of the family are refreshed and strengthened from the stresses of the day. If we calmly deal with crisis, conflicts, and misunderstandings instead of yelling and screaming, then our children will more likely reflect our approach. We set the tone of the home. **All the communication skills we develop as a couple are handed down to our children just as we inherited the communication skills of our families of origin. When we practice healthy, effective skills, our homes will reflect that in the prevailing atmosphere.** The parents make that decision, not the children—unless we let them.

Respecting the individuality of each family member also fosters harmony rather than dissension. Each of us wants to be loved and respected for who we are and the talents we possess. If we have learned anything over the years, we understand the importance of respecting and appreciating individuality, as a couple and as parents. Although we may share similar goals and values, our interests and talents as well as our approach to situations differ.

Each of our sons is gifted uniquely: intellectually, athletically, creatively, and socially. Although they may be gifted in more than one area, not one of the boys enjoys the whole package. Our challenge and responsibility as parents is to recognize and appreciate our children's individual talents. To expect all our sons to receive all A's or be the 4.0 student is unrealistic, just as it is unrealistic to expect all of them to be athletically gifted. **If we respect and appreciate their individual God-given talents, our sons will more likely accept who they are and what they can accomplish.** We minimize sibling rivalry in our family, a big source of dissension in many homes, because our sons know we love them for who they are. They are not competing with their brothers for our love and attention. They know they are loved for themselves.

We also have to realize that while our children may share some of our interests and talents, they are unique individuals. Parents often expect their children to be carbon copies of themselves. We project our interests and dreams on them, not recognizing they have their own paths to follow. The movie *October Sky* beautifully depicts this scenario. We highly recommend it for parents and children. We need to support our children's dreams and aspirations, even when they are not exactly what we had planned for them. We've seen the effect on young people when they feel obligated to go to a certain college and study a specific major not because that is what they want but, rather, what Daddy and Mommy want. It is hard at times to let go of our dreams for our children, but we need to let them follow their dreams, as long as they are not immoral, illegal, or inappropriate. We shouldn't expect all the boys to be doctors and teachers because that is what we are.

When Tony, our oldest son, decided to pursue a medical career, people were quick to assume that David would follow suit. David enjoys the written word and creative writing; he tolerated math and science. He had no desire to study the sciences in college or become a doctor. David's choices were best for him, just as Tony's were in his best interest.

(Cathy): Joe and I can see a little of ourselves in each of the boys. At the same time we are fascinated at our differences: same parents and ten unique individuals. I became acutely aware of how different a child can be from his parents one afternoon with Danny. Like David, Danny is creatively gifted although in a different vein. Danny loves to draw and create. He can spend hours building with the mass of Legos we have accumulated over the years. As a room freed up with older sons heading off to college, Danny would dump the bins of Legos on the floor of this room and build to his heart's content. Having the Legos all over the floor was a mess, though. We couldn't get in the room for anything else with the Legos strewn all over. I suggested to Danny that we "organize" the Legos by putting them in Ziplocs maybe by color or design. (Remember, I am the "Organizer.") Danny looked at me and cried as he told me that then it wouldn't be fun anymore. "The fun is in looking for the exact piece I want," he sobbed. I assure you looking for pieces would not be fun for me. I like things in their place. I realized what different thought processes Danny and I preferred. The solution to the

problem took some creativity on both our parts. We (the "we" here actually meaning Joe and Danny) built a box the width and length of the bed for the Legos to fit into that would slide in and out as Danny wanted to build. Danny was pleased with the solution, and we can all walk in and out of the room again. Respecting Danny's individual needs allowed us to solve the problem instead of create new ones. Likewise, we didn't have to squelch his creativity in the process.

Our children need our love and respect, but they also need to know they are a priority in our lives. Our children want and need our time and attention. In society we hear so much about spending "quality time" with our children. **We believe "quality time" is any time you're with your child.** It is the quality of the interaction between parent and child not just the time factor that determines the value of the experience. We choose to make the time with our children quality time, whether we're working on a homework assignment, giving baths, driving in the car, preparing dinner, or walking around the block. Think of the hours, weeks, probably years we would've wasted if we had not chosen to make diaper time quality time. We know that changing a diaper became so much more than a mundane chore by laughing, talking, smiling, and playing with the baby.

(Joe): Quality is defined as "the degree of excellence which a thing possesses." Quality is also that modifier of the time that society says we must give to our children—quality time. The more we think about this, however, the more we realize that parents are the actual modifier of the time we give to our children. I would suggest that quality time is the time a child spends with a parent; we the parents are the modifiers. One of my first challenges as a "modifier" of the time spent with my children came when I had to make the choice of turning off the television set and reading to my sons. Bedtime for them was eight o'clock—a definite conflict with Monday Night Football. If I was going to read to them, then it meant

not getting involved in the football game. It was hard at first to make that choice. However, as I realized what it meant to them and experienced the joy it brought to us all, the easier it got for me. To be sitting on the couch reading with Tony cuddled up on one side and David on the other and enjoying the book was a reward that a parent can only receive from his or her children.

(Cathy): Your children feel special when you are an active part of their lives whether they are three months old, three years old, thirteen years old, or twenty-three years old. We know that our sons appreciate our attendance at soccer games, school programs, and honor society inductions. Playing Sequence with Timmy in the afternoons when all his brothers are at school or grocery shopping with him are meaningful, "quality" events if I choose to make them so.

I remember Chris's first college soccer game at Trinity. The game was scheduled on a September Tuesday evening in San Antonio. I could tell he hoped one or more of us would attend, even though he was a freshman and uncertain whether he would see any playing time. I debated whether or not to go. San Antonio is three hours away and it was during the week. Finally my heart won out over my head, and I decided to take Timmy to see the game. An hour or so outside of Houston, I began questioning the sanity of what I was doing: driving three hours to San Antonio, watching a two-hour soccer game, and then driving three hours back to Houston. Was I really crazy? We arrived at the game as the Trinity soccer team was warming up. When Chris saw us, he ran over to give us big hugs and kisses. I will always remember the smile on his face that afternoon. That smile made the three-hour drive there, the two hours at the game, and the three-hour drive back worth every minute. There was no doubt in my mind he appreciated Timmy and me being there. As a bonus Chris did play that game, but even if he hadn't, the smile was reward enough.

Our children do need and want our time and attention. If we're too busy chasing the American dream, wanting the more, the bigger, and the better, our children quickly realize where our

priorities are. *"Remember, where your treasure is, there your heart is also" (Matthew 6:21). Too often parents shower their children with "things" as a substitute for their love, time, and attention. I know that as a wife I want and prefer Joe's love, time, and attention to the material gifts he can buy me. Our children are no different. Make them a priority in your lives, a part of your short-term and long-term goals.*

Our home life must reflect the values we hold. Do we spend time together as a family? What is the quality of our interactions? Are we eating dinner together or do we all eat whatever, whenever, and with whomever? Do we spend time together as a family or is everyone in their own rooms doing their own thing? Is the television our main source of interaction? What are we watching on television? Answers to these questions provide an insight into the quality of our family life.

*(Cathy): One spring break a friend of the boys who was home from college stopped in for a visit. I was the only one home at the time, so he sat on one of the kitchen stools and we talked as I prepared dinner. The conversation led to the topic of family. The young man shared that there were three things he wanted to emulate when he had his own family that he had observed in ours. First, he wanted a big kitchen table like the one we have. Our table is often compared to the one on the TV series the Waltons. I wanted to know if he intended to fill the table as we had. He wasn't sure about that yet. Second, he said he wanted his family to eat together as a family. He shared how at his home each of the family members grabbed their dinners and then retired to their own rooms to watch television or pop something into their VCR. He was disappointed that his family didn't eat together. Dinnertime is such an important time in the Garcia-Prats' day. **Dinnertime is not just a time to feed our bodies—it is also a time to feed our minds and our souls. Too many families ignore the fact that we need this time together to reconnect and be family.** If we are letting other commitments keep us from eating together, we need to*

reexamine our priorities and refocus on who we are as family. Third, this young man wanted only one television in his home, as we have. He saw how having televisions, VCRs, and computers in every child's room was pulling the family apart. We observe how more and more parents are building mini-apartments for their children instead of building a home. Then society wonders why we aren't family anymore?

Make your family a priority in your life of your love, time, and attention. We can't enjoy being family if we don't spend time being family. A integral part of our time being family is sharing our faith. Sharing our faith may be the times we read from the Bible or discuss teachings of the church or prepare for the sacraments. Our primary way of sharing our faith, though, is by our example. **If we want our children to understand the integration of faith in our lives, we have to integrate our faith into the choices we make, the values we embrace, and the lifestyle we live. Faith is part and parcel of who we are, not something we practice for an hour on Sunday (or not at all).**

The integration of faith into our family life enables us to overcome the hurdles we invariably face as well as appreciate the blessings that are richly bestowed on us. Our faith keeps us focused and anchored. We can't imagine getting through the day without God by our sides. **Knowing we are not alone provides us with a sense of peace and security. We know God gifted us with our children yet did not leave us alone to raise them. We just have to seek His guidance and rely on His wisdom to help us in our efforts.** We remember the comment made about our last book by an individual who felt we relied too much on prayer and trust in God. She needed case studies to show her the way to parent. We assure you all the case studies in the world will be of no assistance if God is not part of your family. We don't sit back and pretend that God will do it all. We know good families and good marriages don't just happen. We realize that we must choose to be responsible parents and spouses. We do not deny or apologize that our choices are influenced by our belief in God and what He wants for us as individuals, as a couple, and as a family. Psalm 127:1 echoes our belief: "Unless the LORD builds the house, those who built it labor in vain."

It is our beliefs and faith that helps us determine the choices we make for our children as well as the values we teach them. We determine right and wrong, appropriate and inappropriate, moral and immoral from our beliefs. Which programs the boys watch on television, the movies they view, the activities they participate in as well as our discipline and where and how we educate our sons, are all decided based on our beliefs. Faith is an integral part of our lives.

We also believe in the power of prayer. Prayer is our lifeline to God. We pray as a family at meals and in the evening. At dinner time after we say our formal blessing, each person at our table, family and friend, has the opportunity to offer a personal prayer. We pray for family members who aren't with us, for family or friends who are sick, for guidance on our work and play, for someone going through a rough time or needing to make a decision. We all remember Timmy's prayer the evening of his first day in preschool. He asked us to pray for all his girlfriends. Timmy's prayers have matured since then. How touching when we pray for one of his friend's grandmother who died and his friend who is sad. At the end of the day before the younger boys go to bed, we come together as a family to say our evening prayers. The boys stop whatever they are doing—whether it's homework, shooting the basket, reading a book, talking on the telephone, or playing a game. We say the traditional prayers of our faith. (If we want our children to learn their prayers, they need to hear their prayers.) We end our prayers by saying: "Thank you, God, for this day. Please, bless Mommy, Daddy, Tony, David, Christopher, Joe Pat, Matthew, Mark, Tommy, Danny, Jamie, and Timmy. Help them to be good boys and Mommy and Daddy good parents." Each and every day the boys hear us ask God for His help and guidance.

We encourage you to embrace your faith and live it. One's faith strengthens, guides, and enriches the family.

Raising Responsible Children

Family life is meant to be enjoyable. When parents decide to have children, they don't do so with the intent to make their lives miserable, but, all too often, that is exactly what happens. Parents end up with unruly, undisciplined children who are not pleasant to have around. If we don't want our homes run by our children, then we have to establish expectations and responsibilities in our homes.

What do we do to make enjoying our sons an integral part of our parenting? **We establish expectations of their behavior (guidelines, rules, boundaries, and standards) not only to allow them to develop and mature but also to avoid chaos and frustration in our home. We provide responsibilities for the boys to fulfill not to be taskmasters but to teach them to be trustworthy, dependable, and self-reliant.** We begin when the boys are young and continue to provide them with firm, loving, and consistent guidance as they grow and mature. We establish our expectations and responsibilities together, as a couple, so we're both on the same page—and our children know it. **Children inevitably drive a wedge between parents when they realize their parents do not agree on expectations, responsibilities, and consequences.**

The expectations and responsibilities we establish for the boys must be age-appropriate. We can't expect the four-year-old to act like a ten-year-old or vice versa. The twelve-year-old's responsibilities will differ from those of the five-year-old. A child's physical and mental abilities must also be considered when considering both expectations and responsibilities. What may be appropriate for one son at age three may not be for another son at the same age.

When an expectation is not met or a responsibility not fulfilled, a parent must be ready to implement consequences. In other words, parents must discipline their children. Discipline has a punitive meaning in our society, but actually discipline means to teach or to train. **Our ultimate goal in disciplining is for our sons to attain self-discipline. Self-discipline does not happen overnight. It is a gradual process that we, as parents, must initiate and follow through to fruition.** When parents question the necessity of establishing responsibilities for their children, we remind them that a child does not wake up on their fourteenth birthday and decide to be responsible. If we want well-disciplined, responsible, and respectful children, then we must provide the environment for our children to develop these characteristics. To quote Plato: "And the beginning, as you know, is always the most important part, especially in dealing with anything young and tender. That is the time when the character is being molded and easily takes any impress one may wish to stamp on it."

We have learned that it is to our advantage as parents to establish rules and guidelines for our sons as well as to provide them with responsibilities. We find that the time we invest in our sons' early development facilitates our parenting efforts as they move into the teenage years. The expectations and responsibilities have been established; the boys understand the consequences when expectations are not met or responsibilities remain unfulfilled. We don't want to spend all our time hassling with discipline. What fun is that? Like the other areas of our relationship, we needed to decide what we wanted and then determine how to attain our goal.

(Cathy): **People often ask, "Cathy, how do you do it? How do you take care of ten boys and stay sane?"** *I can honestly answer that it is not a "me" but a "we" that makes our family run smoothly—Joe, the boys, and me. I assure you that I would not have had ten children if Joe had not chosen to play an active parenting role, and I would not have had ten children if our parenting efforts had not been fulfilling. For our family to function effectively and enjoyably, we must all work together.*

When I talk about responsibilities, some parents complain that it is a constant battle because their children don't want to help around the house. Our children prefer to do other things, too. They don't enjoy taking out garbage or straightening up the bathroom; however, they also realize that it is part and parcel of how our home functions. They understand that if Mom or Dad is going to be available to drive them to soccer practice, then they need to do their share as well. Mom and Dad can't do it all and still be pleasant parents. Our sons don't relish their responsibilities; they are normal children. They don't, for example, jump up from the dinner table on their night to clean the kitchen and enthusiastically yell, "Yes! It is my night to do dishes!" They simply put a CD in the player and face the music.

(Joe): We happened to be at a school-sponsored dinner one evening, having a good time talking with other parents. The topic of conversation at our table of parents turned to how hard it was at times to get the children to help around the house. One father mentioned that it was a chore to get his boys to mow the lawn each weekend and that he had finally resorted to paying the boys to do so. He turned to me and asked, "What do you pay your boys to take care of the lawn at your house?" I replied, "After they do the lawn, I usually let them eat at our table for dinner and sleep in our home that evening." He responded, "Oh."

We want to point out that responsibility is threefold. **We teach our sons that they are responsible for themselves, responsible for others, and responsible to God.** Responsibility for themselves entails taking care of their personal well-being, schoolwork, and personal belongings. Responsibility for others encompasses family, friends, and society at large. Responsibility to God means they follow His law of love: love God with your whole mind, heart, and soul and love your neighbor as yourself. They learn to be responsible in all three areas through their responsibilities at home and with our family.

We've learned that one reason our sons usually do what is expected is because they understand that we will impose consequences. If children don't think anything will result from their lack of fulfilling their responsibility or acting appropriately, then they will continue to do what they choose. When the boys don't fulfill their responsibilities, we have to determine appropriate consequences. Consequences, much the same as expectations and responsibilities, must be age-appropriate and age-realistic. To place a two-year-old in their room for two hours is inappropriate, whereas having a fourteen-year-old work out in the yard for two hours could be an appropriate consequence.

We've discovered parents have a hard time meting out consequences. Sometimes it is an inconvenience for them—either because deciding on the consequence itself is a nuisance or because the consequence causes them to be inconvenienced. Others simply don't want their darlings to "suffer." Parents continually rescue their children from the consequences of their actions. Note the mom who races back across town because her son forgot his soccer shoes. Consider the father who rushes the forgotten homework to school so his child won't get a detention or receive a poor grade. Witness the parents who blame the teacher or school for their child's low grades even though the child hasn't turned in assignments all semester.

(Cathy): When I gave a presentation at a middle school in Houston and spoke about the issue of rescuing our children, the principal shared with me that she now has parents who "fax" the forgotten homework to school. She then chuckled as she told me that she then walks the faxed homework over to another one of their office machines—the shredder!

(Joe): I have a very good friend at work who enjoys talking about parenting and kids' issues with me. One day this friend mentioned that her child was being very obstinate about his spelling assignment. He would return from school with words misspelled on his assignment and then insist that they were correctly spelled. My friend would argue firmly that they were spelled incorrectly and that he would not do well on his spelling test if he persisted in misspelling them. This usually resulted in a battle of wills about the assignment and hurt feelings for both parties. She asked what she could do. I pointed out to her what a successful individual she had become because she had learned over the years what to do to be

*successful. Moreover, she learned how to become successful through
some failures along the way. Maybe it was time for her son to taste
some "failure" by spelling those words wrong on his exam and
suffering the consequences. I also pointed out that it was important
for her to have him succeed and that she might have to tolerate
some poor grades on his tests for the problem to remedy itself.*

It may be hard not to run up to school and help your child, but
is it really helping him or her in the long term? If we want our
children to learn to be responsible, then we must let them learn
from their mistakes and forgetfulness as well as accept the consequences of their actions.

The same holds true regarding expectations of our sons'
behavior. We expect the boys to treat not only us with kindness and
respect but also their brothers. We do not allow them to call each
other names or use inappropriate language. We remind them that
each of us has our weaknesses, faults, and distinct physical characteristics. Just as they don't want or need anyone pointing out their
faults and lesser qualities, neither do their brothers. We expect them
to be sensitive to the feelings of each other. If they aren't kind to a
brother or won't behave, they spend some time alone or have a
privilege revoked. If the boys start arguing over the computer or a
game, the computer is shut off and the game removed. If they don't
make curfew, they lose their driving privileges for a period of time.
When they argued about where to sit in the car years ago, we
assigned seats. When they wouldn't cooperate in the car riding to
and from school, they rode the bus for a week. When they didn't
put their clean, folded clothes away in their drawers, they washed
their own clothes. Parents need to think about how they want their
children's behavior to change and then determine the best way to
make it happen. We had few hassles in the car after they had to ride
the bus for a week. Computer problems are minimized. We don't
yell, nag, or argue. We are firm, loving, and consistent.

If we want our homes to be loving, caring, peaceful, and
enjoyable, then we need to set the standards for what is acceptable

and unacceptable in our homes. Our children need and want limits and guidelines, and they depend on us to provide them. We enjoy our children and our home because each one of us understands that we must work together so we can all enjoy a home filled with laughter and love.

Recognizing Family Is a System

Family is a system, a system of varied parts that need to work together to operate effectively. When we married, a new family system was formed made up of the two of us. We brought the expectations and assumptions of how our system would develop from our families of origin. We had to move beyond the expectations and assumptions of our parents, though, and meet our own expectations. **We had to establish a family system that would work for us and that is what we have nurtured for the past twenty-six years. We have blended the attitudes, behaviors, expectations, and assumptions of both our families to create the Joseph and Catherine Garcia-Prats family. As our family grew, we adapted the system to incorporate our children's need to grow and reach their full potential with our continuing need to grow as individuals and as a couple.**

Recognizing that as a family we are a system of interrelated parts is important. "A family is more than the sum of its parts. It is a dynamic and developing system whose members are radically interdependent" *(A Family Perspective in Church and Society).* Like the ecosystem Joe described earlier, each person in the family plays a pivotal role in preserving the balance of the system. We have to acknowledge that there are certain characteristics that foster and strengthen the family system, and that each event in family life impacts the lives of all the family members.

In *A Family Perspective in Church and Society,* the following characteristics are identified as being family strengths.

> "They include the ability of the family to: appreciate and respect each other; spend both quality and

quantity time together; develop and use skills in communication, negotiating and resolving problems and differences in a positive and constructive way; develop a strong sense of commitment to stay related during times of transition, difficulty, or crisis; possess a solid core of moral and spiritual beliefs; and rely on other resources such as the social network, which includes family, friends and kin, as well as community resources such as churches and other helping agencies."

Our experience of marriage and family supports the characteristics outlined above. As we developed them in our relationship, we were able to integrate them into our family. By doing so we didn't eliminate the challenges, demands, constancy, and fatigue of parenting. Instead, we learned how to effectively manage them as we enjoy our children and the fullness they bring to our marriage.

We encourage you to enjoy your children. Don't look at parenting as drudgery. Look at parenting as another adventure in your marriage along the road of life. You can travel this road by skipping over the tree roots and rocks while appreciating the sunshine and flowers, or by tripping and stumbling over the same tree roots and rocks while complaining about the dark and gloomy path.

Laugh and play with your children as you care for them. Show them your loving heart. Read to them as often as you can. Children treasure story time. **Don't let the hours and days slip away without your children knowing you love them.** We know how quickly the years fly by, although some days, we must admit, don't fly by fast enough. As we look at our older sons, we can truly appreciate what we have accomplished. They are fine young men who in turn are touching many lives around them.

Share your time, your love, and your faith with your children. By doing so, you will all be enriched. That's what we mean when we say: The Garcia-Prats are richer by the dozen!

Unless the Lord build the house,
they labor in vain who build it
—*Psalm 127:1*

Prayer is in all things, in all gestures.
—*Mother Teresa*

Eye has not seen, ear has not heard
what God has ready for those who love Him.
—*1 Corinthians 2:9*

Chapter Ten

Living Your Marriage for the Greater Glory of God

Spirituality, faith, and prayer are unique to each individual, even to those who share the same religion. We accept and respect the fact that our beliefs, practices, celebrations, and religious holy days may differ from other couples'. The emphasis in this chapter is on the importance and integration of each couple's faith in their marriage. Mother Teresa always encouraged Muslims to be better Muslims, Jews better Jews, Hindus better Hindus, and Catholics better Catholics while never denying her own Catholic faith. Likewise, whatever the tenets of your faith, we encourage you to embrace and practice them as you build the foundation of your marriage.

Our faith is the foundation of our marriage. Who we are, what we do, and the choices we make evolve from our faith. Our faith is interwoven into the fabric of our marriage. In Ecclesiastes we read:

"A three-ply cord is not easily broken." We know that for our marriage to strengthen and grow we must remain a three-ply cord of husband, wife, and God. We are confident that with God by our side we can handle the challenges of married life as well as appreciate the joys.

We consider ourselves blessed to have grown up in families where religion was an important component of family life. We observed the value our parents placed on their faith and how they integrated their beliefs into everyday life. Faith is still an important part of their lives. Knowing what we know about our own marriage, it is hard for us to imagine how both sets of parents could remain married over fifty years if God had not been an integral part of their individual lives and their life together as a couple.

As we got to know each other during the first months we dated, we found the faith connection we shared a wonderful addition to our relationship. We enjoyed attending Mass together either at The Newman Center at Tulane University or at Loyola University's chapel. We appreciated the understanding of faith in each other's life without the need to constantly defend our choices and attitudes. Our faith is a constant in our relationship, like the three-ply cord, strengthening us as we maneuver through the challenges, demands, and joys of marriage. Our marriage is more than a piece of paper that declares us husband and wife. Our marriage is a commitment to each other as well as a commitment to God.

When we decided to get married, we wanted a Christian wedding because we wanted a Christian marriage—specifically a Catholic Christian marriage. We were not just signing some papers and entering into a civil contract. We were embracing the sacrament of marriage, which is a covenant—an unconditional and permanent commitment. Our commitment to our faith, as individuals and as a couple, confirmed our marriage as a sacrament. **Having the wedding in a church doesn't make the marriage a sacrament or a Christian marriage; rather, it is the faith commitment of the couple that affirms the covenant.**

Our faith and spirituality is an active part of our life, not something we put in a drawer and pull out only as we need it. We realize that for faith to have meaning we need to live and express it in our day-to-day interactions and experiences. Our faith and love of God is expressed in the love, respect, and commitment we demonstrate to each other, our children, and those around us. St. James tells us: "What good is it to profess faith without practicing it?"

Society compartmentalizes all the facets of our lives. People want to believe that, although we attend church on Sunday, our choices and decisions the rest of the week are irrelevant to our spirituality. People want to believe that their personal spirituality shouldn't affect their business decisions, their relationships, or their lifestyle and choice of activities. Sadly, many people are comfortable with their faith until it interferes with societal values and personal decisions. Faith isn't integrated into their lives; it is a separate entity.

In respect to our marriage, our faith is reflected by the quality of our relationship with our spouse. Is our relationship loving, mutually satisfying, and mutually beneficial or is it wrought with anger, discontent, and selfishness? If we want our relationship to develop where "two become one," faith must be a part of the equation. A faith-filled relationship is one where spouses speak and treat each other with respect, are loving, forgiving and compassionate, and establish priorities that place their marriage first—even when they don't feel like it or want to do so.

(Joe): I have come to realize that our relationships teach us so much about God in ways that I did not expect. These relationships have added a deeper appreciation of the meaning of loving as a spouse, as a father, and as a friend. As a boy in grade school, when the Gospel proclaimed "there is no greater love than for a man to give his life for his friend," I truly did not comprehend what was being said until I developed mature friendships. Likewise, when the Gospel

referred to Christ loving His Church like the bridegroom loving His bride, the passage did not really have the same impact on me until Cathy and I were married and had developed a mature love for each other. When there was a reference to God as our Father, it was only after the birth of the boys that "fatherhood" took on the meaning that was intended by the writers of the Gospels. In each instance, it was my relationship with Cathy and my children that gave so much meaning to the Gospel teachings as well as indicate the direction in which to continue to develop each of these relationships.

Likewise by nurturing my relationship with Cathy, God has taught me much about myself through our relationship. Realizing that Christ, as a bridegroom, would do nothing hurtful to His bride, the Church, so should I, as a good spouse, not be selfish or proud in my day-to-day dealings with Cathy but strive to be loving toward her. When I find myself affecting our relationship in a hurtful way, I have to sit back and remember the love Christ shows me every day. He so lovingly gives Himself to His bride, the Church, while He maneuvers His Church through the ups and downs of daily life. I must do the same. In my relationship with Cathy, I must do my best to be loving, considerate, honest, and forgiving just as Christ is for me. If He is that way toward me, how can I not be that way toward the individuals I love?

(Cathy): My faith development, as in every dimension of my life, has been a gradual process of learning, understanding, and integration. I never fathomed that my marriage to Joe would provide such a rich opportunity for me to grow spiritually. I've actually been amazed at the correlation between my relationship with Joe and my relationship with God. As I've grown in my appreciation and understanding of the impact of love, respect, and commitment in our marriage, I've grown spiritually closer to God. This growth didn't always happen when Joe and I were the perfect lovers and spouses but, significantly, during our times of struggle and discontent.

A Christian marriage, the love between a husband and wife, is compared to the love of Christ for His Church; therefore, it makes sense that my love of Joe and my love of God are closely related. How can I say I love God and then speak or treat Joe disrespectfully? If I'm not forgiving and compassionate toward Joe, I cannot expect God to be forgiving of my indiscretions. When I am at peace with Joe, I find that I am at peace with God. When I am not at peace with Joe, I struggle with all areas of my life, including the spiritual.

I highly recommend the book The Mystic, a book recommended to me by a dear friend, Fr. John Payne, S.J. The author, David Torkington, uses a marital analogy in relating the development of an individual's prayer life. I could identify with stages in both my marriage and my relationship with God throughout the book. During the times in our marriage when we have struggled or been "married singles" (a term we first heard during our Marriage Encounter weekend to describe couples who are married but living separate lives), it is my commitment to Joe and to God that has given me the strength to keep going even when I've felt confused, lost, and alone. It is this love and commitment that enables Joe and me to grow through the hard times and appreciate and relish the good times. The words Torkington uses to describe what happened in the relationship of the couple likewise describe what has transpired in our own marriage: "The love my parents had learned and continued to learn grew with the years, not in spite of but because of the sacrifices they both had to make. It grew and blossomed into a love that continued to sustain them through many difficult times that they had to face together." Torkington beautifully relates how we, the husband and wife, are the ministers of the sacrament of marriage—not the priest—and we continue to minister to each other when we love unconditionally and selflessly. It is our everyday interactions and expressions of love, from the simple touches and acts of kindness to our complete giving to each other through sexual intercourse, that reaffirm our marriage. **Through our daily acts of love to each other, which are also expressions of our love for God, we continually renew our marriage vows.**

Why do we struggle in our relationship with each other and with God? Why does attaining the peace we so desperately crave demand so much? I've come to realize that most of our struggles in both relationships are due to our pride and selfish natures. To overcome this, we must continually strive to give without counting the cost and to pray for God's love and guidance.

Likewise, we must continually develop our relationship with God. **Like our marital relationship that grows stagnant with lack of time and attention, our relationship with God will not grow and mature unless we make it a priority in our lives.** We have noticed significant changes in our faith development during the years of our marriage both as individuals and as a couple.

(Cathy): With marriage came new developments in my faith. The whole concept of self-giving and sacrificial love takes on new meaning when you are in a marital relationship. As we began our family, the meaning intensified even more. I often felt, though, that I couldn't love and give the way I was expected to. The Holy Family was held up as the model family to emulate. Yet I knew that my family of origin, although a loving family, was not exactly the Holy Family. Even in my early years of parenting as our family quickly grew to five sons, I often found it hard to relate to the Holy Family. I couldn't envision Mary and Joseph ever having a disagreement, a frustration, being angry, impatient, or stressed out, or Jesus not being the "perfect" child who did everything He was expected to do and with a smile on His face. Plus Mary and Joseph had one child. By contrast, we faced the needs and demands of our first five children.

Fortunately, nineteen years ago shortly after the birth of our fourth son, Joe Pat, I began visiting a perpetual adoration chapel one hour a week. Although my initial motive for visiting the chapel was self-centered (I saw it as an hour, a whole hour, of peace and quiet), I quickly realized that that one hour was fostering and strengthening my prayer life. *During these hours alone with God, I grew in many ways. One of them was in my understanding of the example of the Holy Family. It was their love, devotion, commitment, and support of each other that I needed to emulate on a daily basis. Mary became, and still is, a source of real strength to me as I strive to mirror her attitude, choices, and acceptance of what life brought her. I had to choose to love and support my husband and my children. My attitude and approach to loving would make a difference in their lives and, ultimately, in mine. I could wake up each morning and throw up my hands at all that needed to be done taking care of Joe and the boys, or I could wake up and thank God for Joe and our sons and ask for His love and guidance in handling the demands of the day. **I've learned that when love is in my heart the activities of the day are filled with joy, whether I'm washing eight loads of clothes, cleaning bathrooms, running the boys to soccer, or meeting the individual needs of one of our sons. I took to heart Mother Teresa's words: "It is not how much we do, but how much love we put into the doing."***

Likewise, the example of the importance of the Holy Family's faith life encouraged me to strengthen my prayer life. To this day when I find the emotional and physical stresses and demands of my life overwhelming and affecting my relationships, I have to reexamine whether my prayer life is adequate or if I have pushed it aside due to the stresses. When I refocus and reinstate God first in my life, everything—and I mean everything—falls right into place. I've learned that when I have God, I have everything that I need. I share with you one of my favorite quotes: "It is not the absence or presence of problems that determines our peace of mind; it is the absence or presence of God." (Regretfully, I didn't write down which book this quote came from or the author.)

In our marriage and in our family life, we have found that when we are at peace as a couple and at peace with God, we are able to handle the challenges and difficulties that arise. We are not, we assure you, a marriage or a family without problems or challenges. We are a couple, though, who determines how we will resolve a problem, whether it revolves around us as a couple or one of the boys.

(Cathy): I remember the time I was extremely worried about two of our sons, for two very different reasons. I could feel the worry eating me away. I knew what they each were going through, and my heart ached for them. I knew all I could do for them was pray and be loving and supportive. Yet I found praying wasn't easing my worry or my pain. One morning I went to Mass and after Mass sat in the church alone. During this quiet time, I finally handed my worries and concerns over to God. How often do we say we believe or trust in God only to turn around and try to handle everything on our own? That was what I was doing—not trusting in God or handing over my burdens to Him. "Come to me, all you who are weary and find life burdensome, and I will refresh you" (Matthew 11:28). Once I accepted His offer to come to Him, I was "refreshed." The concerns didn't just disappear, but I was able to accept them and trust that God would see the situations through.

When I trust in God and accept His plan for me, my days are more peaceful. Like most people, though, I question "why" and often don't really want to be challenged by His demands or have my life disrupted or rearranged. When Joe and I were first approached to write a book on family, we initially rejected the idea for many reasons. With much encouragement and support from Claire Cassidy, who had written an article on our family after Timmy, our tenth son, was born, the book came to fruition. After the book came out Joe and I, individually and as a couple, were invited to speak on family and parenting by church, school, and community groups locally, nationally, and internationally. Speaking in front of a group of people was never a dream of mine. Teaching a classroom of children was the closest I wanted to get to speaking to a group of people. Yet today I enjoy and appreciate the opportunity to share our experience of family with other families no matter the size of the audience. Joe and I have learned a lot in our years of parenting and feel called to share what we have learned with others. Many days I still question why, especially when I feel pulled in myriad directions. I would like to go back to being "just" Mom, but I have to trust that this is where God has led Joe and me. I find it interesting, too, how on days when I feel as if I'm changing hats every few hours or I'm trying to convince myself that I've had enough of the juggling, I receive a phone call or a note in the mail expressing appreciation for the book or the words I shared at a presentation. These angels pull me back on track. We have to trust in God and His plan for us.

We also need prayer in our lives. Prayer is an important part of our faith development. Our present experience of prayer is very different from when we grew up in our families of origin. Prayer for us then was primarily the traditional prayers of our faith. Prayer now is so much more of a personal listening and talking with God.

(Joe): My faith was a gift from God and, in a sense, my parents. I was determined in the course of my faith development that my faith would be a practical faith, a faith that is interwoven into my everyday life. Cathy and I have shared that faith from the beginning of our relationship. This faith guides my day and guides our lives and that of our sons. It is a faith that is practiced not just on Sunday while I am in church. I practice that faith each day through how I treat Cathy and the boys as well as how I treat the people around me—my patients at the hospital, the staff, the nurses, and the ward clerks. Cathy and I practice it at home in our thanksgiving before meals and before we put the boys to bed each night. We want our sons to feel the guidance and integration of our God in their lives. We show our children God when we treat everyone we come in contact with in a respectful and compassionate way.

For us to live with God as our Father who shows us daily His love for us, for us to live with God as our Father who has a plan for each of us, I believe we must look for His help in two ways. Mother Teresa, in her book No Greater Love, tells us of the importance of silence, external silence as well as internal silence, in order for us to be able to listen to God. She says: "In the silence of the heart God speaks. **Silence gives you a new outlook on everything. The essential thing is not what we say but what God says to us and through us. In that silence, He will listen to us. There He will speak to our soul and there we will hear His voice.**" This passage has touched me deeply, for I realized that there was not much silence in my life. Yes, we have ten boys and a very busy schedule. At the same time, think of the noisy interventions we are surrounded by—TVs, computers, the internet, radios, and CD players. I love to drive to and from work with the radio on, listening to the traffic, news, and weather reports. Now I shut it off and drive to work and then back home in silence. I have been impressed in what my mind has heard in these periods of silence. I encourage you to take the time each day to have a period of silence and to work on bringing about internal silence as well.

Mother Teresa also reminds us of the importance of prayer in our lives. She uses two analogies to emphasize this importance. She says that we are like the wires in an appliance. Some of the wires are thick, some thin, some short, while others long. But these wires are useless unless electricity runs through them to make the appliance work. Prayer is that electricity that ties these wires together. Likewise, she tells us how we are like lamps trying to show our light to the world. Prayer is the oil that keeps our lamps burning. So let love, respect, commitment, and faith guide each of us in our choices each day. Let silence and prayer keep our feet on the right path.

(Cathy): My days begin and end with prayer, and many minutes in between are filled with prayers. I've learned that all we do becomes a prayer when done with love: the cooking, the cleaning,

the diapering, the bathing, the reading of stories. I've also learned that my prayers don't have to be eloquent dissertations. Simple words suffice for praise, thanksgiving, and petition: "Thank you, God, for the beautiful day." "Please protect the boys on their way to school." "Bless Joe, the babies he cares for today as well as their families." "Please help me find the patience and the time to get done what I need to do today." "O Sacred Heart of Jesus, I place my trust in you." "Lord, make me an instrument of your peace"(from the Prayer of St. Francis of Assisi).

While I realize the importance of praying for Joe and the boys, I find the need to pray with them is equally essential. From the earliest days of our relationship to the present, prayer has been an integral part of our marriage. During the times we struggle, praying keeps us going even when we question whether God is listening to us.

Our family prayer times bond us together. We started praying as a family when Tony and David were toddlers. We just added another child to our prayer circle as each came along. The boys have never refused to be a part of family prayer time. We believe they don't reject it because we're not just saying words but striving to live the words in our daily lives.

Our prayer time, whether as an individuals, a couple or a family, helps keep us focused on what we believe God wants for us. Through prayer we strengthen our faith. And it is our faith that guides the choices we make regarding our lifestyle, the clothes we wear, the schools where we educate our sons, the activities in which we are involved, our commitments, and even our choice to have a large family.

I read an article that asked this question: "When someone visits in your home, what does your home life tell them about you? Will they know that God is a part of your family?" We can display religious articles and crucifixes in our home, but if the family members are not treating each other with the dignity and respect they each deserve as children of God, then the religious symbols mean nothing. We must make our homes and our relationships *reflections of our faith. There is a line from a hymn we sing at church that states: "They will know we are Christians by our love." Do people know we are Christian, or whichever faith we practice, by our love? We must ask ourselves if people will recognize we are faith-filled individuals by the way we live our lives.*

Several years ago Joe and I attended a pediatric dinner. One of the wives at the table asked me if I would change my religion for my husband. I said "no" because my Catholic faith was very much who I am and that I believed in Catholic practices and teachings. My "no" led to an intense questioning of the validity of our Catholic beliefs and teachings, not only by this one wife but by others at the table. Joe and I answered their questions as best we could. Finally, one doctor who was well respected by his colleagues, entered the discussion. He leaned back in his chair and as he looked around the table, he calmly said, "I don't know anything about the theology of what you're talking about, what is true or not true. I just know one thing, just one thing. Cathy and Joe—they live what they believe. And that's enough for me." No one said another thing. These words were spoken by a man who doesn't practice any formal religion or even outwardly acknowledge the relevance of God in his life, yet his understanding of faith was more profound than most of the adults at the table that evening.

To this day no one has ever said anything that has touched us more. We strive very hard to live what we believe. We know that each of us is called to be a light in the world. **We must shine that light first to each other in our marriage, then to our children who, hopefully, along with us will create a brighter light to shine for all the world to see.** We are pleased if people know we live what we believe. We want them to know as well that our faith is not a binding, restrictive experience as often portrayed by society but, rather, one that brings us peace and joy as a couple and a family.

We don't hesitate to tell you that our faith is an invaluable source of strength, inspiration, and guidance in our marriage. Dr. Ed Young tells us: "If love is to survive in an atmosphere of change, it must be rooted in something that is changeless." We encourage you to embrace and live your faith, to rediscover it if it hasn't been a priority in your marriage. Your faith will provide the foundation to build and to strengthen your marriage as well as the grace you need to fulfill your wedding vows.

The most wasted of days is that in which
one has not laughed.

—Sebastian R. N. Chamfort

You will find, as you look back upon your life,
that the moments that stand out, the moments
when you have really lived, are the moments when
you have done things in the spirit of Love.

—Henry Drummond

People who really and truly love each other
are the happiest people in the world.

—Mother Teresa

Chapter Eleven

Laughter, Memories, and Traditions

*H*appiness is integral to God's plan for each one of us. No matter what God has chosen for us to do or by what means He has chosen for us to accomplish it, our happiness is interwoven into His plan. On the challenging days of our marriage, we questioned why God bound us as a couple. On the other hand, we have marveled at His wisdom on the good days. For many reasons, both mortal and divine, the combination was right. When we began dating, we enjoyed being with each other and sharing many experiences such as studying together and attending parties. We made each other happy. Inevitably, our relationship deepened into love and led to marriage.

Our marital relationship continues to reflect that happiness despite the many bumps encountered along the adventurous road.

We acknowledge that making a marriage succeed takes effort, time, and mutual dedication to this goal on the part of each spouse. We especially stress the importance of our effort being a daily one. As we strive toward our goal, we should not preclude the crucial component of laughter in the relationship. A daily openness to playfully embrace joy is vital to a healthy marital relationship.

Married life is meant to be fun. We should wake up each morning and be glad to be a wife or a husband, a mother or a father. We need to keep life's stresses and demands in perspective so we appreciate the joy of living. Laughter is at the heart of a family. Without laughter, every day becomes drudgery. With laughter, our days are filled with peace and joy—and the obstacles we face we just dance around.

Creating Memories from Our Time Together

We are always fascinated by couples and families who have story after story to tell about some funny or interesting event that occurred to them. The stories, conveyed with such feeling and emotion, usually relate happy consequences or endings. Think of the many stories that you have heard from couples about their special experiences dining out, camping, hiking, taking in a movie, or traveling. As we listen to these stories, we share in those memories and maybe even conjure up similar experiences in our own minds. The common thread intertwining them is that time spent together as a couple and as a family creates opportunities for memories. Unhappy memories surface for the same reason—the result of people interacting with each other. What determines whether or not the memories are happy is the quality of the relationship that exists for the couple relating the incident. When spouses are on the same page and are effectively communicating, they place themselves in a position to appreciate mutual fun and enjoyment. If a couple isn't happy with their relationship, they are less likely to be open to enjoying those wonderful moments when they avail themselves. We both know how much drudgery it is when we are forced into attending a function that we don't particularly want to go to. No memories there. We are not open to allowing the experiences to be fun-filled, not malleable to letting the moment shape the time into a good memory. So, when you as a couple enjoy each other and respect each other and include fun into each day, memories will become part of your spirited and fun time together.

(Joe): When I was in my last year of pediatric residency training, I had the luxury of having a whole weekend off after finagling some schedules. Neither Cathy nor I could remember when that had last occurred. Another pediatric resident and good friend agreed to take the beeper for me and assume my call responsibilities. Cathy, afraid the hospital would find me and I would feel obligated to go in, insisted we leave town. So on the spur of the moment we drove to San Antonio to enjoy the weekend. Little did we know when we left Houston that both the last cold front of the year and a national child psychiatry convention also intended to visit San Antonio. We arrived in San Antonio with spring clothes and no reservations only to find cold weather and no hotel vacancies. We bought sweatshirts to deal with the cold, finally located a hotel room in the northern outreaches of San Antonio, and proceeded to have a memorable weekend together. Our memories of our first of many excursions to San Antonio are special.

(Cathy): On another trip to San Antonio we attended a pediatric convention. We were expecting our fourth child at the time ,so a few days respite were welcomed. When we arrived at the hotel, the receptionist at the desk greeted us with a warm congratulatory smile. I wondered how she knew that I was expecting since I was only a couple months along and not yet showing. When we arrived in our room, we realized the congratulations were not meant for the pregnancy—the receptionist thought we were newly married. Joe's

secretary, knowing we were looking forward to a few childless days away as well as wanting to ensure that we would have a nice room for the weekend, told the receptionist when she made the reservation that we were on our honeymoon. We were in the honeymoon suite. We enjoyed the room, the extra smiles we received, the quiet time together, and the memories of our second honeymoon, pregnant with Joe Pat.

San Antonio continues to garner memories for us: the trips for Tony's USS swim meets and high school state championship meets, the high school and club soccer games, and now the college soccer games at Trinity University with Chris.

Observing Traditions

National holidays and religious holy days lend themselves to establishing numerous traditions. Many of the traditions that we currently celebrate or participate in originated with our families of origin. Each special holiday and holy day brings the opportunity to experience special times spent together either as a couple or as a family. Our approach to these holidays and holy days should be one of openness to the occasion. This attitude enables us to share and create our connection with those we love and to enjoy the themes of the national holidays or relish the religious significance of the holy days. The key word is "connection" with our spouses and family. For without that bonding, the importance of such a holiday pales. Likewise, our appreciation and involvement with these holidays and holy days as well as the events they commemorate rekindle in each of us the special theme celebrated. Our memories of Fourth of July family picnics, exchanging Christmas gifts, Easter egg hunts, Christmas tree-cuttings, and Thanksgiving Masses all remain in each of us and continue to bring us joy and laughter. We've picked up the baton of tradition that was handed down to us by our families of origin and reworked it to fit us. We enjoy our newly formed traditions with our spouse and family just as we remember our old family traditions with fondness.

(Joe): Thanksgiving has become a very memorable time for our family, especially as our older sons began attending colleges out of town: Tony at St. Louis University, David at Creighton University in Omaha, Chris at Trinity University in San Antonio, Joe Pat at Regis University in Denver, and Matthew at the University of San Diego. Thanksgiving is the first time since August that our whole family is together. The laughter and interactions for the entire weekend are fun-filled and memorable. Although each Thanksgiving has its own special memories—morning Mass at Strake Jesuit College Preparatory, our special friends who share dinner with us, and the postdinner soccer games—I will always remember one Thanksgiving in particular for the kindness of our friends and the laughter these memories generate.

About ten years ago, our thoughtful friends, George and Misty, invited our family to their home for Thanksgiving dinner. Now you need to remember that with a large family like ours, the invitation itself shows much kindness as well as courage. The meal proceeded normally until halfway through dessert when two of the boys began vomiting profusely—not due to the cooking, I might add. We headed home where the domino effect took over. By Friday, I was the only one not sick. Cathy and the baby stayed in one room while I set up an infirmary for all the other boys in the den with their buckets. Fortunately, the virus waited until Cathy and the boys recovered before striking me.

A few months later, George and Misty actually invited us to dinner again. This time George was prepared. As the boys, Cathy, and I walked into their home, George greeted each one of the boys with a brown paper bag. He wasn't taking any chances this time. Not all the boys understood the significance of the brown bag, but the rest of us appreciated George's humor. George and Misty hold a special place in our hearts for their kindness, laughter, and bravery in having the Garcia-Prats over twice in one year.

(Cathy): Birthdays are special events in our home—and we have our share of them. For Joe's fiftieth birthday, the older boys and I decided to throw a surprise party for him. (We never told the younger boys because we knew they wouldn't be able to keep it quiet. They ended up just as surprised as Joe that we were having a party.) Joe's birthday is in mid-December, but there was no time to celebrate a surprise party before Christmas. We picked a date during the holiday season and decided to have the party at our home. For weeks the planning ensued with neighbors and friends storing decorations and food. The evening of the party Joe and I went to dinner with our good friends, the Taylors. Joe suspected nothing. We left the house with the boys eating pizza and talking about going to the Strake Jesuit Christmas basketball tournament. As soon as we left for dinner, the boys and friends brought everything out from hiding and transformed our house into a party scene. When we returned home, Joe walked in the door and immediately noticed our kitchen's transformation. A look of anger crossed his face—not one of surprise. His initial reaction when he saw the food and decorations was to assume that the boys were having a party and didn't tell us—the nerve of them—only to be shocked when Joe realized it was his friends throwing the party for him.

Establishing Our Own Traditions

As we have said over and over in the course of this book, each couple and family are unique unto themselves. That being the case, some traditions which may have been a mainstay for your family of origin may not have the same meaning for you as a couple and as a family. Or you may discover that a tradition that was quite special for your family of origin can be made equally special for your own family by tailoring it to this new relationship. Similarly, **since you are a new family, create your own new traditions.** It is what you and your spouse find special and what you make of it that will give it meaning with your distinctive touch.

(Joe): Cathy and I have always enjoyed going out to dinner. It affords us a time of quiet for each other. That was true even before we had the kids. So it seemed perfectly in order for us to celebrate our anniversary by going out to dinner. Celebrating our anniversary also brought about a few challenges we had not foreseen. Our anniversary is at the end of May, as are most proms and graduations. To find a restaurant that is not filled with high school students is a challenge. Timing became everything—we have late anniversary dinners!

As one might expect, getting away for a nice dinner as our family grew took some planning on our part. We realized dinner out during the week was unreasonable, even for our anniversary. We prefer waiting until the weekend when we can relax and really enjoy the time together. One anniversary my brother, Vic, called in the evening to extend his best wishes to Cathy and me. Vic is very sensitive and the true romantic. After he wished us a happy anniversary, he stated that he wanted to call early in the evening before we went out to celebrate a wonderful meal, eaten in candlelight with romantic music in the background. I very much appreciated my brother's considerate thoughts. However, if he could have seen me on the other end of the telephone, he would have seen me in shorts and sneakers as I had just returned from picking up the boys from soccer practice. Cathy and I also had much to finish that evening before we could take a breath and have a quiet moment. Vic's vision for us sounded wonderful but not on that particular Thursday night. Vic continues to be sensitive, warm, and thoughtful. We are glad that our boys have had the chance to see his kindness and consideration.

(Cathy): Our second anniversary dinner was quite memorable. We were enjoying our evening, the dinner, the atmosphere, the reminiscing of our wedding, when Joe realized he had forgotten his wallet at home. Usually that wouldn't be a problem; I would pay the dinner tab. Except on this particular night, I had specifically

told Joe I wasn't bringing a purse. And so we had no money or credit cards between us. Joe had no alternative but to return home and fetch his wallet. It was the longest wait of my life! The waiter was beginning to feel sorry for me. I could sense he thought that Joe had jilted me. What a relief when Joe returned! I have never enjoyed a cup of coffee and a dessert more.

(Joe): Dressing up for Halloween is a lot of fun in our household. Finding the right costume for each of the boys is always a challenge. The younger boys enjoy digging through the costume box, examining all the costumes we have accumulated over the last two decades. The other Halloween tradition that has become as much fun as dressing up is carving our pumpkin with a scary or funny face, depending on the boys' mood that particular Halloween evening. On Halloween eve night we transform our carefully chosen pumpkin into a "work of art" replete with candle. The boys enjoy designing the kind of eyes and mouth the new jack-o'-lantern will have as well as seeing the transformation when the candle is put inside. We have a collection of pictures of these jack-o'-lanterns surrounded by our boys.

We Are What Memories Are All About

We should remember that the reason all of our experiences are so special is because we are the fabric of each memory. We are the slate upon which the traditions are written. Without each other, the experiences don't seem to be "stackable" in our memories nor have enough Velcro to stick in our hearts. Without the person we love to share the experiences with, they just seem to slip away. **Traditions and memories connect us to the past. They are the form of oral history that keeps us close in our hearts with our families of origin. They are the wires that will connect us with each other and let our children connect with us for the future.**

(Joe): Matthew, our fifth son, graduated from Strake Jesuit College Preparatory in Houston in May 2000. His brothers before him—Tony, David, Chris, and Joe Pat—have also proudly graduated from Strake. As I sat with Cathy at the graduation ceremony, I felt much pride as they read the academic scholarships that Matthew had received. The pride returned when he received his diploma. This moment of pride and love for what he had accomplished welled up inside of me. I also realized that half of our ten sons were now graduates of Strake Jesuit. What an accomplishment and an honor for them for their persistence and hard work! Ultimately, however, it was a moment that only Cathy and I could fully appreciate in that we both understood all that had gone into our reaching this point in our lives and the life of our family. This was a memory that meant so much more for having shared it with her. With five more sons to attend Strake, we anticipate savoring similar memories a few more times.

(Cathy): We continually make deposits into our memory bank as a couple and as a family. Our sons add one memory after another. They always have a tale to tell or a story to weave. Like twins, they speak a language all their own. Their laughter permeates the rooms of our home, and the rooms of our hearts. Our sons definitely know how to have a good time and share that good time with others.

Each year our family sponsors and works the soft drink booth at our parish bazaar. Over the years, the boys have been a big part of our ability to successfully manage the booth by either working shifts or taking care of their younger brothers. Recently, a bazaar was held not long after Joe had been ill and his father had died. The boys understood that we would need their help more than usual in managing the booth. They not only accepted the responsibility—they made it fun. Saturday night of the bazaar the boys hooked up a CD player in the booth and entertained themselves and the crowd with their laughter and antics. We had no trouble manning the booth with volunteers because the young people wanted to be part of the fun.

Taking a mundane, boring activity and transforming it into an enjoyable one is what we need to be about in family. The boys tease me when I play music and bop along while doing household chores, but the music and dancing at least remove some of the drudgery from the routine for me. How interesting for me now to watch the boys as they pop in a CD while they wash dishes in the evenings.

It's our daily interactions that create the joy in our home. The nicknames the boys have for each other alone add a special touch of humor. Timmy has more names—and he answers to all of them. One of the names is Bor (Bor is shortened from Tibor and we're not even sure where or how he received that nickname). On the summer swim team, the other swimmers in his age group know him only as "Bor." One morning at practice, Coach Chris (who is also his brother) tries to get his attention by yelling: "Timmy! Timmy!" One of his new friends looks at him and asks, "Why is Coach calling you Timmy?" Timmy in turn calls Joe Pat "Paddy." The name remains. Tommy is "Chop," Jamie is "Hans," Tony is "T." If someone new visits our home, they may begin to think we have more than ten children due to all the names they hear. I do know there are many days it sounds as if we have more than ten children in our home.

The interaction of the boys with each other and with us adds the greatest memories to our memory bank. Each experience, the good and the not so good, the rewarding times and the tough times, all mean more because of the sharing of them together as a couple and as a family. How I'll always remember Timmy asking on the day Joe was in the hospital and Joe's father died: "Mommy, is this what they mean is a 'bad' day?" Or the boys' willingness to drive twelve hours to El Paso for their grandfather's funeral so we could be together.

The laughter and the tears are all a part of our memories. Memories and traditions are only as meaningful as our relationships with our spouse and our family. Time invested in our spousal relationship pays so many benefits for both husband and wife, mother and father. Build the relationship and reap the rewards of memories and traditions. We can honestly say that our greatest joys and rewards are seeing our children together and being family.

From good parents come a good son.
—Aristotle

A happy childhood is one of the best gifts
that parents have it in their power to bestow.
—Mary Cholmondeley

This is my commandment: love one another
as I have loved you.
—John 15:12

Chapter Twelve

The Boys Talk: Our "Ten" Cents

By Tony and David Garcia-Prats

*G*rowing up we assumed every family was much like ours. We have two loving parents who provide for us, who love and care for us and one another. As we grew older we began to see how lucky we truly are to have the parents that we do, parents who place family first, who put an emphasis on faith, love, and respect. We took this for granted for so long. We have had the chance as we've grown older to meet people who don't feel the same pride and love for their family as we do for ours, and it makes us sad. Our home life was a pleasant, nurturing one. Though our home life wasn't always perfect, we have always felt welcome and happy when we are with our family and still look forward to being home. We could never understand why some of our friends didn't want to go home. It made us sad to find that so many people's family lives, if not abusive, were less than loving. We could not understand why marriage and family life are so often disparaged, by both media and friends, when we saw it as something to look forward to and to cherish.

When we step back and take a look at why our views are different from so many others', we can't help but realize that it all begins with the marriage of our parents. **From the joining of these two people comes the family life that we know and love. Together and individually they are an example of what a relationship, specifically a marriage, should be like. We learn from what they say and what they do; we take their example and attempt to carry it over into our lives.**

When taking a look at our parents' marriage, the first thing that comes to mind is love, the essential building block for any relationship. **We have come to realize that love is an everyday choice that must be made. It is a conscious choice to make the marriage and family work. It is a conscious choice to make marriage and family a priority. It is a conscious choice to make time for the things that are truly important. Yet all these choices are not as difficult when they are all based on love.** They choose to love each other; other decisions follow in suit. It is out of love for my mom and family that Dad opted to work in an academic setting rather than in a more lucrative and time-consuming private practice. It is because of love that my mother chose to stop teaching first grade and stay at home to raise her sons. We benefit as individuals and as a family because of these decisions. We see these difficult choices being made so seemingly easily by our parents, and we do our best to follow in their footsteps. We make choices to help the family out because of our love for them. When our parents needed some time to themselves to relax and to finish this book, it was no trouble for us to take the entire family to the beach for the weekend. In fact, it was actually our pleasure. But the small things, when added up, make a big difference as well. My dad's daily calls home from work just to say "Hi" to Mom, the delicious meals my mother cooks daily, and coffee in the morning for us are all things that we observe, admire, and try to emulate. Likewise, taking time to drive a younger brother to a late practice so Mom or Dad can address other more important things, washing the dishes with a smile, and mowing the lawn are all things that are done out of love.

We see our parents choosing to do these small things, and we follow their example. When we choose to love our parents, brothers, family, and friends, the other choices become simple.

When we watch our parents on a daily basis, the respect that they have for each other becomes all too obvious. **They share a mutual respect as a couple, being as equal as possible as a couple and as parents. They divide household tasks that need to be done without worrying about traditional gender roles within the family.** Dad cooks when he needs to and now makes delicious fajitas and a chicken dish that is actually requested from time to time. Mom enjoys going to soccer games and practices as much as any dad would, and she can even be found doing the yard occasionally when one of the younger siblings is unavailable. They do whatever is necessary to keep the family running smoothly and to keep their marriage a happy one. We follow their example and do our part around the house and with each other as well. The dishes are cleaned nightly by one of us. We have all learned to cook (which is a great benefit in college). We do our best to watch our brothers' activities whenever we can, and many times the whole family can be found at a soccer field cheering loudly for the brother who happens to be playing. All of these things are based on respect for each other. The respect we learn through their example carries on in each of us outside the home to our friends and those we see every day at work and school. When we treat those around us with respect, that respect is reciprocated.

More specifically within the marriage, my parents respect and celebrate each other's individuality. **Although they are a married couple, they are still two very unique and different individuals. They have their own strengths and weaknesses, likes and dislikes.** The intense nature of our mom is perfect for dealing with many situations, while other situations may call for the calm demeanor of our dad. When going to the movies Dad may want to catch the next James Bond, while Mom would rather sit through a light-hearted, more sentimental movie. We're sure there are times when Mom didn't want to see Bond, James Bond, again and times when Dad could do without another romantic comedy. But they respect these differences, enjoy them, and celebrate them out of love for each other. They have always shown this same celebration of individuality for all ten of us. How else could the oldest five have chosen such different colleges and majors? (Tony a biology and chemistry major at St. Louis University and at Baylor College of Medicine in Houston, David an English major at Creighton University in Omaha, Chris an education major at Trinity University in San Antonio, Joe Pat an international business major at Regis University in Denver, and Matty a business major at the University of San Diego.) Five different schools in five different states with diverse areas of study, from medicine to English, education to business, and five even more original choices yet to be made by the five youngest brothers. Although my parents have much in common, their differences compliment each other and strengthen rather than weaken their relationship. They are not afraid to ask for or give help when needed. We celebrate the differences in the members of our family and in our friends. **In the relationships that we have made and are making, we look for friends who share many of our ideals, yet challenge us with their uniqueness, friends who enjoy our differences as much as we enjoy theirs.**

One aspect of our parents' relationship that they share and celebrate more vehemently than any other is their strong faith in God. Beginning with their wedding vows and continuing in big events such as baptisms, first communions, first reconciliations, and confirmations as well as beginning their twenty-fifth anniversary celebration with a Mass, our parents have made their faith the center of their marriage and the family. They set an example in their daily lives by attending Mass with the family, going as a couple to weekly adoration, and sharing in family prayers every night and at the dinner table. All these moments of shared faith have become our own. They made faith important in their lives, and now we make it important in ours. At dinner we recently began to go around the table and individually offer up intentions and thanksgiving before beginning to eat. The intentions that we share give us time to think about each other and those around us as well as the importance of God in our lives. Just as Dad and Mom go to Mass with each other and the family because of the importance of their faith, we similarly find ourselves going to Mass with friends we have made. These moments in our relationships are especially memorable and meaningful because we are able to share with our friends such an important part of who we are. **The importance of faith to our parents' relationship influences us to seek out friends who share similar views about the importance of faith in our lives.** Our faith brings us together with those we love, thereby enabling us to share with each other these moments with God, whether at the dinner table, around the den floor and couches at night reciting our family litany, or holding hands during the Our Father at Mass.

The importance of the marriage of our parents will never be truly understood by any of us. **At least in some sense every relationship we have had or ever will have, whether it be acquaintance, friend, girlfriend, or future spouse, is influenced by the relationship our parents have. This is an incredible responsibility for a couple. Luckily for us, one which our parents took very seriously.** We may touch on things here and there, but the values they instilled and the examples they set are things that we'll carry with us forever. Because of their love and commitment to each other, our family lives have been blessed. Relationships that we have had and people whom we have shared things with have all benefited from the example of our dad and mom. We can only speculate what our marriages (when/ if they happen) will truly be like. But if we use our parents' marriage as an example and love and respect our spouses as much as they love and respect each other, then we can only assume the best. **The two greatest things our parents have given us are their love for each of us and their love for each other.** What an amazing gift to us, one which we hope we are also able to pass on.

*The sound of a kiss is not so loud as that of a cannon,
but its echo lasts a great deal longer.*
                                        —Oliver Wendell Holmes

*Life is short and we have not too much time for
gladdening the hearts of those who are traveling
the dark way with us. Oh, be swift to love!
Make haste to be kind.*
                                        —Henri Frederic Amiel

*It is not how much you do but how much love
you put into the doing and sharing with others
that is important.*
                                        —Mother Teresa

Chapter Thirteen

Keeping Love Alive!

*A*ll couples, whether newly married or seasoned, need to understand that all friendships, marriages, and relationships demand time and attention to grow and flourish. A good marriage doesn't just happen because we want it to happen. When we look back at the beginning of our relationship, we recognize how we invested a great amount of time doing the "little" things to make an impression on the other and to show each other we cared: the special phone calls, the acts of kindness and appreciation, the extra primping, the compromising, and the exhibition of model behavior. We consciously thought about what we said and did. We wanted to spend as much time together as possible laughing, talking, and sharing—sometimes with friends, but more often alone. Although we became comfortable with each other and realized we didn't always have to look our best or put on a happy face when our world disintegrated around us, we still wanted the other to desire our company and to enjoy our time together. In short, we made our relationship a priority in our lives.

What too often happens in a relationship is that the uniqueness and the "passion" wear off. We spend less time meeting the needs and wants of the other. We simply coexist. **We assume or think the small touches don't matter as much anymore when, in reality, they matter a great deal. Renee Locks wrote: "Friendship isn't a big thing—it's a million little things." Those million little things continuously nourish and strengthen the relationship; without them, the relationship grows stagnant, boring, and unfulfilling.**

(Cathy): How easily we get caught up in the day-to-day activities and let the little things slide. We become so busy, stressed, or tired that we often neglect or ignore the special people in our lives. Yet all of us want and need to feel special on a regular basis. I want to know and feel that I hold a unique place in Joe's life, and I want him to realize how much he means to me. If I want Joe to understand how special he is to me, then I need to demonstrate my love for him through my words and actions. To paraphrase John F. Kennedy: Ask not what your spouse can do for you; think what you can do for your spouse. We must consciously think of ways to express our love, always remembering that marriage is an active process. It takes continuous effort, keeping in mind that we reap what we sow.

The "little" things I do for Joe may not seem like much to an observer's eye, but I know they mean something to him. I prepare his favorite dinners or desserts. I send the sentimental or funny card or write him a letter. I assume some extra household responsibilities when he has additional responsibilities at work or outside commitments. I take the time to freshen up before he arrives home—what a difference a little lipstick and blush can make in my appearance. I provide as calm a home as I can with ten children. I listen to the events of his day. I express my love and appreciation in words. I am his friend and lover.

You may have noticed I did not mention material gifts. There are times when a gift does express my feelings, such as a framed picture of us or the boys or maybe a book Joe mentioned he wanted to read. I may be at a store and see a sweater or tie I think Joe will like. **Thoughtfully chosen gifts can make a person feel special, but when the gift is given as a replacement for your love, time and attention, the gift is an extremely poor substitute. The daily expressions of love and appreciation are more important.** I am reminded of the words of Sir Humphrey Davy: *"Life is made up, not of great sacrifices or duties, but of little things in which smiles and kindness and small obligations, given habitually, are what win and preserve the heart and secure comfort."*

(Joe): In professions such as medicine, law, and education (just to name a few), there is usually an annual requirement for mandatory educational hours in order to maintain an adequate fund of knowledge and, in some instances, licensure. These educational hours in medicine are called CME hours (Continuing Medical Education) and may focus on updates for physicians concerning new medications, new medical treatments, new surgical treatments, ethics, etc. An added benefit of attending the programs and mastering this new educational information is the invigoration of the physician to become a better doctor and, hopefully, a better healer by incorporating this new information into his or her practice of medicine. A third sidelight of this endeavor is the camaraderie when one attends these meetings. Many times the physician reestablishes old friendships by meeting colleagues who are also in attendance and taking this opportunity to discuss common problems encountered during one's management of patients.

It is interesting that prior to and after our marriage we are not required to demonstrate proficiency in communication, accepting responsibility, fidelity, etc. Likewise, we are not required to obtain any CME (Continuing Marital Education) hours to maintain our proficiency in our *"spouse-ship."* **Yet Continuing Marital Education should be required each year to revitalize our spousal relationship in order for us to be "remarried" to our spouse for another year.** *This approach sounds rather far-fetched and radical;*

however, without some form of CME hours each year, our relationship stagnates just as surely as our professional prowess.

So how does a married couple obtain their CME hours? We can only reinvigorate our relationship through time spent together, learning more about each other and about ourselves through each spouse's feedback. This time may include an evening out enjoying dinner or sharing a dessert, conversing while we fold clothes, or just having that cup of coffee at the dinner table after the boys have finished and gone out to play. It is this time that affords each of us the opportunity to learn more about our spouse and ourselves. Moreover, it is the celebration of our intimacy and sexuality that strengthens the marriage. Time spent listening and sharing revitalizes each spouse's love, respect, commitment, and faith. Ultimately, it is a time commitment that we must consciously make happen.

I can vividly remember two years ago when school for the boys had just started as well as all the accompanying homework and five different soccer practice schedules. In addition, we had just returned from taking Joe Pat to Denver for college. Cathy and I seemed to have some obligation every time we turned around. One evening as we were talking after dinner, we realized that we had not been on our much appreciated "date" for over three weeks. How had that happened? **Our obligations seemed like a powerful ocean wave that had swept us away from the time we needed. We had to refocus on what was important—our relationship. Without that foundation being solid, it is so hard to make the other important elements in our life transpire smoothly in the direction desired. Indeed, marriage requires CME.**

One of the earlier versions of *For Better and For Ever*, the marriage preparation program we use with engaged couples, requires participants to answer the following query: Name three ways you have demonstrated your love for your financé(e)/spouse this week. The first night they are asked to respond, couples usually can't recall three instances. However, knowing the question will be repeated at every session encourages them to thoughtfully express their love to each other during the upcoming week. This lesson thus reinforces the importance of actively and consciously nurturing your marriage, whether you have been married a year or twenty-six years. Little things matter!

People often ask us: "How do you find time for each other, especially with ten children?"

We have to make time for each other. It truly is a conscious choice we make. Too often couples tell us that they will reconnect once their careers are established or the children are grown. Gradually, such couples become "married singles." That is, they inhabit the same house but pursue separate and distinct objectives. Unfortunately, when couples haven't maintained their relationship over the years, they find they don't know each other anymore or don't share any interests. We witness too many marriages that dissolve after the children are grown. In these cases, their children rather than their marital bond held the "marriage" together.

We emphasize again how important it is to make your marriage—after your faith—the number one priority in your life. Focus on each other, enrich each other, buffer each other from the stresses of the world. Be loving, forgiving, accepting, and respectful. Foster healthy communication, intimacy, and sexuality in your relationship. Don't look for life to remain the same but expect and relish change. Whenever a spouse tells us in a negative tone of voice that his or her spouse is not the same person he or she married so many years ago, we reply that we hope not. If change hasn't taken place, then growth and maturity haven't taken place either. We are not the same couple or individuals we were on our wedding day. We believe we are much better now than then. After twenty-six years of marriage, we frequently find ourselves viewing the same situation differently. As we considered stories to share for the book, our perspective on some events were disparate.

(Cathy): I remember the day a friend asked Joe and me whether the summer months were easier for us than the school year. Joe answered in the affirmative very quickly: We didn't have to get up

quite as early. We didn't have to rush around getting breakfast and lunches prepared. The evenings were less hectic without homework, school, and athletic responsibilities. Meanwhile, I sat there dumbfounded by his response. As far as I was concerned, one wasn't necessarily easier than the other—just different. During the school year breakfast and lunches for most of the boys are prepared and finished by 7:30 A.M. whereas during the summer breakfast and lunch often overlap because of the boys' varied schedules. The summer evenings may be less hectic, but the summer daytime hours are noisier and busier for me. Quiet time is a much harder commodity to find with ten children home rather than just two or three. Joe hadn't thought about the dramatic changes in my day until then. I must admit that he became much more understanding and appreciative of what my summer days entail.

As a married couple we must learn to appreciate and celebrate our differences as well as our similarities. Relish the uniqueness that each of you brings to your marriage: your family of origin, your faith, your personality, talents, and interests. We are better individuals and a better married couple because of our similarities and differences.

We know without a shadow of a doubt that we are a better "one" than we are a separate "two."

(Cathy): **Joe makes me a better wife, mother, lover, friend, teacher, and speaker/author.**

(Joe): **Cathy makes me a better husband, father, lover, physician, and friend. We also know we are richer by the dozen because of the gifts of ten sons.**

Marriage is the ultimate adventure—full of laughter, sorrow, smooth sailing, and rough waters. Enjoy, enrich, and nourish your relationship. Make time for each other and God in the midst of everyday demands. The joys and rewards for your efforts last a lifetime and beyond.